ELLEN B[illegible]

I Could Live Here

A Travel Memoir of Home and Belonging

First published by Abhuta 2023

First edition

Cover art by Ute Hagen

ISBN Ebook: 979-8-9892889-0-8
ISBN Paperback: 979-8-9892889-1-5
ISBN Hardcover: 979-8-9892889-2-2

For Hank

"Sometimes I don't know who I am." Said the boy. "I feel lost."
"Everyone feels a bit lost sometimes," said the mole, "I know I do. But we love you, and love brings you home."

—CHARLIE MACKESY, *The Boy, the Mole, the Fox and the Horse*

Contents

Prologue

Peru

The last light of a July evening cast shadows dancing across the aged wood plank floor of the rental apartment. We were in the high Andes, perched atop a steep Inca passageway, in the historic heart of Cusco, Peru.

I stood before a large picture window cupping a steaming coca tea and looked out across the now-familiar labyrinth of cobbled streets and terra-cotta rooftops winding down to the bustling Plaza de Armas below.

The cathedral's massive stone façade stood illuminated in the warm blush of evening light. And, at the heart of the square gleamed a spotlit fountain with a golden statue of Inca king Pachacuti, hand raised and fierce gaze fixed on the surrounding mountains.

Some ninety miles in the distance, the snowcapped 20,945-foot peak of Ausangate, a mountain sacred to the Andean people, towered overhead, bathed in the faintest pink light of alpenglow.

Cusco had gotten under our skin. This was our third long-stay in six years. A migratory nest—this UNESCO World Heritage city, gateway to Machu Picchu and the Sacred Valley—that embraced us, again and again, in its eclectic vibe.

Hank joined me at the window. We watched until the final tinge of color faded. "Not a bad view, huh?"

"Yeah. Not bad at all. I could live here," I replied with a smile, knowing my response would trigger the same. And though the often-repeated sentiment had evolved from an inside joke into a way of life, I still chuckled.

But that didn't mean I wasn't surprised by the journey we'd embarked upon. I was fifty-four, Hank eighty-one. We'd been loose in the world without a permanent home for nearly a decade. We'd wandered and roamed and stayed across the Americas and Europe—from Mexico and Nicaragua to Colombia, Peru, and Portugal—navigating the heartbreak of recurring goodbyes, the humbling effects of displacement, the pleasure of foreign words, and the magic of new friendships, with little stability beyond a few months. An uncertain journey to an unknown future.

As the sky darkened to a velvety navy blue, I savored the moment, storing away its magic in my heart like a souvenir. Though, what good was a souvenir without a home to return to? Nothing to display on a wall or a shelf. No physical evidence to share with friends and family. It was as intangible as our itinerant life. Or was it?

For us, home was a moving target. It was a path initiated by circumstance yet seeded across decades, one *I could live here* at a time. A way of life I'd arrived to in confusion and doubt and hope. One that straddled the life I'd lived and the life I wanted. A life that balanced wanderlust with temporary homemaking.

A nomad's life.

I was about to turn away when a sudden burst of light illuminated the sky, followed by the deafening crack of fireworks. A shower of golden sparks cascaded downward, painting intricate patterns against the now-dark sky. We watched, transfixed by the scattered bursts of color and light, each more spectacular than the last. Reds, blues, and greens exploded in front of us, so close, it seemed, I could reach out and touch them. Echoes of applause and cheers reverberated across the thin, high-altitude air until the sky was once again dark and tranquil.

A knock at the door broke the spell. It was Ana Maria, the Peruvian adventurer who owned the rental apartment and lived upstairs. We opened the door to find her holding a small brown bakery box. "Would you like some tres leches cake?"

She knew Hank had a sweet tooth and that tres leches was one of his favorites. He had accepted the box and was headed for the kitchen before Ana Maria and I finished hugging hello. By the time we got to the kitchen, Hank had plated three slices. Ana Maria chuckled and sat on a stool at the kitchen counter while I filled the electric kettle with water for tea.

With a deep understanding and affection for her country, Ana Maria filled us in on the meaning behind the celebrations. *Fiestas Patrias,* Peru's national holiday. Like the Fourth of July in the United States, Peruvians celebrate their independence from Spain on July 28th with parades, bands, and fireworks.

I sat and listened, watching the animated movements of this small, restless woman who had become a cherished friend. For a moment, I was back in 2012 on the Inca Trail when Ana Maria was our trekking guide, listening to her talk with passion and knowledge about the *apus,* the mountain spirits or deities considered sacred by indigenous Andean communities. Then, her soft voice transported me back to a 2015 adventure and a weekend at a crumbling country house, expropriated by the government a half-century ago but recently restored to her family.

Would there be more adventures together? Would we ask to stay, to apply for residency like so many of the foreigners we'd met who'd traveled to Cusco and never left? Maybe time would tell, but when we said goodbye that night, it was with a warm sense of connection that came from time immersed in this special place, in the exuberance of its celebrations, the flavors of its food, the feel of its land beneath our feet, and the warm hospitality of its people. It was a physical feeling, an understanding born from hard-won experience and unknowable possibilities.

Later, I sat alone, content in the darkness and took in the city's sounds— a vibrant cacophony of life. The lively chatter of people passing by the house, the random clap of fireworks, car horns and motorcycle engines, the steady beat of drums, and the unique deep, resonant tones of Andean flute music.

We'd been homeloose for 2,734 days, winging it, two people of no fixed abode. We were 4,000 miles from our homeland, 11.000 feet above sea level, south of the equator, where summer is winter. And life felt exciting and rich and fortunate.

Was I finally home?

I

Part One

Growing Pains

1

The Phone Call That Changed Everything

New Mexico, USA

We were reading when the phone rang. New Mexico sunshine blazed through the three-story windows that fronted the leased house we called home. The homeowners, friends and former neighbors, were on the other end. We put them on speakerphone and listened to the unexpected news that they had a buyer for the house and wanted to close by the end of the month.

Their words hung there, darkening the sunny room.

I could tell they wanted to honor the sixty-day notice we'd agreed to in the lease. But I also heard hope in their voices and knew what a financial boost a quick sale would be for them. I turned to look at my husband, Hank. He paused, then nodded his acceptance. It mirrored my feelings. We wouldn't fight it.

"No problem," I said, trying to sound more buoyant than I felt. "Don't worry about the timing. We'll figure something out."

One minute, we had half a year before the end of a three-year lease;

the next, twenty-eight days.

• • •

I didn't sleep well that night, still rattled by the call, its unexpectedness, and the harsh reality we couldn't afford to counter the $600,000 purchase offer. I lay awake, cursing the years spent traveling instead of saving, freelancing instead of working a salaried job, and racking my brain for a palatable solution. I tried to imagine myself going back to teaching math, my original career. I tried to summon the energy to stop freelancing. But it left me too paralyzed to breathe. I berated myself for the choices I had made, for prioritizing freedom over security, for my stubbornness, and for lying awake at four in the morning with my heart drumming in my chest.

I looked over at Hank, my partner of twenty years, happily retired from a thirty-five-year teaching career, sleeping beside me—a sound, peaceful sleep. I rolled over and lay there watching his chest's gentle rise and fall, the wispy eyelashes usually hidden behind glasses.

I glanced around the moonlit room.

Every item was a reminder of the past: The landscape photograph of a rugged California coastline with jagged cliffs plunging dramatically into the Pacific Ocean and waves crashing against the shore below, captured during a summer road trip. A vintage Moroccan Berber blanket, sourced on travels through the Middle Atlas Mountains, draped across the chair that I liked to sink into at the end of the day. The carved-wood bedroom furniture we'd purchased thirteen years ago when we relocated from Pennsylvania to New Mexico to begin a new life chapter. And the hand-woven Mexican rugs we'd brought home over the years scattered across the floor, picking up the tiles' varying hues of reds, oranges, and yellows.

I asked myself if I believed in a sense of security and contentment that came from comfort and familiarity and knew I didn't have an honest answer.

My rational mind told me to let it go. My rational mind said this loss was an opportunity. But I wouldn't listen. Instead, I crawled out of bed, curled up on the living room couch with a lambswool tartan blanket from Scotland, and brooded.

Finally, I fell asleep and dreamed I was in an airport, watching a plane take off, its bright silver wings tipping and turning over an unfamiliar horizon.

• • •

"None of this is necessary— the four-bedroom house, the three-car garage, the ten acres of land," Hank said over coffee the next morning. "It's much more than we need. More than we can afford. We've been fortunate, but we always intended this house to be transitional."

"I know." The words came out weak and defeated, and a raw, bitter taste lodged in the back of my throat.

At forty-seven years old, my freelance travel writing and photography business had been well-established for thirteen years since leaving teaching. I attracted exciting opportunities to explore the world and had built a robust client base. The profession, however, was rapidly evolving, saturated with younger, eager digital influencers. Life had gone off track at some point in recent years—the American Dream of financial security and upward mobility no longer seemed assured.

"We can find another place here or move to Mexico like we talked about when we sold our house," Hank continued. "Mexico is a place we know well and love. We have good friends there. And it's affordable. You could still freelance. Improve your Spanish."

"We could," I said halfheartedly.

"It's warmer," he added, trying to lighten things.

It was February 2011. We were in the kitchen drinking dark-roasted Guatemalan coffee. Outside, the morning's gray and gloom matched my mood. A strong arctic blast blanketed much of the Southwest in snow, and the thermometer hadn't inched above freezing in twenty-four hours.

I turned to the window. A thick layer of snow covered every surface, including the roof of the bird feeder, swaying gently from the sturdy branch of a towering ponderosa pine tree. The fluffy white powder had piled up on the top, creating a graceful curve. Western scrub jays, dark-eyed juncos, and house sparrows flitted to and from the feeder, sending a cascade of snowflakes down in a gentle flurry.

Hank reached across the table to refill my coffee, and the porcelain cup felt as heavy as a hammer. Questions buzzed inside my head. *Do we want to stay here? Should we move permanently to Mexico? Somewhere else? What about our stuff?*

I looked at my husband and saw he was happy—chatty, upbeat, and energized. Hank and I are opposites. He rises to exercise every morning at six a.m., can toggle between reading and conversation without irritation, and is in bed by ten every night. I sleep late and head straight for the coffee machine in the morning. I am terrible at multitasking and still pull all-nighters. I'm a chronic worrier with a contrary temperament. For me, every new venture is tainted with self-doubt. In comparison, Hank never takes life too seriously.

"Think about it," he said. "We don't have to decide today but should book the movers. Make sure they're available."

"Right," I told him as though I was already on it. Calling a moving company is a good thing. I knew this but still couldn't face the sinkhole of uncertainty that loomed before us. I wanted it all. I wanted this rented house. I didn't want to let go. It was ten a.m., and I was still in my bathrobe.

I got dressed and searched Google for the mover's phone number when there was a knock at the door. A glance out the kitchen window revealed a silver Toyota Tacoma pickup in the driveway. So unexpected that, at first, I didn't recognize it until I spotted our friends Corinna and Don on the front porch with Hershey, their chocolate-colored Australian shepherd, running circles in the snow.

I put down the phone and followed Hank as he made his way to the door. I watched Hershey peering in one of the tall, narrow windows framing the front door. His snow-covered nose pressed to the glass, his lively amber eyes searching until they locked with mine. My worries evaporated, and I felt myself smile for the first time that day.

• • •

"How many days did you say you have?" Corinna asked, scooping almond flour into quinoa pancake batter and then onto a hot griddle, my Nicaraguan lace apron tucked neatly around her trim waist.

"Twenty-eight," Hank said, filling in the details of our predicament.

That Corinna ground flour from raw nuts and seeds and prepared gourmet meals in the dilapidated sixteen-foot camper trailer she and Don inhabited while they built their dream home was impressive enough. But that they'd lived in it for five years—as they cleared timber, built roads and retaining walls, and laid the foundation on seven acres of raw mountain land—and were still happily married was, as we judged it, a miracle.

"You could move into our guest house." Don joked, referring to the private guest quarters of a house that only existed in an architect's blueprint.

We'd fallen into the convivial habit of using our kitchen to prepare and enjoy communal meals with Corinna and Don. It was an arrangement that got them out of their cramped trailer. But given Corinna's culinary talents, we suspected we got the better of the deal.

Friendship came easily with the two of them. Intelligent and creative, they'd met and married in New Zealand, where Don, an American entrepreneur, was traveling between projects and Corinna, a German expat and artist, had a ceramics gallery. After a few years in New Zealand, they got itchy feet and moved to the States, living for a time in the Pacific Northwest before settling in New Mexico.

As I stepped over a sprawling Hershey in search of a bottle of barrel-aged maple syrup, I overheard Hank tell Don he always thought four houses would be ideal: One in Mexico, another in the Caribbean, and a third in Central or South America, with a home base in New Mexico.

I'd heard Hank lay out this scenario before and had always dismissed it as a crazy, wistful dream, especially for two retired teachers eking out a creative's existence—Hank writing young adult action-adventure novels, my freelancing. But this time, something clicked, and the whisper of an idea took form.

"That's it!" I said, brightening as I pulled the syrup bottle off a pantry shelf.

"What? Buy four houses?" Hank asked.

"No. Rent them. We could put our stuff in storage and move from one place to another like nomads—staying as long as a visitor visa allows. And maybe find a new home along the way."

Hank poured us another mug of coffee. I could tell he was letting the idea sink in.

"Breakfast is ready," Corinna announced. She handed us each a plate stacked high with pancakes, and we headed to the dining table, a beautiful piece of solid hardwood with seating for eight. I passed around small bowls of fresh berries sprinkled with lemon juice, vanilla, cinnamon, ground almonds, and grated coconut.

The dog snored, we ate, and the cozy aroma of hot spices filled the open-plan kitchen where we dined when Hank announced, "Let's do it. Put it all in storage, explore for a year or more as we decide what's next."

Nothing had changed. We would still be homeless in less than a month. We would still be leaving behind friends and familiarity, yet the tightness in my chest had been replaced by excitement.

2

Where Now?

"Where exactly will you go?"

It was a good question, and our friend Dave was not the first to ask it. We'd been asking ourselves the same question, with no firm answer, throughout the hectic weeks that followed our decision to wander.

We lounged on the back deck of Dave's house, enjoying one of those magical New Mexico winter days when the sun creates heat so warm and welcoming it feels like you're beneath a gigantic heat lamp with the air-conditioning cranked high.

This was the same house where I worked when we first arrived in New Mexico. Then, it had contained a thriving, home-based photography agency owned by Dave and his now ex-wife Jan. Here is where I'd learned the business of travel photography back before the agency was sold and dismantled. And now, after moving out of our beloved home, Hank and I were temporarily ensconced in its master bedroom while a newly divorced Dave slept in the guest room across the hall.

Faye, the sweet twelve-year-old Siberian husky with one brown eye and one blue that had remained with Dave after the divorce, rooted around in the snow, her bottom high and her nose down. Now and then, she looked over at Dave, an invitation to play, but he was too preoccupied with his heartache to notice.

There was no need to probe. As friends and colleagues, we'd been privy to much of the path that had led to the recent end of Dave and Jan's marriage. And I recognized his anguish from a terrible, broken time in our marriage when tearing love apart had seemed the only way to reconcile it. Pablo Picasso said any real act of creation is first an act of destruction, and in my fourth decade, I was just beginning to perceive the truth of that fact—that sometimes lives and hearts and homes are destroyed before they can be made new.

"Sometimes I think about doing what you're doing," Dave told us. "Packing up the RV and just driving." His eyes revealed a wistful longing.

"What's stopping you?" I asked.

He walked to the grill to baste a pork loin, and sizzling meat released a sweet, smoky aroma tinged with the spicy heat of grilled green chiles, reminding me I'd forgotten to eat lunch.

"I'm too old to go chasing around alone," he said.

This surprised me.

In his early seventies, Dave was healthy and fit and still traveled the globe on assignments for the many magazines and newspapers that published his self-illustrated travel stories. But the word *alone* revealed just how destabilized he still felt.

I knew what he meant, though, and in his fears, I saw my own. Hovering around the excitement of our decision to wander was a greedy part of me that desperately wanted nothing to change. A cowardly part of me that only saw all there was to lose: a familiar life, established routines and friendships. Not for the first time, I wondered if Hank and I were running from or toward something. I had no idea.

Before freelancing, before New Mexico, there'd been an advancing sense of restlessness brewing in our household. And the itch to wander was not an unfamiliar one. Almost two decades earlier, Hank and I spontaneously eloped during a three-month summer vacation. Two years later, we set out in a Subaru Outback towing a pop-up tent camper, only to return home after over a year on the road. Within fourteen months, we'd relocated 2,000 miles away to start a new life. And for much of the past decade, we'd traveled the world, content in the knowledge that travel and home were two distinct and separate realms. The familiarity of home balanced the thrill of adventure. But this time, there was no home to return to.

After we sat down to dinner, Dave leaned back in his chair, balancing his margarita, and asked again: "Seriously. Where will you go?"

"Mexico," we replied in unison. Mexico was an easy choice, but we hadn't realized we'd both already made it.

3

New Beginnings. Familiar Places.

Mexico

We'd arrived yesterday in Ajijic (ah-hee-HEEK), a quirky lakeside village an hour's drive from Guadalajara, where Hank and I had stayed off and on for the last fifteen years. It was early afternoon: June sun streamed in through glass patio doors. I sat on a large, slipcovered sofa in our German friend Ute's Ajijic studio, surrounded by walls and easels alive with color. My bare feet curled beneath me, a hand-painted Talavera teacup in my hands. The room smelled of paint and turpentine—the tools of Ute's trade. An edgy track of Arabic dance beats played from an iPod on a Bose music system.

Ute's work awed me. On the surface, her paintings were impressionistic representations of Mexican village life. Fiestas. Mariachis. Vaqueros. But when I really looked and let my perceptions fade—when I went beyond the glorious color and surrendered my ideas and memories—the magic and mastery appeared. The bold colors. The textured layers. The luminous light. Ute doesn't just paint the world around her; she paints emotions and experiences.

It felt good to catch up with Ute in her creative space—to be together again in Ajijic.

Steeped in pre-Columbian roots, Ajijic (also written Axixic) is a Nahuatl word, the native language of the area, meaning "the place of water," a reference to the abundant Lake Chapala, which anchors the town. With the arrival of the Spanish, Ajijic became part of the colonial tapestry of Mexico. Spanish architecture and traditions remain in the town's buildings, picturesque courtyards, and the Catholic church. By the mid-twentieth century, as word of Ajijic's natural beauty and allure spread, a wave of foreign artists and writers arrived, bringing a bohemian burst of art and culture that persists. The creative community suited Ute perfectly.

"Where's your rental?" Ute asked as she settled onto the studio couch and leaned across to pour me more tea. She'd brought a teapot and fresh mango slices with crushed mint and almonds from the kitchen. The snacks were on a ceramic platter in blue and black and white with a distinctive fish motif that I recognized as a purchase from a road trip we'd taken together a few years earlier to the village of Tzintzuntzan near Lake Pátzcuaro in the state of Michoacán.

"We've rented a two-bedroom townhouse on Calle Galeana," I said. "A block-and-a-half up from the *Carretera*."

"That's great. You're close by. Do you need the lounge chair you left with me the last time you were here? Carsten can help us strap it to the jeep's roof when you're ready, and I can drive you home."

I first met Ute during a visit to Ajijic without Hank. A friend of my friend Jan was in the midst of an ugly divorce and needed an affordable, creative place to heal. I'd suggested Ajijic, thinking its daily sunshine, welcoming community, mountain hiking, lush gardens, and lake views would provide a supportive and immediate solution.

Soon afterward, the three of us—Jan, her dejected friend Sandra, and me—had crammed into an overpacked Volkswagen Jetta and made the two-day drive from New Mexico to Ajijic. Once there, we'd camped out in a shared hotel suite at La Nueva Posada and searched for a rental. Within a week, we'd settled Sandra into the lovely guest house of an elegantly restored village home owned by a California divorcée. And then, once we knew that Sandra was safely nested, Jan and I returned to New Mexico.

In the course of that search, we'd ended up at Ute's unassuming house on a quiet street just up from the *malecón,* the town's popular waterfront promenade. Someone had suggested she might know of a rental, and we'd just shown up on her doorstep. She was living alone then. Her husband, Carsten, still worked in Vancouver. Inviting us in, she'd led us through a simple home decorated in an artistic mix of styles and colors with big, bold paintings everywhere. And then, out onto a sunny, tiled patio with brightly painted pink-and-yellow walls, a bubbling fountain, a koi pond, and a café table. I knew I wanted to be friends immediately.

• • •

"Are you glad to be back?" Hank asked.

He'd just finished carrying the lounge chair from Ute to the rooftop terrace of the rented house when a ferocious thunderstorm, the first of the summer monsoons, exploded to life. Outside, the rain beat on the windowpanes, sending torrents of water gushing down the slopes and streets to the awaiting lake. The sweet smell of rain rose around us. The deluge was so fierce that his question was barely audible.

I stared at a trickle of water flowing through the uneven gap beneath the carved wood door, tempted to let the storm drown out the conversation.

Yes. I was glad to be back. Over the years we stayed in Ajijic, I'd come to love this village that blasted its celebrations and humanity outside our windows. The old-world charm of its cobblestone streets and colorful buildings. The warmth of its people. The art galleries, lively local market, and leafy plaza where foreign and Mexican residents gathered. And now, I opened my eyes every day to the pleasures of a blessed life—the love of a good man, independence, health, and a welcoming community. And I was grateful.

Still, I had this sense we were on the cusp of something I didn't yet understand. Not escape as much as a reassessment of life as we knew it.

Ajijic was a comfortable beginning, I told myself. It was a launching pad where, snug in the sunshine of the familiar, I could learn to sit in the shadow of the unknown.

"Are you all right?" Hank asked, pulling me out of my thoughts. "I didn't mean to stump you."

His tone was teasing, but there was a look of tender concern in his eyes.

I tried to conceal my qualms with a smile, but my mind froze. I didn't know how to tell him there were things I couldn't yet articulate.

4

Baby Steps

It was an odd sensation to open my mouth and hear gibberish spill out.

Nos vemos nuevamente el miércoles pasado. See you again last Wednesday.

Ella no viene con nosotros. She no come with us.

After years of visiting Mexico, my Spanish was shameful. I could mostly understand our friends and neighbors, the wait staff and baristas, the merchants and housekeepers. But when it came to speaking, I sounded like a toddler.

I chided myself for not enrolling in Spanish classes. Though the best I could manage after six years of high school and college French courses was a preposterous concoction as incomprehensible as Inspector Clouseau.

Thanks to Hank's fluency as a former Spanish and English teacher, I had a live-in tutor. But I was a resistant student, and he'd pretty much given up trying to teach me. I was a quick study for social courtesies and daily vocabulary—especially food. But I got cranky whenever he tried to move me into more advanced topics like irregular past tense and future subjunctive.

"Why don't you ask Elena María if she'd like to practice her English in exchange for helping you with your Spanish?" Hank suggested one afternoon.

"Good idea. She is going to Sunday dinner with her family and offered to bring me back some of her mom's homemade *mole*. I'll ask her then" I said.

Elena María was our neighbor. Married to a Canadian expat, she was a stylish, black-haired beauty from Guadalajara who looked to be about my age and, unlike many of our Mexican friends, was not a fluent English speaker.

She agreed immediately, and we started meeting on Tuesday and Thursday afternoons at El Jardin, a bustling café on the plaza. Over margaritas and a budding friendship, I soon stopped thinking about how hard it was to trill my Rs and assign the correct gender to an inanimate object. I forgot how bad I was with languages and worrying about sounding like the village idiot. I started to squeal *increíble* (een-cray-EEE-blay) at the shenanigans of Elena Maria's philandering brother-in-law and say *ciao* when we said goodbye without feeling like a total poser.

However, a month and a half later, Elena María's husband accepted a teaching position in the Dominican Republic. And soon, they were gone. Without our café sessions, my progress stalled.

"It looks like you're stuck with me again," Hank said one morning at Café Grano, the Ajijic roastery where we went most mornings for coffee. "Verb Conjugation 101 begins at six a.m. tomorrow."

I looked up from my cappuccino and groaned.

"Seriously," he said. "You're doing well."

"Really?" I asked though I was secretly pleased by this.

"Yep. I haven't heard you tell anyone you're pregnant in at least a week."

That made me smile.

In Spanish, the word for pregnant is *embarazada,* which I'd mistakenly used for *embarrassed* until Hank corrected me.

"A week or so back, Rodrigo asked me if you were taking classes," Hank said as the barista handed him his second cup of coffee, a crisp, dark roast from Chiapas in southern Mexico. "He thought your Spanish sounded better."

I thought back to the previous weeks. It was true. I was having an easier time with the language. I no longer had to ask Francisco at our local *fruiteria* to repeat the price of my bill. And in place of a frozen stare of confusion when the hairdresser asked me a question, I now rattled off an answer, even if it was ridiculous.

"It was easy with Elena María," I told Hank. "No rote memorization. No boring drills. No classes. I just listened to her funny stories about her family, asked questions, and used the translation apps on our phones when we didn't know how to say something."

"Well, it helped," he said. "Your pronunciation, in particular, has improved."

It felt good to imagine that my Spanish was getting better.

The reality, however, was that I still understood very little. People talked, told jokes, and swapped insults in a language alien to me. But it was a strange sort of peace from the subversive inner voice that had traveled with us to Mexico. *What are you doing here? If you were a grown-up, you'd get a real job.*

5

On Mexican Time

Summer in Ajijic is a stunner. The mountains, usually brown and brittle after months without rain, transformed into a luscious green as soon as the monsoons started. Watery sunshine bathed the lake and village, the aroma of ripened guava and blooming jasmine floated through the air, and children squealed as they splashed in puddles, sights and sounds that converged to create a pleasant backdrop to the day.

We quickly settled into a summer routine of rare freedom—no plans, no commitments, and few responsibilities. With downsized expenses, we could almost afford to relax for a little while. I maintained my blog and a few writing projects. Hank was at work on a new novel. We had all the hours in the world to drink coffee, hike the mountain trails above the town, see friends, and generally work out what we wanted to do with the rest of our lives.

Despite my reluctance to let go of the New Mexico house, the loss had set us free.

• • •

"This will make you laugh," I said. "I've decided to write a book."

Hank was napping in the sun on the terrace. He turned toward the patio table where I was writing in a journal. His eyes squinted into the sun. He looked genuinely surprised. "Really? What about?"

"About this. Our adventure. It's just an idea. Nothing too serious," I said, playing it cool. "Maybe a coffee table book with photographs and vignettes of the places we'll live."

"Do it," he said, rolling over onto his back, hands clasped behind his head. He smiled, his eyes meeting mine, and for a minute, I could see the man I fell in love with two decades earlier when I was twenty-seven and he was fifty-four. A solid man with a stern expression that masked a gentle disposition. He was a man of few words, at ease with himself and the world. A man who, when I'd told him, all those many years ago, I'd nearly convinced myself to marry a man my age, had asked me the one simple question that forever sealed our relationship: "Do you love me?" I did. I do.

We sat beneath a deep azure sky in companionable silence until Hank asked if I'd had any luck finding a rental house in Nicaragua. It felt like we'd just gotten comfortable in Ajijic, but a vague plan had taken shape over the summer, a vision similar to what Hank described to Don back in New Mexico: Four houses. One in Mexico. The others, in Central and South America. We would spend three months in each place, the duration of most visitor visas. And Nicaragua, like Mexico, was a place we gravitated back to again and again. Three visits in the past decade. A familiar next step.

Yet, I felt myself grappling with the same questions here as in New Mexico: what I wanted, what I needed, what I could let go of, and how much loss letting go would require. It was tempting to stay put, but I was determined to give this nomadic experiment a try. To go all in.

I told Hank Nicaragua was proving elusive and all the rentals I could find online already had bookings. Not for the entire ninety days we planned to be there, but a week here, a couple of days there. Just enough to make them unavailable for our purposes. Plus, the rates were surprisingly expensive. "North American prices," I said, "geared to cold-weather escapees prepared to splurge on a luxurious vacation house—not long-stay travelers like us."

I gazed at the view, taking in the red-tiled roofs, towering mountains, and shimmering lake. "This will be tough to beat," I said. "Finding a comfortable rental on our budget might not be so easy elsewhere."

Hank shrugged as if these things couldn't be helped, then rose and walked over to the table to take a swig from my water bottle.

"Maybe we should do what we did when we first came here," he said, setting down the bottle. "Book a hotel for a week and start the search once we're in Granada. Or we could live in a hotel," he called over his shoulder before disappearing into the house.

It wasn't entirely an unreasonable idea. I'd noticed an inviting boutique hotel on Facebook—a restored colonial mansion with six guest rooms, courtyard gardens, a swimming pool, and a spa. *What the heck?* I grabbed my phone and dashed off an email to the hotel manager asking if they would consider an extended stay.

• • •

The next morning, I stayed in bed while Hank worked out. Later, I joined him in the kitchen for our latest addiction: a mango smoothie with creamy yogurt and local honey. As the blender whirred, I picked up my iPhone and was reading the day's news headlines—142 Killed in Syria, Obama and Lawmakers Reach Debt Deal; Mexican Federal Police Arrest Cartel Boss, J Lo Marriage Collapses—when a Facebook Messenger alert flashed across the screen. I tapped open the message and read in stunned silence.

Dear Mrs. Barone,

Thank you for your interest in our hotel. Our guest rooms are beautifully outfitted but do not have cooking facilities or a refrigerator, though our on-site kitchen does. If these issues aren't a problem, we're in business, and I can offer you a substantial extended-stay discount if you decide to stay with us.

The hotel also has a private island in the 365 Isletas of Granada with an open-air house, flowering trees, a billiard table, sofas, and hammocks. If you were to stay with us, I could make the island available to you as a beautiful place to write.

Additionally, we promote responsible tourism by donating half of all hotel revenue to a local charitable organization that offers young people personal, educational, and healthcare programs and serves free meals to children and community members of little means.

Whether you end up staying with us at the hotel or not, please don't hesitate to contact me if you need anything while you're here.

Sincerely,

Natalie Hayes

I gazed at my phone and then up at Hank, pouring our breakfast smoothies into two hand-blown glasses. He handed me mine. "Here," I said, giving him the phone. "Check this out."

Even for seasoned travelers like us, to commit to living in a hotel room, sight unseen, for three months was a leap. I couldn't imagine what Hank was thinking.

He sat down and read the email.

"Sounds great," he said. "What do you think?"

"Um. I think it sounds amazing!"

6

Past and Present

Nicaragua

I can't remember at what age I first became aware of tragedies and triumphs beyond my own domain, but from the time I was a little girl, and well after I should've known better, I remained blind to much of the world.

Ours was not one of those families discussing world news, politics, or literature around the dinner table. Schoolwork, music lessons, and social activities were more the standard of the day in my sheltered suburban sphere, where friends in our Newark, Delaware, neighborhood were more or less like us.

The third of four children, I was not the smartest or prettiest, or even the best-intentioned. And yet, I'd managed to do what was expected of me for much of my life. I kept out of trouble, earned a college degree, and went on to support myself.

But just past midnight on December 23, 1972, when a cataclysmic earthquake obliterated Managua, Nicaragua, I was still a ponytailed nine-year-old asleep in a canopied bed. Six thousand Nicaraguans died that night, 20,000 others were injured, and over 250,000 were left homeless. Yet, as far as I can recall, there was no mention of the disaster in my home.

I imagine now that talk of the catastrophe would've made it to the card table of my parents' bridge club or around the water cooler at the chemical company where my father worked. But none of it trickled down to the level of childhood isolation where I resided.

Surely you would think that by my first year in college, as I cast my first-ever vote in the 1981 elections, I would have caught the scent of the greater world and the violence erupting in Central America. Surely you'd think that after Hank and I arrived in Nicaragua in 2000, I would've known that Nicaragua had been at peace for a decade. You would be wrong. Travel still had—and has—a lot to teach me. As Gloria Steinem once said, we learn the most where we know the least.

I didn't know that first trip in 2000 would inspire three more visits to Nicaragua over the next decade. And I certainly didn't guess that in 2011, on a balmy Tuesday morning in Mexico, it would lead us to make the arguably unreasonable decision to move into a hotel that sounded too good to be true.

• • •

What if it's nothing like we imagine? I pondered this possibility one afternoon as I walked in the hills above Ajijic. In the month since we'd emailed off an impulsive *Let's do it!* to the hotel manager in Granada, an edge of doubt chilled my optimism like the cool October mornings we now awakened to.

What if we feel isolated and cut off from the local community in the hotel? How will we build meaningful relationships? What if the whole idea, which seems glamorous now, doesn't fit us at all?

I was in the midst of this worry-fest when I skidded on some loose gravel and nearly lost my footing. As I noticed the beauty surrounding me—the vast sweep of indigo sky, rolling green ridgelines, and shimmering lake below—it dawned on me I was an idiot to imagine trouble rather than the possibility of something extraordinary. I laughed it off and headed back.

Three weeks later, Hank and I boarded a plane for Nicaragua. At the airport in Managua, our friend Adriana greeted us. Adriana was a thirty-four-year-old repatriated Nicaraguan we'd met on that first trip eleven years earlier. Like many of her generation, Adriana spent part of her childhood in exile in the United States when her family fled the Sandinista revolution that overthrew dictator Anastasio Somoza and then the savage civil war that raged in Nicaragua throughout the 1980s. After the 1990 elections, when the Sandinista regime was voted out of power by a nation desperate to end the war, Adriana's family and many Nicaraguan refugees returned home.

"Papa Hank!" Adrinana shouted, rushing across the International Arrivals terminal to envelop him in a fierce hug. A mischievous, five-foot bundle of spunk and enthusiasm, Adriana is one of those rare people who make you feel like family the instant she meets you. She'd always had a special relationship with Hank, like the favorite daughter who gets all his jokes and sees straight through to his soul.

There were more warm embraces, a few minutes of wheeling our luggage out to her SUV, and then news of Adriana's husband and baby daughter, whom we looked forward to meeting later in the week when they would come for a swim in the hotel pool.

On the hour-long drive to Granada, we caught glimpses of a Nicaragua we fondly remembered: Gracious women with colorful bundles perched atop their heads. Roadside stands overflowing with a colorful bounty of tropical fruits, bright pink *pitahaya,* hairy red *mamón,* and green-skinned plantains. The verdant quilt of fertile plots and gently sloping mountains. Cloud-fringed volcanoes and terra-cotta rooftops.

But the pieced-together shacks we passed and the children we saw in the streets hustling packets of chewing gum instead of attending school told another story, one of broken promises, social injustice, and the legacy of a complicated history. A story that made me want to keep my heart wide open to Nicaragua—seeing it not as a stereotype or statistic, or how I wanted or needed it to be, but as a home.

I had no idea then how difficult that would be.

Soon, Adriana rounded Granada's bustling central plaza with its historic buildings painted in faded pastel colors and horse-drawn carriages. Two blocks later, she parked alongside an unassuming blue building. The doorman was already out and unloading our bags when we were greeted on the sidewalk with a cheery hello from Natalie Hayes, the hotel manager whose enticing email was behind this crazy scheme.

"Ellen and Hank, how wonderful to finally meet you," she said. "Welcome to Hotel La Bocona. We hope you'll like it here."

We hugged Adriana goodbye, confirming plans for her to return at the weekend with her family. Then, we followed Natalie through a small lobby to a courtyard garden of the beautifully restored nineteenth century mansion with soaring ceilings and hand-painted tile floors into our room. I stood there staring at a palatial 1,400-square-foot suite with a canopied king-sized bed and antique dining table with seating for eight, and thought, for the umpteenth time since choosing to wander, about how random and unexpected life is when you don't have a plan.

• • •

We unpacked, placed our few belongings in the room's two antique wardrobes, and prepared to go out for a stroll and a bite to eat.

Natalie suggested the Garden Café and sketched a rough map on a page in my pocket journal. A little after four o'clock, we stepped out onto Calle La Libertad and into the thick of a lively Granada afternoon.

The street swarmed with horses, scooters, motorbikes, cars, and taxis. Women in colorful dresses and frilly lace aprons broadcast their merchandise in a singsong sales pitch that I couldn't quite decipher. Men sold shaved ice from pushcarts. Small clusters of giggling girls in matching school uniforms crowded the checkered tile sidewalks, and rowdy teenage boys rode past balanced double, even triple, on their bicycles. The air was thick and steamy with a faint whiff of breeze off Lake Nicaragua, the enormous freshwater sea at the city's far edge. After one block, we both were shiny with sweat.

"I'd forgotten how hot it is here," I said. Hank gave me a quick look, one eyebrow raised, and suggested we skip the walk and head for food.

I consulted Natalie's map, and we crossed Central Park, continuing down Calle La Libertad for another block until we spotted the Garden Café on the corner. Brightly painted in pomegranate red with a chalkboard menu propped against potted palms, the café looked, from the outside, like our kind of place. When we stepped inside, we saw walls of overstuffed bookshelves, cozy reading nooks, simple wood tables with friends sharing a beer, couples chatting, and young people with earbuds and iPods dozing in garden hammocks. I suspected it would become a favorite. After one refreshing sip of pineapple, coconut, and lime smoothie, I knew it already had.

• • •

That first night, I woke up at three a.m. to an explosion of firecrackers, the signal in Latin America of a celebration. I wondered if there was an important Nicaraguan holiday or religious observance going on and climbed out from under the bed's mosquito netting, slipped into a hotel robe, padded barefoot across the suite, and stepped out into the open-air courtyard with the hope of seeing the night sky illuminated with fireworks. But there was only a narrow crescent moon hanging in a swath of silvery clouds.

The fireworks had gone silent, replaced by a chirping chorus of geckos that scurried to hide behind the large canvases of abstract art hung throughout the hotel. Gradually, my eyes adjusted to the faint moonlight and took in the green thicket of bougainvillea, poinsettia, hibiscus, and palms in the courtyard garden. I wandered beneath the wide overhanging roof that sheltered the courtyard terraces. With the pleasant feel of cool tile beneath my bare feet, I paused to study the paintings with their textured swirls of earthy red, yellow, and deep purple. There was a surprisingly complementary relationship between the antique mansion with its graceful stone arches and wood-beamed cane ceilings and the modern austerity of the unframed canvases.

At some point, I settled into one of the wicker chairs that formed a cozy seating cluster on the veranda outside our room. Something floral tinged the warm breeze. I sat beneath the night sky and felt a stinging rush of melancholy as I tried to reconcile the beauty and comfort of this haven with the outer reality of Nicaragua's staggering poverty.

7

Settling In

The first week of November 2011 brought my forty-eighth birthday and national elections in Nicaragua. A glut of giant pink billboards showing a smiling President Daniel Ortega waving to voters amid fluorescent promises of love, peace, and solidarity appeared everywhere. Campaign slogans were spray-painted on walls and pasted to utility poles that proclaimed VIVA DANIEL!

I remarked on the propaganda and the apparent lack of opposition one morning to Arlen, our Spanish tutor. In her late twenties, an attentive and earnest Nicaraguan, Arlen was a freelance teacher who tutored foreign language students and helped Natalie's son with his Canadian correspondence courses.

Arlen and I sat beside one another at an elegant banquet table in the hotel, where she came to help us improve our Spanish, working two mornings with Hank on an advanced refresher course and the remaining three with me focusing on the basics.

"Some people say that Daniel stole the 2006 elections," Arlen said after I remarked about the campaign placards. She spoke slowly in Spanish. Her tone was contemplative, and it felt like she chose her words with great care.

"Some think that he shouldn't be able to be elected for the third time when the Nicaraguan Constitution specifically prohibits presidents from consecutive re-election and from serving more than two terms despite the recent Supreme Court ruling that allows it. *Entiendes?"* Her intelligent brown eyes locked on mine.

"Si, más o menos" (more or less), I said, somewhat surprised by the depth and directness of her response.

Switching to English, she continued. "Living through war is horrible. I was born into it. It was a tough time."

I knew from previous visits about the revolutionary war that ended the iron-fisted dictatorship of Anastasio Somoza, about the Contras, counterrevolutionaries illegally backed and armed by the Reagan administration, and the 30,000 people killed. I knew people fought hoping for a better life, how most of those hopes died in the decade of fighting that followed, and how it drove the country to financial ruin.

We drank coffee and sat quietly. The garden courtyard just beyond the table smelled of the morning's fresh, damp earth. "People want peace," Arlen said, breaking the silence. "The scars of war are still too fresh. Change was needed, and the Sandinistas had good intentions. But war and politics have gotten in the way. Now people just want to have enough to provide for their families."

Later that night, I lay awake in bed, unable to sleep. I kept thinking about Arlen. *What was her life like? Where did she learn English? Was she able to see me as an individual beyond politics and stereotypes?*

I thought about how she gave the impression of great compassion and wisdom. How her kind eyes and tidy appearance conveyed a quiet dignity, and how the horrors of war and her personal experiences seemed to have stimulated her intellect and imbued her with extraordinary grace and a generous spirit.

• • •

On the eve of the election, Hank and I celebrated my birthday over dinner at Restaurante El Zaguán with Tina, a Canadian friend passing through Granada, and Robyn, a fellow hotel guest. Tina was in Nicaragua leading an adventure travel tour. The conversation was lively with Tina's tales of her previous week's coast-to-coast bike tour across Costa Rica. She showed us some photos on her phone. Then the conversation turned to what we were reading. I'd recently picked up a secondhand copy of the book *A Fortune-Teller Told Me: Earthbound Travels in the Far East*, an intriguing travelog by the Italian journalist Tiziano Terzani about a year in 1993 spent traveling across Asia without flying after a Chinese fortune teller told Terzani that if he traveled by air during that year, he would be killed. As he went, he visited fortune-tellers, astrologers, and shamans. The book was a new favorite, and to my surprise, Tina was familiar with it. She looked at me across her grilled tilapia and asked if I'd ever had my fortune told. "You should do it. I've had some pretty powerful readings."

I wasn't exactly sure what to say, so I ordered dessert—*arroz con leche*, a creamy, sweet, vanilla-scented rice pudding—and the conversation seamlessly shifted to Robyn and the online flash sale that had landed her in Nicaragua. We worked our way through dessert and coffee and finished the evening on a convivial tide of goodwill. As we walked back to the hotel, though, I couldn't seem to shake the feeling that there was something vaguely significant in Tina's offhanded recommendation of fortune-tellers.

Back at La Bocona, Hank headed to our room to relax and read, but Robyn and I stayed up talking. The moon was big and bright, not a cloud in sight. It still surprised me to look up from the inside courtyard and see the open sky.

Six years younger than me, Robyn was a laugher, and her good cheer was contagious. We giggled, remembering the bossy American real estate agent who'd marched us across town yesterday on a poorly disguised sales pitch of expensive Granada homes rather than the purported historical walking tour we'd paid for.

"Come on. Keep up. I have an appointment in forty-five minutes!" Robyn barked in a pitch-perfect imitation of the pushy agent. We hooted and tossed back our heads in laughter.

Between jobs, Robyn had arrived at La Bocona a week earlier with her husband Simon to escape a dismal New Jersey winter. At our invitation, the congenial couple had swiftly fallen into the daily habit of joining Hank and me at breakfast or in the cluster of chairs outside our room to swap stories and share the details of their explorations. We'd quickly bonded with the friendly pair in the easy way of travelers.

"Did Simon get home okay?" I asked Robyn as we sat down in the familiar seating cluster. She nodded yes and kicked off her sandals, sprawling her tall, willowy body across a short sofa, her toned brown legs and flowered sundress draping over its end. "He sent a text during dinner," she said, gazing up at the stars. "No problems."

We'd said goodbye to Simon that morning as he'd climbed into a taxi headed for the airport and a flight home to keep a long-ago scheduled appointment for minor eye surgery. When Robyn mentioned a delay in processing the paperwork for her new job meant she was unexpectedly free, we'd convinced her to stay. Though, as my gaze settled on her relaxed form and the mischievous smile on her face, I was fairly certain she hadn't required any convincing. "Silly man," she said. We both laughed.

I'd been savoring Robyn's company, grateful for the laughter and female companionship, and was glad she'd stayed on. Over the past week, I'd learned enough of the details of her life to be in awe. She'd left Jamaica, her country of birth, for the United States at age seventeen, put herself through medical school as a single mother, survived cancer, and moved her elderly mother in to live with her and Simon. Courageous. Smart. Devoted. Being in her company felt like a gift—a twenty-one-day gift until she returned home.

8

Unnerved and Uncertain

One evening, not long after Robyn left, Hank found me alone in the hotel kitchen. The day staff, Ofelia, Marisol, and Natalia had gone home. Only Gustavo, a young concierge, and Louis, the night watchman, were on duty. I was busy snarfing down potato chips from a Pringles can and didn't notice that Hank had come in. He leaned against the stainless-steel counter and stared at me with unusual scrutiny.

"What?" I said, washing down the chips with a swig of Coke. He watched me for a bit longer but said nothing.

"What?" I asked again, tipping the half-empty can in his direction in an invitation to join me.

He shook his head no and said, "Well, whenever you binge on junk food, it usually means you're anxious about something. Talk to me."

We walked out to Natalie's garden table and sat there in the near dark, watching the evening light disappear into the black night. I paused momentarily, reaching for the Pringles can, unsure if I was ready to confess how uncomfortable and out of place I felt.

"I'm embarrassed," I said. "You'll think I'm crazy and judgmental."

"More than usual?" he smiled.

I chuckled, grateful for Hank's ability to make me laugh at myself, then fell silent again.

"No, seriously," he said. "Tell me what's up. It always helps when we talk."

"Well, it's difficult to explain. It's just that the more time we spend here, the less I like it, and I hate that about myself."

"What's changed? You loved it here before."

I felt him studying me in the dark.

"That's the problem," I said. "What I remember most about Nicaragua, beyond its natural beauty, is how kind-hearted people were, how the country seemed to pulsate with warmth and grace. Right?"

"Yes. That's what I remember, too."

"And I recall Nicaraguans as trusting, honest and helpful—the real spirit and charm of the place."

"Sounds right. Go on."

"Well, it's weird, but it feels different now. People seem different. More exploitive. Less genuine."

"Really? That surprises me. Take Ofelia, Marisol, and Natalia, for instance. They couldn't be kinder or more helpful."

"I know. It's true. Adriana and Arlen, too," I said. "So, maybe it's me who is different—perhaps I am more suspicious and less trusting. But why?" *What was wrong with me? Was this trip a mistake? Where was the adventurous spirit with which I'd seen so much good and possibility?* I didn't feel even a whisper of it stirring in me now.

Neither of us spoke for a long time. I was feeling heavy-hearted and dispirited.

"It's odd," I said finally, breaking the silence. "I thought I'd love being back after all those years of returning for brief visits, always leaving wanting more—but I haven't."

As I spoke, Hank held me in his gaze, unwavering. I looked away to the courtyard with its bubbling fountain, waters glistening in the low light, and then met his eyes and tried to explain.

"Somehow, beyond Granada's picturesque facades and brightly painted barrios, I sense an underlying tension with everyday experiences casting me as an interloper—the children who point to empty tummies and grab our wrists, asking for money wherever we go. The machismo catcalls in the streets. The beggars and touts who eye me like a walking ATM. It isn't just the color of my skin or that my body is puffy from too much food or my obvious foreignness: it's as if people can see the uncertainty I carry. The way I avert my eyes. The way I try to shrink and disappear."

I hoped he would understand, but all I saw was confusion on his face. I tried again to explain.

"When we first visited Granada, I remember how we'd breezed in with the small press group. How I'd climbed out of the air-conditioned van with you and the others, all of us with cameras slung across our chests, my shutter clicking, my curiosity buzzing, my place in the world secure and unquestioned. Now, I feel like an impostor—no longer a tourist but still an outsider. Then, there is the fact that we live in a hotel with no home to return to. Is this really our life?"

The moon rose, almost full above the garden courtyard. In the pale light, a flicker of a smile breached his confused look.

"Never fear," he said, rising to leave. "Hank is here."

Despite Hank's familiar reassurance, Granada unsettled me more than I wanted to admit. While the decision to wander wasn't out of character for us, it did, at least for me, feel overwhelming in a way I hadn't expected or remembered feeling before. Perhaps it was because life had been comfortable the past few years in New Mexico, ticking along at a creative clip supported by good friends in a beautiful part of the world. Then life shifted, like tectonic plates, causing the upheaval that had sent us packing with bulging suitcases and comfortable shoes for the unknown and its heady promise of freedom and adventure. And now, to Nicaragua, a place like nowhere else. A place of beauty and poverty and wooden funeral hearses pulled by lace-covered horses, where layer upon layer of life and history resided in vivid Technicolor complexity and questions about justice, morality, happiness, and displacement shoved me up against myself. It was my first glimpse of how little I understood—and how much I needed to learn.

In Ajijic, I'd grown accustomed to feeling like a welcomed guest at a warm and boisterous celebration. The cheery exchange of hellos in the street. The colorful cut-paper streamers fluttering in the breeze. The peppy ranchera music. It gave me a surge of confidence and contentment, during which I'd walked miles each day, learned the names of the neighborhood children who played in the street outside the house, and met up with friends at the plaza for conversation and coffee.

In Nicaragua, however, I felt unexpectedly unnerved and uncertain. Not always, but again and again.

I appeared no different to Arlen and the hotel staff: cheerful and easygoing, a speaker of Spanglish, and the grateful recipient of Ofelia's morning coffee delivery. And though I'd traded jeans for a tropical uniform of sundresses sewn by a local seamstress, I still looked the same. But in truth, I no longer felt like myself. My world had subtly narrowed, depending on the resolve I could summon to make peace with the reality outside our door. Some days I was crippled by cowardice and insecurity, choosing to lose myself in books, work, and distraction rather than exploration. *Perhaps I'm not the adventurous traveler I like to think I am.*

• • •

Somehow, Arlen saw what I needed without my asking and quietly assigned herself to be my cultural guide.

"Come on," she said one morning. "Let's go out. I want you to see what's special about my country."

She moved our Spanish lessons into Granada's bustling streets. She took me shopping and to her home to cook *gallo pinto,* a traditional dish made with rice and beans. Another day, we purchased a pirated DVD of the movie *The Help* dubbed in Spanish from the market and watched it at the hotel. We cried and laughed through it together and analyzed its message within the context of Nicaraguan class divisions. She introduced us to her family and had me read Nicaraguan poetry. Arlen didn't so much tutor us as immerse us in her life, and our hearts swelled with gratitude for her kindness.

During these outings, I realized there are many forms of travel. For years, Hank and I had parachuted into cultures on brief international trips, spending a week or two in a place, sometimes returning repeatedly, as we had with Nicaragua. We'd learn its history, politics, and geographies, visit its iconic landmarks, ask questions, meet people, and form opinions. But I was beginning to understand that this nomadic experiment was about a different kind of exploration—more internal than external. In Granada, a deeper way of engaging with the world was emerging. One that included immersing myself in painful truths.

9

The Big Bitch

The thing about living in another culture—or hanging around long enough to dig into its messy inner issues—is that it forces you to face your own. What Nicaragua offered was a choice, though not a simple one. Could I give my heart to it, even if I felt inept and uneasy? It was a question I didn't have an answer to, but I knew I had to find a degree of trust. So I got busy plotting how to playfully haggle with the market vendors. I got in the habit of not leaving the hotel without putting money in a pocket for those in need. And I learned how to ignore the catcalls with the air of neutral indifference that the local women displayed.

Sometimes it worked. I could look into the vendor's eyes with a friendly smile when they quoted me an outrageous cost for bananas or avocados and pay them a fair price—slightly more than a local would pay but less than the gringo rate. And I'd be rewarded with a knowing smile back. I'd stop in the park to buy ice cream for a few kids, along with one for myself, and enjoy the resulting giggles and glee more than the cold treat itself. Or, I'd buy a trinket from a street vendor I didn't need just because I could and should.

Other times, though, when someone approached to ask for money or to sell me something, I'd recoil with an aggressive shake of my head, thinking I'd already given enough, bought enough, been hassled enough, and then retreat, eyes down, to the haven of La Bocona.

"How do you handle it?" I asked Natalie one afternoon after skulking back to the hotel trailed by an aggressive man demanding more money than I'd already given him.

"Look, don't worry about it," she said. "Once you've lived here a while, it just stops. Maybe they recognize that you belong, or perhaps it's just a vibe you give off, but trust me, one day, you'll notice that it doesn't happen anymore. It helps, too," she added as an afterthought, "to consider that kindness is often viewed as a weakness in this culture."

I waited a minute, thinking she might say more. She didn't. But the concept—of kindness as weakness—nagged at me. It was hard to explain, but somehow it confirmed my discontent.

When I was not anxious—God forgive me—I was lonely. I would recall the creative vibe of Ute's studio, Spanish practice with Elena María, or the sound of Robyn's contagious laugh and feel a deep longing for friendship. Sometimes travel feels that way.

I don't think I ever doubted our decision to wander, but I had fears.

Mostly, I was confused. How could I live each day in a place where people perceived being kind as a weakness?

What does that even mean? When did life become so messy and complicated?

Of course, life's messy and complicated issues had always been right in front of me while I'd bumbled along, too blinded by denial and dumb luck to notice. I wasn't entirely clueless, but I'd always believed I could steer myself out of problems through sheer goodwill. But that presumed I was aware of my feelings.

Later on, it would occur to me that my experiences in Granada mirrored my internal state at the time. Leaving the hotel each day to return overwhelmed, doubt creeping in during fretful nights left me feeling unsettled and vulnerable. However, I didn't understand that straight away. So, I continued to see Nicaragua through the muddied lens of my distortions, attributing sinister motives to things that were part of the country itself and made it what it is, something that, on previous visits, had appeared benign or even charming.

"It's a tradition bred from distrust," I informed Hank one evening after walking past an elderly couple seated in rattan rocking chairs and chatting with neighbors on the sidewalk in front of their house, an evening custom enjoyed across Nicaragua.

"By sitting outside," I explained, "they don't have to invite people into their homes where they might see their possessions."

"It's the same reason," I continued, "that stores, even the tiniest mom-and-pop *tiendas*, keep their goods behind a counter or in locked cases—because Nicaraguans don't trust one another."

Hank looked at me hard, and I realized, with a jolt, there was righteous fury in my voice.

"That's one interpretation," he said after a pause, giving me a long, level gaze.

It was in this frame of mind I decided we needed a getaway.

• • •

The remote ecolodge, an hour's drive from Granada, was a haven of silence compared to the city with its tolling bells, high-volume music, tooting car horns, and exploding fireworks that had been booming for days in boisterous preparation for the upcoming Christmas and New Year celebrations. Yet I tried not to be alarmed as I skidded down a steep, narrow path behind the teenage nephew of the lodge owner, staring at a pistol sticking out of the back of his low-rise Levi's.

I had hoped to find relief from my paranoia in the countryside, not an armed escort in the form of a boy whose macho idea of protection could potentially escalate a perceived or actual threat into a violent one. *Was it even legal for a teen to carry a gun?* The thought of being a foreigner involved in a shooting with an unlicensed youth made me mildly hysterical.

"Better not go alone. Manuel will go with you," the lodge owner had said in a tone that left no room for wiggling when I inquired about a hike at breakfast that morning. Now, it took all I had to shake off my anxiety and keep it together as my imagination ran wild. *Had there been trouble here before? Did the locals resent the new lodge and, in turn, its foreign guests? What could justify taking a gun on a nature hike? Were there jaguars or narcos hiding in these hills?*

My relief was palpable ninety minutes later when Manuel nodded a silent goodbye, and we'd returned to the lodge without incident. For the remainder of our stay, I passed on any more wilderness hikes, opting to follow Hank's lead and enjoy the views of tangled jungle, smoldering volcano, and glistening lake from the safe perch of the hilltop lodge. Soon, the subtle sounds of nature—the screech of a passing flock of parrots, the distinct trill of a kingfisher, the cheery chirps of geckos, and the gentle rustle of palm fronds and giant Guanacaste trees—began to reveal themselves and drown out my mind's fear-mongering chatter.

It helped, too, that additional guests had arrived. A young married couple from Chicago: him a stocky fireman, her a sexy Brazilian school teacher. Along with a friend of the owner, a kindhearted El Salvadoran man living in Miami. At dinner that night, over homemade *nacatamales* (banana leaves stuffed with cornmeal, pork, potato and onion), *flan de caramelo,* and *Flor de Caña* rum, the conversation was riveting as the newcomers spun out the tales of their lives. The pleasures and challenges of forging new beginnings in the foreign language and culture of the United States. The ruins of war in El Salvador, the grief, the displaced families, the complex politics and problems of the struggling nation. Within the laughter, wisdom, and adversities of strangers, I found the unexpected reassurance of commonality and began to relax.

For the next forty-eight hours, Hank and I padded between pool and hammock, drifting around in companionable silence, not unlike the blue morpho butterflies the size of dinner plates that fluttered about the gardens. We napped and read, ate and laughed, existing in the lazy hours of vacation time when time stalls and slips away and the worries of conventional life feel as distant as Mars.

"So, is the Big Bitch gone?" Hank asked as we crawled into bed on the final night of our stay, the night air thick with a chorus of insects, tree frogs, and jungle creatures. In the moonlight, I could see the faintest smile flicker across his face as I curled into his open arms, tucking my forehead into the familiar soft fold of his neck. I laughed, even as I winced at the thought of the desolate and dark cloud that had hung over me during much of our time in Granada, no matter how much I tried to suppress it.

Years ago, Hank bought me a T-shirt that read: I used to be schizophrenic, but we're just fine now. As the shirt suggests, we joke there's more than one Ellen in this marriage. Ellen The Student who spends her days reading, learning, studying, and gathering information. Ellen The Fearful, who lurches between flailing and failing and is afraid to trust in her instincts and abilities. And Ellen The Observer, who watches it all from the sidelines and sometimes offers guidance, reassurance, and encouragement with great sweetness. Other times her words are vicious or filled with blame. Then there's Good Ellen, Bad Ellen, Defensive Ellen, Vain Ellen, and Ellen the Big Bitch, code for those times when I just can't find a way back to myself.

I thought back over the past few days—the way leisure and nature and the easy friendship of travelers had blunted my feelings of disconnection—and with relief, discovered that, yes, the edge of toxic judgment that had infected my thoughts in Granada was silent. I'd found my way back to the feelings of kindness and tender-hearted humanity my soul ached for. The Big Bitch was gone.

10

Welcome Home

"*¡Bienvenido a casa! Nos hiciste falta.*" Ofelia said in greeting when we returned to La Bocona the next day as she warmly embraced us.

I could guess by the tone of the good-natured exchange that she was welcoming us back. But I wanted to improve my Spanish, so as we unpacked our swimsuits and shorts and placed them in a laundry sack, I asked Hank to tell me exactly what she'd said.

"She said: Welcome home. We lacked without you," Hank told me.

"Really? She said lacked?" Affection welled up inside, intense and unexpected. I wanted to find Ofelia and tell her how much we appreciated her and that she'd managed to pierce my stone heart with her thoughtfulness and grace. I couldn't, though, not only because I didn't know how to say all that in Spanish but also because, like Arlen, Ofelia carried herself with a quiet dignity that eschewed such brash emotional displays.

"Don't make a big deal out of it," Hank said, reading my mind. "She was just welcoming us home."

Home.

I suddenly had an idea that the word was far bigger than I'd ever imagined, even if I didn't quite know what that meant.

In the course of our travels, I'd found myself thinking *I could live here* so often over the years that it had become an inside joke, with Hank betting on how long it would take for me to declare it and begin imagining us living in the places we visited. The mental image of us settling down permanently, foraging in local markets, decorating a home abroad with native handicrafts and textiles, and lingering over morning coffee in neighborhood cafés didn't seem remotely imaginary.

What did seem unreal was to equate Hotel La Bocona with home. Yet, for the first time, I could feel the idea of it taking hold.

For a while, the hotel offered sanctuary. But could a life of travel ever supplant one more steadfastly rooted?

• • •

A few weeks later, as Arlen and I climbed the twisting, narrow stairs of the Iglesia Merced bell tower, she asked: "When will you and Hank return home?"

Home.

There it was again.

I pulled my camera out of my purse and told her we didn't know.

The view from La Merced church tower is one of Granada's most picturesque—red tile rooftops, green garden courtyards, the canary-yellow cathedral, and, in the distance, the hazy blue edge of Lake Nicaragua. Below, a tangle of crisscrossed utility wires, cars and bicycles, and horse-drawn carriages rolled past turquoise, red, and yellow buildings as pedestrians navigated crumbling sidewalks.

A puff of cool lake breeze billowed through the tower's open arches, reminding me that it was January, Nicaragua's coldest month, though still sandals-and-sundress weather for *Norteamericanos* like me. I moved around the tight space, photographing in every direction, attempting to control, frame, and portray Granada from a position—I suddenly perceived—as detached and distant from its thumping heart as I'd held myself these past three months.

Arlen leaned against the tower's thick adobe wall and watched me work. With my eye pressed to the viewfinder and the shutter clicking, I explained how Hank and I still had extended stays in Ecuador and Peru planned and that we'd be away for at least another six months.

After a while, she said: "That's a long time." There was sadness in her voice. Confusion, perhaps. I couldn't tell.

Arlen wasn't alone in wondering when we would return to the United States. During a Skype call, my mom had asked nearly the same question earlier that week.

"When are you coming home?" she'd asked. And a surge of memory, like a sudden tide, flooded through me from a time when Hank and I had stayed with my parents before we'd parked our six-year-old Corolla in their gravel driveway in Delaware and left for Latin America with vague promises to return for it in a year, or so. That eight months had passed since then took me by surprise.

"You should've seen the elegant outfits your mother used to sew," Dad said one afternoon during our visit. "Phyllis," he continued, show Ellen and Hank the photograph of you in the dress and overcoat you made for our honeymoon."

There had been pride in his voice and a tenderness that didn't fit the picture I had of my parents' marriage.

My God. He loves her. After all the kids and responsibilities, arguments, and decades, he still loves her!

This was the surprising thought that had flashed across my mind as my mother padded out of the room, unsteady on feet swollen and sore with neuropathic pain, searching for a photograph taken nearly sixty years earlier.

In her late seventies—short and round, with silver hair that used to be blonde, my mother was, and still is, an intelligent woman. She'd stayed active in her church and community, and age had emboldened her. But in my youth, she'd often been overwhelmed by her role as a mother and housewife, and her anxiety had cast a shadow of insecurity over my upbringing.

Only recently had I realized that her anxiety rose from unconfronted fear. Fear that her well-being depended on people and circumstances beyond her control. Fear that she wasn't living up to familial and societal expectations. Fears I now understood.

Seated on the red checkered sofa in the family room of the suburban home of my childhood and where my parents still lived, I'd studied Dad as he reclined in his favorite La-Z-Boy chair and saw the picture-window view of the springtime landscape of my youth—lush green pine trees and flowering dogwoods, azaleas, and rhododendron. Dad wore khaki pants cinched at a shrinking diabetic waist, a striped button-down shirt, and the sturdy brown walking shoes that had replaced the slick-soled leather loafers he'd been wearing when a slip in the yard had broken his neck two years earlier. His glasses looked bigger than I'd remembered, and, like my mother's, his pale blue eyes were almost as faded as his white hair.

I tried to reconcile this gentle and vulnerable man with the often tense and turbulent father of my memories. A man up to his neck in responsibility, strapped and strained beneath the demands of an anxious wife, four kids, and a mortgage. And I was startled to recognize that I'd often experienced similar turbulence in myself and my relationships.

More than three decades had passed since I'd left my childhood home for college and a career, and I saw very little of my family for many of those years. But I'd been thinking about family a lot lately. I'd been thinking about what an erratic and absent daughter and sister I'd been. How I'd once believed I could escape their anger, judgment, and dysfunction, only to discover that I carried the weight of it with me. And how, even now, in middle age, when I'm old enough to know better, I still pitch back and forth between affection and exasperation with my family in ways I don't with other people.

Years later, I am still figuring out what that means and how to accept that ambiguity within myself and reckon it with the ways it might find expression in my relationships with family. I know I want to be more present with my family, gentler, lighter, more searching, and attentive, though I suspect there would never be a point in my life when I wouldn't prefer to do it from a distance.

But on that bright, balmy day with Arlen, who seemed to soften me for others, I believed I might possess the capacity to live and love wholeheartedly within that paradox.

The thought left me with a glorious, emboldened feeling that lasted about halfway through our walk back to the hotel, the amount of time it took me to remember the Ram Dass quote: *If you think you are truly enlightened, go spend a weekend with your parents.*

Suddenly, I let loose a laugh on the pot-holed sidewalk as people and traffic streamed by. A teenage girl in a bedazzled Michael Jackson tank top nervously linked arms with her companion as the pair skirted around the crazy *gringa*.

I was as startled by my outburst as anyone—possibly more. For a second, it looked like Arlen would ask me to explain, but the look in my eyes must've told her something, and soon she was laughing harder than I was. We saturated the air with the crackle of our giggles all the way back to La Bocona.

11

Reptiles, Preservation, and Paparazzi

Ecuador

The following Sunday, Hank and I caught a flight from Nicaragua to Ecuador. A week later, we bobbed aboard a small ship in the Galapagos Islands. Our time in Granada, and its emotional turbulence, felt like another life on another planet. Travel can do that. One week, you photograph from a bell tower in Nicaragua; the next, you're face-to-scaly-face with a lizard in the Galapagos Islands. Mind-boggling.

We'd joined a small group of adventurous travelers who also had crisscrossed continents to view the famed Galapagos wildlife and see the inspiration behind Darwin's theory of evolution. However, since Darwin published *On the Origin of Species* in 1859, the Galapagos Islands have become one of the world's most popular tourist attractions. Too popular. Earlier that month, the Galapagos National Park Service had instituted a new set of travel regulations designed to disperse boat traffic better and help protect the archipelago's unique ecosystems.

Our eight-day voyage aboard the twenty-passenger *MY Letty* put us among the first passengers to experience the new itineraries. This was precisely why I was onboard—to report on the new regulations and create imagery from the altered cruise itineraries. Whenever possible, Hank accompanied me on assignments. He helped with the photography and copy editing, and, like all good storytellers, he watched and listened for the real-life stories, anecdotes, settings, characters, and bits of dialogue that pepper engaging travel tales.

It was early February 2012, the rainy season in Ecuador's famed archipelago, a time of year when the alchemy of short bursts of daily rain and the hot equatorial sun transforms the otherwise parched islands into a blaze of color. Orange and yellow swaths of scrubby vegetation carpeted the islands, and male marine iguanas, usually a dull dark gray, boasted buff bodies emblazoned in shimmering shades of turquoise, red, and green in nature's attempt to impress the girls.

The islands were everything we imagined. The mix was amazing: Animals not found anywhere else. Iguanas that looked like mini-dragons and sneezed out salt. Snoozing sea lions, and coral pink flamingos. Wild creatures that could care less about our presence were everywhere we went. Sometimes we swam with penguins. Sometimes, dolphins played in the bow waves, and pirating frigate birds harassed and chased other birds, trying to steal their food or nesting materials. And, sometimes, blue-footed boobies danced for one another—and us.

There wasn't a day when something didn't blow me away. Maybe it was the scent of a palo santo tree after a rain, with its sweet aroma of pine, mint, and lemon, the iridescent red sheen of the Sally Lightfoot crabs skittering sideways atop the shoreline rocks. Or the serenity of an evening skiff tour through a mangrove stand. All I could do was look around and trust the feeling, trust that there's more to this world than we will ever understand.

Coming from Nicaragua, a country with a serious trash problem, the pristine condition of the islands was impressive. No floating plastic. No stray Cheetos bags tumbling across the beach. No mounds of discarded garbage. No rusting washing machines hidden away in weed-tangled ravines. Just pure raw wildness, up close and personal.

The new regulations were working. Rarely during the voyage did our shore explorations or snorkel adventures in prime wildlife zones coincide with other cruisers.

"There used to be a dozen boats at this site," said naturalist guide José Luis Castillo one afternoon as we'd anchored alone off Punta Suarez at Isla Española.

• • •

"Don't you need an assistant for your next gig?" someone joked one evening, as someone almost always did after they'd learned that my work as a travel writer and photographer regularly involved trip-of-a-lifetime experiences like this Galapagos cruise.

I thought about giving a light-hearted *it's-a-lot-more-work-than-it-looks-like* answer.

I thought about explaining that while they would enjoy a cold Pilsner and swap stories with fellow passengers at the end of a hot day in the equatorial sun, I would be in the cabin, bent over a laptop, downloading and meta-tagging images onto a hard drive, and then again to a backup drive.

Instead, I responded with a friendly chortle that seemed to satisfy.

But the interaction got me thinking about Susan Sontag's astute argument, which mirrored my growing suspicions that photography is *"an aesthetic consumerism, to which everyone is now addicted."* That vacation photographs are now meant *"to offer indisputable evidence that the trip was made, that the program was carried out, that fun was had."* That travel photography was a way of *"certifying experience"* ... but also *"a way of refusing it by limiting experience to the search for the photogenic, by converting experience into an image, a souvenir."*

I remembered the rush of excitement I'd felt thirteen years before when, for the first time, an editor had said yes to a story pitch and given a green light to join a small media tour in southern Utah to collect research and take photographs. I'd carefully packed my Lowepro camera bag with a dozen canisters of Fujichrome Velvia film and nervously stood with Hank in a hotel lobby that first morning as we'd chatted with the other photographers, all of us slinging dual SLR cameras with serious glass, my Moleskine notebook ready, our possibilities expanding, my spirit soaring.

In hindsight, I'm astonished at the unlikely way a handful of assignments snowballed into hundreds of adventures spanning the globe: A camel trek in the Moroccan Sahara. River cruises in Myanmar. Rafting the mighty Colorado River through the Grand Canyon. Cycling in Italy, walking in Provence, and much more. It now seemed like someone else's life, as if I'd been an actress playing their Cinderella story. And yet, as I stood on a rocky precipice in the Galapagos Islands, with the majesty of sea and sky, land and light, splayed before me in a hot tropical sunset, the ocean air strong and briny, it was impossible not to marvel at the fact that this was my life—my work.

For the first time, though, I was beginning to understand I'd been straddling two lives since we'd become itinerant—the life I'd lived and the life I wanted to live. And yet, I found it impossible to imagine the future.

If not this, then what?

An unsettling numbness had set in recently—that feeling you get when doing the work, but your spirit isn't in it. I no longer pitched stories with the fire and competitive zeal that had once fueled my career. I wasn't alone in this. I knew other freelancers were also stymied by the rapid-fire editorial turnover as magazines and newspapers attempted to adapt to the mysterious economics of online publishing.

But this wasn't just about work or the travel industry. I could feel a difference in myself. I didn't have a vocabulary yet for my feelings, but I was starting to think differently about success and accomplishment and what other people think.

I was mulling this over when a passenger blustered up beside me, a congenial Brit with a sharp eye for landscape photography and the crisp lenses and pro cameras to match it.

"Glorious view," he cheered. "Ah, but you must see beauty like this all the time with your job and all," he added absentmindedly, setting up a tripod.

The sun was low in the blue sky, and I squinted despite the Maui Jim sunglasses and the polarized lenses that saturated the turquoise waters stretching out to the horizon. I wondered how many times I had stood like this at the precipice of one of the world's natural wonders, at sunset, with spare camera batteries and a small notebook in my pocket, chatting with a fellow traveler. It must have been hundreds of times.

I glanced at *MY Letty* anchored in the distance and the passengers chatting animatedly around me, capturing memories with their smartphones, their lives and stories concealed. Each trip, each assignment, was a new experience. This was just one of the many extraordinary moments that shaped me as a photographer and a person.

Taking a deep breath, I raised the camera, feeling the weight of it in my hands. I adjusted the settings and carefully framed the beauty that unfolded before me. Each click of the shutter was already in the past. The future, unimaginable.

If not this, then what?

12

Starting Again at Starting Over

Ecuador

I opened the door to an empty refrigerator for the third time that day. It was a large stainless-steel model, as sleek and conventional and North American as the rest of the furnished three-bedroom, high-rise condominium we'd rented by email from an online listing in an English-language newsletter for Cuenca expats.

After the cruise, Hank and I relocated to Cuenca, Ecuador, a UNESCO World Heritage site nestled in the southern Andes—a new city for us but a place on our wander list for years. We'd chosen Cuenca for its reputation as a small historic city and cultural hub with a pleasant climate and made the twisting four-hour ride between the high Andean city and the Guayaquil airport via a private van service. From the gridlocked traffic of Guayaquil on Ecuador's Pacific coast, the route traveled a two-lane highway strewn with fallen rock and corkscrew switchbacks ascending into lush green cocoa and banana plantations and then the cloud-shrouded teak and bamboo forests of the Andean foothills, until the high stark landscape of Cajas National Park with its free-roaming alpacas and barren beauty about twenty miles west of Cuenca.

As I looked around the condominium kitchen, at its gleaming white marble floor, white IKEA-style cabinetry, and white swing door that opened into a laundry room with matching white LG appliances, it was obvious—the rental was comfortable but not a home.

Still, it was close to the Tomebamba River and within walking distance of a newly opened SuperMaxi grocery store, where we planned to solve the problem of the empty refrigerator.

After a stop in the building lobby to ask the doorman for directions, we exited onto Avenida Ordoñez Lasso, the busy four-lane boulevard that linked the upscale residential district to El Centro, Cuenca's historic center.

The sky was cloudy and gray with a threat of rain that made me glad I'd worn a jacket, but I wished I'd brought an umbrella. Yellow taxis, blue buses, shiny SUVs, and compact cars sped past as I stopped to scribble down the details of a nearby hair salon with a Facebook badge and phone number in the window. Across the street stood the Hotel Oro Verde, an upscale hotel and restaurant where we'd eaten most of our meals during the brief turnaround before the cruise. Beyond the hotel flowed the Rio Tombebamba, its banks lined with silver-hued eucalyptus trees. And though the street buzzed with heavy traffic, we had the wide sidewalk to ourselves.

Had we made a mistake in choosing a rental in such a residential area on the city's modern edge? We'd always liked our creature comforts, but after nearly nine months of car-free living in Latin America, we'd grown accustomed to living in El Centro with the city center on our doorstep.

We hadn't traveled to South America to live a North American lifestyle, had we? And yet, we were headed for SuperMaxi, where we could buy Washington State apples and Louisiana Tabasco sauce purchased with U.S. dollars, Ecuador's official currency.

It seemed incongruous in so many ways. The luxury high-rise. The American currency. The strip mall grocery store. But there was also something vaguely reassuring in the neatly manicured lawns and the flower-lined driveways with well-maintained vehicles that we glimpsed through elegant wrought-iron gates as we passed.

These people don't need anything from us, I thought, and felt a bone-deep jolt as I considered the tangled and complicated feelings behind such a thought.

For a moment, surrounded by the tidy accessories of civilization, I almost yearned for Granada's decay and chaos: The crumbling grandeur and faded facades, the roving groups of Catholic schoolgirls and their carefree laughter.

I hoped we would be happy here; maybe we'd discover how we fit in and fill the condo with new memories. I imagined us inviting friends over for dinner. Laughing so unexpectedly, I'd snort wine through my nose (as had happened once with Robyn) and become shamefully addicted to some silly sitcom on one of the gazillion Satellite channels that streamed in from Hollywood on the condo's plasma TV.

An hour later, we emerged from SuperMaxi laden with grocery bags and hailed a taxi from the waiting queue for the brief ride home.

Back at the condo, we filled the empty refrigerator and cabinets with our purchases: ready-made ceviche, shrink-wrapped veggies, and commercially baked bread. We placed a plastic tub of Tide in the laundry room, then sat side-by-side on the sofa, grabbing the remote to flick on the TV—something we hadn't done since leaving the States—and watched an episode of Modern Family. Afterward, we unpacked toiletries into his-and-her vanity drawers in a spacious en suite bathroom and collapsed into a king-sized bed.

I tried to fall asleep but found myself listening for the chirps of geckos, the constant, soothing night song of Hotel La Bocona, and I was filled with nostalgia. I wanted to be back in bed where I could push back the veil of mosquito netting and wander out into a balmy night to curl up in a terrace chair and sit beneath the moon and stars. I wanted to awaken in a familiar place to the sound of familiar voices—Ofelia, Natalie, and Arlen—and to feel the tingle of the hot afternoon sun on my skin after a dip in the pool. We'd been part of the La Bocona family, and its tranquility had helped to soothe the sting of displacement.

But we were here now. Tomorrow we'd look for a cozy coffee house, a local market with fresh food grown in Ecuador, and a café with a strong WiFi signal where we could work when we needed to get out of the suburbs. We'd get an Ecuadorian mobile SIM card, call Ruth, an American expat, a friend-of-a-friend who'd moved to Cuenca from Ajijic, and start again at starting over.

13

Lingering Doubt

"Ellen! Hank! Hello!" Ruth called out and waved as she stepped into the open-air courtyard at the Kookaburra Café where we had arranged to meet. It was a fine February day, sparkling and fresh at Cuenca's elevation of 8,200 feet, with blue sky reflected in a small courtyard pond. I recognized Ruth from her Facebook profile: attractive and trim, with short-cropped gray hair and a warm smile. As she made her way to the table, I took in her energetic stride, friendly manner, and slightly muted American accent.

"How are you getting settled?" she asked after introductions, and we had passed along greetings from Lois, a mutual friend in Ajijic, where Ruth had lived for more than two decades before moving to Cuenca a few years ago.

We were filling her in on the condo and the Galapagos cruise when the café owner, an affable Aussie, arrived at the table.

"How long will you be in Cuenca?" he asked after Ruth explained that we were newly arrived. When we told him three months, a smile flashed across his face. "That's great. We hope to see you often then," he said warmly, leaving with our order.

Later, after he'd returned with the meals, I sipped the apple, celery, ginger, beetroot, and carrot juice and knew this was our kind of place. The feeling solidified when the chicken tamales arrived wrapped in steaming banana leaves and filled with carrots and raisins with a zingy mango chutney. The tasty combination reflected the café's casual fusion of its Australian owners and Ecuador's agricultural abundance.

"Did you make it to the market on your way here?" Ruth asked, referring to her recommendation that we stop by the Mercado 10 de Agosto, one of Cuenca's biggest indigenous markets located only a few blocks up Calle Larga from the café.

"We did," I said, pointing to a canvas shopping bag propped against the café table bulging with fresh, organic fruits and veggies, herbs, and local honey.

She smiled. "I wanted to introduce you to the Kookaburra first, but let's eat at the market next time. Isn't it a wonderful place to roam and browse? The upstairs food court, especially the juice bars and pork plates, are delicious and inexpensive."

I knew then that I liked Ruth. A fellow foodie with an easygoing manner, she could be a doppelgänger for my favorite Aunt Dorothy, a woman who still played golf well into her nineties, never forgets a birthday, and makes everyone she meets feel at ease.

Ruth told us about her life as we ate, and we conveyed our details as best we could. She filled us in on the town gossip—the newest restaurants and hotspots, the city's controversial electric tram system under construction and making a mess of roads and traffic—and tipped us off to upcoming exhibits and festivals, concerts and causes.

"Do you like football? A group of us watch the games most Sundays at the Inca Bar. No? Well, perhaps you'll join our Tuesday night gatherings at DiBacco Italian Restaurant, where we meet up for cocktails and dinner. There's also the symphony. It's fantastic and free."

I felt an unexpected tug of envy. I admired Ruth's obvious sense of belonging. Her tribe. Her certainty about her place in this world.

She seemed content with her life here. Could I?

It wasn't that I wanted to live Ruth's life. But I liked the familiarity, the lightness, the ease, and rapport she radiated, and I wanted that feeling for myself.

The thought I might never find that feeling of belonging was something I hadn't considered. Could I stop the doubts and comparisons and just start living? I hoped so.

There had been a time, a decade ago, when a similar malaise—a period of chronic doubt and confusion—had infected my thoughts until it gradually suffocated the joy out of our marriage. We'd separated and put the house we owned together on the market. Hank went to Mexico. I sought refuge on the Maltese island of Gozo, where I quietly, desperately tried to deny the unbearable grief that had shredded my heart. Six weeks later, I'd returned home, broken, sad, and confused, to heal alone while we waited for the house to sell.

I'd turned inward then. And guided by a skilled therapist and the support of a wise husband, I gradually learned to perceive love and life differently until somehow, without fixing words to it, Hank and I stepped together into a new chapter of our story. And here we were again, making another fresh start. How could I have forgotten how painful and destabilizing that can be? The signs were all right in front of me. But I wasn't paying attention.

During dessert, a lusciously moist carrot cake, I listened absentmindedly while Hank and Ruth chatted about mutual friends in Ajijic, Cuenca's climate, and places in Ecuador worth exploring. I was struck by how easily Ruth brought out Hank's talkative side. He wasn't like that with many people. It took a good conversationalist who listened and asked questions with genuine interest and curiosity. Ruth had that. I sat there for some time in Andean sunshine, quietly lost in the rhythm of their voices when I glanced over to find Hank staring at me with a concerned expression.

"You okay?" he asked after Ruth left for the restroom.

"Yes. Why?"

"You'd gone quiet."

"So?" I replied.

"It's unlike you," he said with a sly smile.

We were laughing when Ruth returned.

"What did I miss?" she asked as we stood to leave.

It was nearly three o'clock when we said goodbye on the sidewalk outside the restaurant. A sudden cloudburst sent us scrambling into the backseat of a taxi with promises to get together again soon.

14

The Sting of Leaving

Over the following months, we got lost in work. Hank confronted the task of editing his latest novel, a perilous adventure tale set in the wild jungles of Chiapas, Mexico. I processed and captioned photographs, completed a Nicaragua story commission, and worked on the Galapagos article. I traveled solo to Chilean Patagonia for a conservation photography assignment, dabbled with my book (still a very nebulous idea), and plowed through the daily deluge of press releases and story pitches that continued to fill my inbox. But when we stepped away from our computer screens, we discovered what a remarkable city we'd landed in.

Most mornings, we went out for coffee and breakfast, often heading back to the Kookaburra. Or, we simply let serendipity lead us somewhere new in search of Ecuadorian d*esayuno* (breakfast): Green plantains, potatoes, *tortillas con queso, huevos,* and *zumos* (fruit juices.), fresh local coffee. Other times, we went to Café San Sebas, a popular eatery owned by an Austin, Texas, transplant whose Southwest-style burritos indulged our New Mexican taste buds.

At night, with moonlight flowing in the condominium's glass balcony doors and the shadowy crags of Cajas National Park looming in the distance, we read, played cards, shared our writing, and watched movies and TV sitcoms.

In the afternoons, I explored alone. The months in Granada were still on my mind. They'd changed me and got me thinking about what it meant to be a traveler in my own way. Not just navigating the cultural differences or figuring out how, exactly, I fit in, but exploring in a manner that allowed me to be me. A manner that said it was okay—that I was OK. So I walked the city without a map or a plan.

Wandering Cuenca's historic district was a little like stepping back in time. The streets were wide and clean, and the cafés and shops were mostly family owned. The buildings were grand and elegant, with European-style, wrought-iron balconies. And overhead was a colorful skyline of blue domes, pastel bell towers, arched windows, wood-beamed eaves, and terra-cotta roof tiles set against a deep, Andean sky—Windex blue one minute and steel gray the next. Locals walked past dressed in jeans and stylish leather boots. Some wore suits and dresses. Indigenous women outfitted in billowing skirts, woolly cardigans, and stovepipe hats carried babies and belongings on their backs in hand-woven *mantas* knotted tightly across their chests. Small crews of street sweepers in matching colored coveralls swished giant brooms made from tree branches over cobblestoned streets, and playful packs of school-uniformed kids ran up and down the streets. In Parque Calderon, Cuenca's central park, older men dressed in Mister Rogers-style cardigans and wool caps sat on park benches watching tourists snap selfies before a fountain.

But mostly, there was a sense of busyness, of *Cuencaños* purposely going about their lives with little interest in mine. I could've been invisible. At least, that's what it felt like. And for a while, before I turned fifty, being invisible felt safe and liberating—like I'd gained a sudden Super Power. Until it didn't.

• • •

One morning, toward the end of April, Hank and I were seated on a bench in Plaza San Sebastian, our bellies full of coffee and burritos. The sun, which had been hiding, warmed our faces. We sat there most days after breakfast at Cafe San Sebas, sometimes for only a few minutes. Other times, we lingered on days like this one with the sun shining, stretching out the time.

It was our final week in Cuenca. The three months had gone by at lightning speed, though by now, I knew the small leafy plaza by heart. I knew which bench had a broken slat that snagged my clothing. I knew the smiling guard with a limp who worked the morning shift at the Museum of Modern Art, which fronts the plaza. I knew that on Sundays, Boy Scouts dressed in khaki shirts with colorfully embroidered badges and yellow neck scarves learned to march, salute, and carry flags on whistled commands. It was Sunday, and we had a perfect view past the fountain to the church steps where scouts, frisky as puppies, chased and poked and squealed, waiting for practice to begin.

We recognized familiar faces from other Sundays in the plaza, perhaps the scouts' families. They recognized us, too, as they passed by in dappled sunshine and greeted us with a friendly smile and *Buenos días.*

I don't know when exactly, but gradually as our months in Cuenca passed, the urge to stay, to settle in, the *I could live here* scheming and dreaming that had gone dormant in Ajijic and Granada, was back. It came in waves—stronger, then weaker, and then strong again—a longing to stick around, to peel back the layers and make this place ours. The well-kept plazas. The afternoon rainstorms, the crack of thunder, the flash of light, the pounding rain against the windows, and the shimmering rainbows that followed. The taxis that flagrantly defied speed and space. The ceviche, the *empanadas,* the *mangos con chile.*

It was true I wanted to stay, but it was also a lie. It was too soon. I wasn't ready to settle down yet. It was odd, but the thing holding me back from asking Hank if he wanted to extend our stay wasn't the fact we'd already booked flights to Peru. It wasn't the bureaucratic challenges and expense of a visa extension. It wasn't even fear that we had no plans beyond a one-week hotel reservation in Cusco. It was potential. It felt like I would never realize it if we stopped now.

I'd come to perceive this journey as something bigger than an adventure, bigger than a lifestyle experiment, or the search for a new home, and I hadn't anticipated the depth of emotion it would provoke. It surprised me, the push and pull, the longing to stay, and the lure of leaving. If only I knew where it would lead.

I flashed back to Tina's words at my birthday dinner in Granada: *"Have you ever had your fortune told?"* and thought of the tarot card reading I'd had last week.

I thought about how unlikely it was that a friend of Ruth's visiting from Ajijic would ask me at lunch one afternoon if I'd had a reading with TC, a local tarot card reader. And how we'd run into TC on the street as we'd exited the restaurant. I thought about how I'd felt there'd been something vaguely significant in Tina's offhanded recommendation about a fortune teller. So I booked a reading. And that's when something unexpected happened: The cards painted a picture of a future that seemed too good to be true.

"Wow. This is uncanny. I wish this were my life," TC had said as card after card, deck after deck, pointed to a future that was fortunate and blessed—more than I could ever have imagined.

I pulled from my purse the small black notebook I carried and flipped to the pages from the session to read my notes. Could the fortune teller really have drawn such a positive reading for me?

The Ten of Cups in the future position indicates that emotional contentment is coming and that your goals in life are worth pursuing despite any current struggles.

The Nine of Coins foretells seeds sown are coming to fruition.

The Eight of Cards predicts an artisan making money doing what he loves.

It seemed too good to be true, and it didn't stop there.

The Seven of Cups indicates many opportunities to choose from the heart.

The Wheel of Fortune shows that the universe is conspiring for fortune. As long as you don't go backward, you can't go wrong.

The Page of Wands shows a future of new adventures, creative expression, and partnership.

My thoughts drifted, running toward hope. Could this be my future? There must have been a dozen more positive sentiments telling me of a creative, peaceful, playful life of new adventures.

"Ellen. Ellen? Aren't you going to answer?" Hank said, pulling me back into the present moment.

"Huh, what? I'm sorry. I was daydreaming," I said, tucking the notebook back into my purse. "What was the question?"

He gave a slight shake of his head and then smiled. "Dreaming about your favorite husband?" he asked wryly.

I laughed and felt a sudden flash of affection. "Of course," I said, leaning over to plant a kiss, his lips warm with sunshine.

He smiled sideways at me as I rested my head against his shoulder and said: "I wanted to know how much time we had to find an apartment in Cusco before the walking tour."

I'd received a last-minute assignment with a luxury outfitter inviting me and Hank to join a walking tour to Machu Picchu in Peru's Sacred Valley of the Incas. It departed from Cusco shortly after our arrival. We were excited about the trek, but it also meant we'd have less time to hunt for the apartment.

I told Hank we had nine days. He nodded. "Good. Maybe we'll find something through the South American Explorers Club. It'll be a start anyway."

"Let's hope so," I replied, surprisingly unconcerned.

I thought of how little we knew about Peru, about Cusco, a place we seemed to have picked from the ether. From our little research, we knew it was the gateway to Machu Picchu. It was the oldest continuously inhabited city in the Americas and one of the highest, at a heart-pounding 11,000 feet in elevation. But we had no idea how difficult it would be to find a furnished short-term rental within our budget.

We knew no one in Cusco. No one would be there to greet us or to help smooth the way. Not very long ago, that might have unnerved me—having no safety net, no fixed abode. But instead of feeling unsettled, this felt more like independence and resilience, like being alone in the world with only each other, our wits, and the kindness of strangers to rely on. Somehow it was all that and more.

We sat for a time in silence. I had the strong sensation we were both feeling the sting of leaving. We hadn't made deep personal connections in Cuenca as we had in Mexico and Nicaragua, but saying goodbye, even to a place, had become increasingly complex: the letting go of memories, experiences, and a sense of familiarity. But I was beginning to understand that in letting go, you open yourself to the wonder and gifts of the next place, the new friendships and insights, cuisines and cultures, languages and landscapes.

After a while, a sudden breeze rustled the trees, and the sun slid behind a cloud. In the distance was the familiar rumble of thunder. I could smell the rain coming—the earthy scent of humidity, eucalyptus, and damp Andean soil.

Hank stood and held his hand out to me. "Ready?"

"Yes," I said, slipping my hand into his.

15

Oxygen Deprivation

Peru

On the morning of the walking tour to Machu Picchu, Hank and I awakened in Cusco, high in the Peruvian Andes, to the sounds of fireworks, car horns, Andean flute music, and the steady beat of drums. A glance out the bedroom window of the fourth-floor apartment revealed a lively procession in the street below. A small dance troupe dressed in feathered headdresses, red robes, and blackstrap sandals had traffic knotted up for blocks as they stomped and twirled in rhythm with the music.

No doubt there'd be more mornings like this one. On our first day in Cusco, a similar troupe swirled past as we walked across Plaza de Armas. I hastily snapped a few photos on my phone, thinking we'd stumbled upon a rare and fortunate encounter. Only later did it occur to me that traffic and pedestrians had paid little attention to the small procession, drifting past the dancers like river water flowing around a rock. After that first sighting in the plaza and another a few days later on Avenida El Sol, I'd begun to suspect such things were the norm rather than an anomaly in this surprising city.

I shivered, a chilly reminder I was barefoot and wearing only a nightshirt. The mornings were when we felt Cusco's cold the most. May in South America is at the edge of winter, and we could see our breath condense on the window as we watched the dancers. Indoor heating is rare in Cusco, and most residents remained swaddled in coats and hats inside their homes.

The travel clock on Hank's bedside table buzzed. We'd set the alarm for seven a.m. to ensure a leisurely start before joining the tour group at nine. I walked over and silenced the alarm. A glance at the clock's display revealed a room temperature of fifty-two degrees Fahrenheit, and I scurried back to bed, pulling the heavy layers of alpaca wool blankets over my head as Hank headed to the bathroom, the apartment's sole source of running hot water, for a shower.

At the airport in Guayaquil, before we'd left Ecuador, I'd groused about the heat, sweat dripping down my back, the airport AC defunct or too expensive to run. Fool! If only I'd known it was the last time I would be warm in months.

The bathroom door squeaked open.

"All yours, babe," Hank said, returning to the bedroom. He was chipper, as he is most mornings. I grumbled but crawled out from under the blankets and brushed his lips with a kiss as I staggered past on my way to the kitchen to make coffee. Then, only with the scent of it brewing did I head for the shower.

When I emerged, Hank was seated on the sofa with a steaming mug of coffee, admiring the view—a broad valley crowded with red tile-roofed buildings pushed up against steep barren mountains. The phrase *Viva El Peru* etched in gigantic letters onto one of the hillsides.

I poured a cup of coffee and snuggled beside him on the couch.

"Not bad," I nodded toward the windows.

"Not bad," he replied, wrapping an arm around my shoulder, his eyes still on the view.

Morning sun flowed through the wall of single-glazed windows fronting the apartment. And even though we were wearing goose-down jackets indoors, I loved it. Despite the chill in the air, for the first time in a long time, I felt happy for no reason.

As Hank had predicted, it was through the South American Explorers Club that we'd discovered the apartment. The director, Eleanor, a thirty-something American married to a Peruvian, had just resigned from her position to open a new Cusco restaurant with her husband. It was her final week on the job when we'd shown up at the rambling adobe clubhouse tucked away on a quiet pedestrian alleyway in San Blas, the artsy bohemian district where galleries, boutiques, cafés, and organic restaurants had gradually transformed the area into one of Cusco's most popular neighborhoods.

"Wait! I might know of a place," she'd said after we'd completed the membership process and were nearly out the door. "Gimme' a minute. I need to make a call." She waved us back to the chairs in front of her desk as she pushed through a call on her mobile.

Earlier, when we'd asked if she knew of a well-equipped, furnished, two-bedroom rental in the historic district, she'd thought for a minute, shook her head no, and told us she couldn't think of any place like that available.

The club had been our last hope after almost a week of classified ad dead-ends and unearthing dismal hovels for outrageous rents. Our hotel reservation expired in two days, and the walking tour departed two days later.

I eavesdropped on the telephone conversation, catching a few words in rapid-fire Spanish, but when Eleanor pulled the phone away from her ear and asked: "Could you be available this afternoon at two p.m. to see it?" We eagerly nodded yes. *Did we appear as desperate as I felt?* I wondered.

"I'd forgotten about this place," Eleanor explained after hanging up. "It's been under construction. But my friend, the one I called, was an advisor on the project, and she mentioned the other day that it was nearly finished. When my friend called the owners, they said it still needed a few things but that you could go and see it. It's a penthouse apartment in a great location with fabulous views and a rooftop terrace for the sun." She handed us a slip of paper with the apartment's address and a roughly sketched map. "Good luck. I hope it works for you."

It felt like our luck had turned when we looked at the paper and saw that the address was only a block from the San Blas hotel where we were staying.

"It sounds too good to be true," I told Hank as we walked back to the hotel. "Do you think it'll be affordable?"

"Let's hope so," he said. "Time is running out."

• • •

Cusco had completely surprised me. Despite our stays in Mexico, Nicaragua, and Ecuador, I'd been unprepared for the mystical Inca capital perched high in the Peruvian Andes. The cold, the altitude, the oxygen deprivation, the tiny taxis that swarmed like bees along steep stone streets, and the long-lashed llamas that trailed behind bow-legged grandmothers in bowler hats were just part of it. There was also the fierce sun, the ornate Spanish cathedrals that squatted atop Inca temples, the children with their soulful eyes and rosy cheeks, the hippy-dippy foreign New Agers draped in crystals and dreadlocks, the sturdy backpackers with their insect-bitten legs, and the adventure travelers dressed like Indiana Jones. The food—simple, pure, and flavorful.

And the sounds, so many sounds to decipher. The crazy clang

of a cowbell that tells you to get your garbage down to the corner *muy pronto* before the trash truck passes by, the high-pitched whistle announcing the man who comes to sharpen your knives. All day, car horns and barking dogs, and all night, the neighborhood watchman with a traffic whistle he rarely stops tooting.

With its juxtaposition of chaos and culture, tourism and mysticism, Cusco demanded total attention. I didn't understand its magic, not then anyway, but in that ancient Inca city, I felt glad to be alive, glad for the circumstances that had brought us there. Though it could've been a lack of oxygen I was feeling.

16

The Sacred Valley of the Inca

At eight o'clock, we grabbed the small duffle bags and day packs we'd prepared for the trek, locked the apartment door, and descended the building's four flights of stairs. We passed the third-floor apartment where Max, a young American veteran of the Iraq and Afghanistan wars, lived sequestered with his demons and PTSD. We continued past the second-floor apartment, home to a large and happy Cusqueñan family, or so it seemed, from the baby giggles and pleasant tones that filtered up through the air ducts. Then, past the ornate first-floor home of the Espinozas, the multigenerational artisanal family of woodcarvers who owned the building. At the intricately carved entry door, we stepped past the granite puma sculptures that framed the building's entrance and out onto the bustling sidewalk of Calle Lucrepata.

A passing taxi tooted its horn and slowed hopefully, then sped away when we waved it off. A scraggly pack of free-roaming dogs trotted purposefully past in a manner oddly reminiscent of hurried urban commuters with places to go and people to see. And across the street, a young woman climbed a concrete staircase with an infant slung across her back and a lurching toddler clasping her hand. Both children wore *chullos,* the traditional Andean knitted hat with tasseled ear flaps—their coal-black eyes and mahogany faces beautifully framed in the colorful wool. The toddler navigated the staircase with quiet determination, each step nearly as tall as he was. The woman's patience was admirable. No hurrying the child along. No picking him up to make the climb faster. No nervous hovering. She just made the slow climb, her steps in sync with his, and something inside me melted at the sight of such a simple act of love.

When we first started traveling in Latin America, I noticed how well-behaved the children were. Kids were everywhere—in the streets, buses, plazas, and stores—as ubiquitous as Coca-Cola. Children were so omnipresent here that you might not even notice them if it weren't for their curious eyes and playful smiles. Or the way they contentedly entertained themselves with little more than their imaginations. It was rare to hear a child cry or complain.

If I could choose a childhood, it would be a Latin American one. Families are more interactive in this part of the world, with more time and more relatives—siblings and cousins, aunts and uncles, grandmothers and grandfathers—to tend to a child's every need. How much easier it would be to love and be loved as an adult with that foundation.

Still, I wondered if all that family would eventually serve to asphyxiate the flickering pulses of independence and individuality necessary for maturity.

I turned at the sound of a motorbike stopping in front of the house next door. Two battered propane gas canisters hung off the bike's back tire, the kind people use in the United States to barbecue. The rider grabbed one, slung it atop his shoulder, then stepped up to the door and pressed a buzzer. Just yesterday, we received a similar delivery to replace an empty tank in the kitchen that fueled the stove and oven. After climbing four flights of stairs with the replacement tank over one shoulder and a backup tank over the other, the delivery boy hadn't been the slightest bit out of breath after climbing four flights of stairs. The thin, high-altitude air was natural for him, no effort at all. Would we ever stop wheezing and gulping for air each time we returned to the apartment? I'd hoped the months we'd spent in Cuenca, living at 8,200 feet above sea level, would've better prepared us.

The sun had come out while we were standing there, and the temperature rose quickly. I'd shed my jacket and stuffed it into the duffle bag when Hank tapped his watch and said we should go. I nodded in agreement, and we set off toward Plaza Nazarenas, the pretty little square where we would meet the small group of travelers we were to join for the assignment with the luxury outfitter.

We turned onto Calle Tandapata, the narrow stone alleyway framed by crumbling adobe walls and whitewashed houses with painted blue doors that winds its way across San Blas. Hank mentioned we had time to stop for a slice of banana bread and a coffee at Pantástico, a neighborhood bakery where we were daily customers after only a week in town.

We said *"Buenos días"* to Irma, the girl behind the counter who was already familiar to us. *"Buen día,"* she smiled and then asked in perfect English: "Your usual?"

A half-hour later, we stepped into the gilded lobby bar of Hotel Monasterio, the arranged meeting point for the walking tour. The parquet floors were polished to a shine. Gold-framed colonial paintings of various saints provided a nod to the hotel's former function as a sixteenth-century Spanish monastery. Etched glass lamps and the flickering flames of silver candlesticks cast a golden hue across the room. A carved wood bar ran the length of one wall. The room was quiet at this hour, but it was easy to imagine it alive with guests sipping *pisco*, the grape-based brandy claimed equally by Peru and Chile as a native drink. Precisely the sort of elegant comfort that luxury adventure travelers would expect after a week on the Inca Trail.

We were about to ask the doorman about our group when a young man, bearing an uncanny resemblance to the actor who played Peter Brady on *The Brady Bunch*, crossed the room to greet us. His broad smile and unbridled energy immediately pegged him as a guide.

"I'm Tristan. Are you with the group?" He was American, with the ease and confidence of someone accustomed to taking charge.

"Of course, the travel journalist," he said when I told him our names. "Let's keep that between us," he winked and leaned in conspiratorially. "Hank," he continued, "glad to have you along. Headquarters tells me that you and Ellen will be in Cusco for a while. Lucky you. I love this place. Have you met Ana Maria, our Peruvian guide, or the others? We're out this way," he said without waiting for an answer and turned toward the front entrance. "Can I help you with your bags?"

His tone was light, but I couldn't tell how he felt about having us along. I knew that it mattered a great deal to his success as a guide to be the perfect host and dazzlingly enthusiastic, no matter how things really were beneath the surface.

We loaded into one of the tour's two Mercedes Sprinter vans and were soon en route to the Pisac ruins, a hilltop Inca citadel an hour's drive from Cusco. I listened to the bits of conversation of our travel mates, a clutch of five women traveling together from Manhattan, each as fit and polished as supermodels. They wore top-brand yoga wear—Lululemon and Prana—and on the seats beside them were outdoorsy accessories, sun hats, hydration packs, and telescoping hiking poles that looked as if they'd been purchased for the trip. I could see they were a self-contained group as they laughed and chatted casually, sharing photos on their iPhones with mentions of children, husbands, and nannies back home.

Theodore Roosevelt once said that comparison is the thief of joy, and I had a sense of what he meant when I thought of how I might appear to our travel companions. I glanced down at my shapeless hiking pants, shabby boots, and quick-dry travel shirt, an ensemble I'd worn on mountain treks on five continents, and felt suddenly self-conscious. I wished that I'd upgraded my look before the trip. I knew it was childish and futile, but a part of me wanted to be seen by these women. But who would they see? The events of our nomadic year had irrevocably changed me and shaped the way I now viewed and interacted with the world. The alteration reverberated in every cell of my body, though I had no idea what to do with it.

I turned my attention to the view outside the window, a dense forest of eucalyptus trees. The van slowed as the driver navigated a series of switchbacks. The scent of eucalyptus wafted in his open window, and the pungent aroma filled the vehicle. It was a perfect sunny day. The high-altitude light was luminous, and thick cottony clouds punctuated a deep blue sky.

"Can you see the snow-capped peaks?" Tristan said, peering over his shoulder from the front passenger seat. I followed his gaze to a clearing, and a serrated ridgeline of Andean peaks and Inca terraces shot into view.

"Isn't it gorgeous?" Tristan said. "Look how green it is. You're fortunate. This is the best time of year to be here."

His enthusiasm was contagious and worthy. The view was spectacular: deep green valley, snaking river, steep mountain slopes, and imposing stone terraces in every direction.

The morning slid into afternoon when we arrived at the Pisac ruins, ready to stretch our legs. The hilltop Inca citadel is perched on a triangular plateau high above the valley with a plunging gorge on either side.

We piled out of the van and joined our fellow hikers, who had gathered in a small huddle around Tristan. A lean middle-aged man with an American accent and confident manner stepped up beside us. "I'm James. This is my son, David," he said, gesturing to a young man standing beside him. The son nodded hello and extended his hand. There was also an older Canadian woman in a Tilley hat traveling alone and a young Japanese-Brazilian couple, financial analysts from São Paulo.

After a few minutes, Tristan called us to order and introduced our Peruvian guide, Ana Maria Meneses. She was slim, somewhere in her mid-fifties, I guessed, with kind eyes and humble energy rare in a guide. We learned that she grew up in Cusco, was the first female guide on the Inca Trail System, and had lived and worked throughout Central and South America, Europe, and the United States.

"Okay, gang. I know you're itching to hit the trail," Tristan said as he unfolded a tourist map. "Here's the route for today's hike."

A path highlighted in yellow wound its way through the archeological complex, down curving agricultural terraces that cascaded down the mountainside. Then to the valley floor some fifteen hundred feet below to the village of Pisac. The route looked manageable. I was relieved that the first day of the four on our way to Machu Picchu was mostly downhill. Then, a sudden recollection of screaming thighs, aching knees, and blackened toenails— memories from previous mountain treks—reminded me that descents could be more painful than climbing.

"Downhill can be challenging," Tristan announced as if reading my thoughts. "So, we're going to take it slow. Grab a hiking pole from the vans if you haven't already. They can help with stability and balance, especially if your legs feel heavy and sluggish."

"The plan," he continued, "is to take a couple of hours to explore the ruins and get to the town, where we'll wind down over lunch and have time to browse the stalls at Pisac's famous handicrafts market. After that, we have a special afternoon ceremony with a local *paco*, a guardian of Inca religious traditions. Sound good? Is everyone ready? *Vamanos!"*

We set out with the Manhattan women falling in fast on Tristan's tracks, the Brazilian couple next, then father and son and the Canadian woman, with Hank and me bringing up the rear and Ana Maria positioned last to sweep for stragglers. After a few hundred yards along a dirt path, we came to an Inca doorway, the unmistakable trapezoidal shape with a single stone lintel common in Inca architecture, marking the entrance to the main temple complex.

The Manhattan Five stopped to photograph one another framed in the doorway. It looked like they'd stepped off the pages of an outdoor clothing catalog: perfect white-teeth smiles and trim figures in colorful activewear with the legendary Inca stonework and vast valley views forming a stunning backdrop. No one seemed to notice me taking photos of them taking photos, though I sensed Ana Maria quietly taking it all in. I looked over at her and wondered if she knew that I was writing an article and creating photography for the outfitter. Her bright, observant eyes revealed nothing.

"Where do you live?" she asked us once we'd moved on.

We were climbing a steep stone staircase, and I suspected the question was intended to get us talking and help steady our breathing or distract us from the precarious drop-off on our left.

"We're homeless," Hank answered cheerfully without a trace of the shame I felt in my gut at his choice of words.

The Oxford Dictionary defines homelessness as *"a person without a home, and therefore typically living on the streets."* Listed synonyms include: *"of no fixed address, without a roof over one's head, on the streets, vagrant, displaced, dispossessed, destitute, down-and-out."*

I resisted an urge to clarify our nomadic status as Ana Maria processed Hank's response.

"So you're traveling then? Cool. How long have you been away?"

Her tone was excited, not judgmental, as I had feared.

I realized it mattered to me, more than it should, that she understood, and the revelation troubled me. I didn't want to be a person who yearned for validation or felt compelled to defend or explain myself, but I carried that in me for better or worse.

"I think you're brave," Ana Maria said after Hank had filled her in. "The way you've let go of everything: possessions, security, friends, and family."

Were we brave?

I hoped so.

17

Mixed Blessings

"So, what did you ask for?" I whispered to Hank.

We were crouched on canvas camp stools in a ceremonial circle on the dirt floor of an Inca ruin. Victor, a Peruvian shaman, was on the ground before us, bent over a small square of wool cloth, arranging tiny bits of candy, money, rice, corn, flowers, and coca leaves on a large sheet of paper as part of a *despacho* ceremony.

I watched the shaman and his wife, Paulina, both small and dark-skinned with strong-boned faces and sinewy muscular legs. They were swaddled in layers of wool clothing in brilliant shades of yellow, pink, and green and elaborately decorated with buttons and sequins. He wore an ornate beaded *chullo* hat with large multicolored tassels. A yellow, floppy-brimmed *montera* secured with beaded straps covered her head. Carefully, they selected various offerings from a collection of miniature clay bowls and vessels and placed them neatly on the paper.

"Victor and Paulina," Ana Maria explained, "are constructing a *mesa*, or healing bundle, as an offering of gratitude to Pachamama, Mother Earth, and the a*pus, m*ountain spirits, in honor of our journey. You can place prayers of gratitude or requests into the offering. These prayers will then be dispatched to the Guides and Spirits when the offering is burned or buried."

When the *mesa* was ready, Victor folded the offerings into a bundle and held it, one by one, above our heads. Ana Maria instructed us to close our eyes and to hold our intentions in our minds. I looked around the circle of canvas camp chairs, noted that our travel companions seemed to be drinking it in, and then closed my eyes.

After the ceremony had ended, Hank quietly confided to me that he'd asked for younger legs.

"I don't have high hopes," he added with a mischievous grin, "but I'll take any help I can get. You?"

I looked over at my husband and was overwhelmed with tenderness for this man I love. Hank was in incredible shape for a man of seventy-five, and I often forgot that he was as old as he is, but the thought that he might be struggling or in pain worried me. I thought of how I'd seen him lean hard into the walking pole on the hike down to Pisac earlier that day, the way he'd stumbled a few times, his legs rubbery with fatigue. I didn't want to discourage him by smothering him with my concerns—Hank was his own man, always had been. But I couldn't help worrying. It was an old reflex.

"I sent a prayer of gratitude for the life that has brought us here," I said after a pause. "And I asked that what I need to learn will be revealed."

I realized how flaky I sounded as soon as the words left my mouth.

Hank chuckled and shook his head. "You're my favorite wife," he said, "even if you are crazy."

It was an old joke between us, and there was affection in his words.

"But be careful what you wish for *mi amor*," he said, his mood now somber.

It was his way of reminding me that the experiences which reveal what we need to learn are sometimes brutal.

I felt a sudden panic and found myself thinking the unthinkable: *What if Hank died?* I know that death is inevitable. I know this intellectually, the way I know that death is happening right now inside my body, with old cells dying and being replaced by new ones. But my eyes pooled with tears every time I thought of losing Hank. In a sudden flash of clarity, I realized I was terrified of losing him—which terrified me.

I was dimly aware that David, the adult son, had wandered over to talk with Hank. Their conversation was muffled as if I was underwater. I wanted to be alone with myself to get a handle on my feelings, but instead, I walked over to thank Victor and Paulina.

"Will you come back?" They wanted to know when it was time to say goodbye.

I looked at them, surprised.

"I don't know," I said, "though I'd very much like to."

It was true. Peru had gotten under my skin. I wanted more.

It struck me that I had no idea about Victor and Paulina's lives. Where did they live? Did they have children? What had they experienced? How had they learned what they knew? Did they see us as curious or ridiculous? Why were they willing to share their blessings and customs? I felt a twinge of guilt at how one-sided the experience had been.

For me, people and their life stories, not churches, ruins, or museums, make a place real. I thought of Arlen and her family. Arlen growing up in a war. Arlen always saying goodbye to the foreigners who visit her country. She would be in Granada now helping someone learn her language and better understand her culture, as she had with us, as Victor and Paulina did today. What had I given in return?

The sun was a faint red glow when we climbed into the vans for the short drive to the hotel that would be our base for the next three nights. As we rode along, I quietly asked Tristan about the shaman and his wife.

"They're from a small mountain village about eighty miles southeast of Cusco in the Ausangate region. You may have noticed Ausangate in Cusco: a 20,945-foot snow-clad peak towering high above the clouds."

We had, I told him. "But I had no idea it was so far away."

"Yeah, it's massive," he said. "And not only is Ausangate the highest peak in southern Peru, but it's also a mountain spirit, an *apu,* held sacred since Inca times. For the Quechua, the indigenous peoples of the Andes, direct descendants of the Inca like Victor and Paulina, it's the reason we exist: they give offerings to the *apu,* and it gives everything in return."

"Wait," I said. "I thought Quechua was a language. It's also people?"

"It's both," Tristan said, laughing. "I'll explain more on the walk tomorrow."

Just then, the van turned off the main road onto a narrow road. We were at the hotel.

18

It Wasn't the Job, It Was Me

The hotel sat like an oasis amid the rough-cut mountains with its landscaped gardens and beds of flowers in all colors. A porter swept our bags away and led us along a flower-lined flagstone path to a private bungalow plush with Andean art and textiles and a sprawling bed loaded with pillows. There was a sitting area with a leather sofa, alpaca throws, and a wood fire flickering in a stone fireplace. The massive bathroom had a large soaking tub and marble shower. Outside, cushioned lounge chairs and a table beckoned from beneath a covered veranda.

After a leisurely soak in the tub, I dressed for dinner. I studied myself in the full-length mirror. I'd put on weight. My skirt pinched at my waist, and I was thankful that the new alpaca shawl I'd purchased in Cusco covered my blouse, which stretched too tightly across my chest.

"You look fine," Hank said as I tried on every possible clothing combination from the few items in the small duffle bag.

We walked a dim pathway to the restaurant, the sky brilliant with stars above us.

"I wish we could've stayed in tonight," I told Hank. "How do these adventure tour guests do it? Up at the crack of dawn, busy all day, with lengthy and elaborate dinners every night, only to return home and boast that they need a vacation from their vacation. That they can sleep when they were dead."

I looked back on the day. The early wake-up. The van ride from Cusco. The cartilage-crunching hike down the Inca terraces at Pisac. Afterward, the catered gourmet lunch in a private garden and browsing the handicrafts market. Then the *despacho* ceremony. And now, a late dinner beneath the stars.

"I'm exhausted," I said, "and it's only day one."

What's wrong with me? Don't you know how lucky you are?

I stared up at the twinkling sky, my eyes searching for the Southern Cross, and it occurred to me that rarely was I myself on the job, though any evidence of that fact remained mostly hidden—even from myself. The feeling of never being enough, doing enough, the fear that I couldn't keep up with the incredible opportunities I'd been given, that I would let myself and others down, was so overwhelming that I rarely relaxed. I was an introvert working in the extroverted world of small-group adventure travel. I had everything I'd asked for in a job—travel, creativity, a supportive network of clients and colleagues—and yet temperamentally, I was better suited to work with less stimulation and more solitude.

In my quiet moments, I wanted to give in to it, let go, be at ease, and feel at home. I wanted the capacity to belong to myself. But my mind kept circling back to the same thoughts: *What's wrong with you? Don't you know how lucky you are?*

It wasn't the work. It was me. And I was repeating a pattern.

That realization took me back to fourteen years earlier when I'd announced my pending retirement to my high school math students. I was thirty-five then, ancient by adolescent standards, but still young enough for them to recognize that it was unusual for someone my age to retire.

Initially, they objected and offered reasons why I should stay: *You can't leave. My sister was hoping to have you for Trigonometry next year. I hated math until your Geometry class.*

I considered their words high praise, and had I been vulnerable to them, I might have been swayed to stay. But when I explained, half-joking, that I simply wasn't cut out to be institutionalized—which was how I'd come to perceive our educational systems—they immediately understood and wistfully wished me the freedom they yearned for themselves.

What I hadn't told them was how exhausted I was. That after twelve years of teaching, I simply couldn't foresee a way to sustain the amount of energy I put into the job: the late nights spent grading papers and preparing relevant and engaging lessons, tutoring students before and after school, showing support and interest outside the classroom at sporting events, musical and theatrical performances, the continuing professional education. Because, of course, it wasn't sustainable. Not for me, anyway.

Again, it wasn't the job. It was me.

I had to change. I was not meant to live this way, floundering in self-induced exhaustion, stress, and anxiety. This I saw now with tender clarity.

• • •

Dinner was at the casual dining venue of the hotel's two restaurants. Over drinks and hors d'oeuvres served on the restaurant veranda, the group chatted with the chef as he prepared our meal, a *Pachamanka* feast: a traditional Peruvian dish of Andean vegetables and meats infused with regional herbs baked in an earthen oven.

Neither Hank nor I are at ease in social gatherings like this. I discussed Myanmar with Tristan and the Brazilian couple, who were well-traveled and savvy about the world like the others in the group. Hank kept quietly to himself, as was his habit.

"Burma, as Myanmar was formerly known, is an extraordinary country largely undiscovered," Tristan said, holding court.

He filled us in on the tours he guided there: cycling among golden temples, cruising the Irrawaddy River, and visiting sacred sites. The conversation then turned to the news that Aung San Suu Kyi, the Burmese opposition leader who in 2010 was released after nearly twenty years of house arrest over her outspoken criticism of the country's military leaders, had recently been elected to a seat in parliament.

"It represents a massive act of hope for the people and a significant step toward democracy," Tristan said passionately.

Hank and I had been following Aung San Suu Kyi and the political developments in Myanmar with keen interest since our first visit there more than a decade earlier, but I said nothing of our experiences. I said nothing of a return visit the following year. I didn't mention the Burmese guide, a quiet physicist who'd been a student in Yangon during the 1988 Uprising when pro-democracy protests ignited a brutal military crackdown and the house arrest of Aung San Suu Kyi. I didn't share what the guide had shared with us: that he'd had to find the meaning of the word democracy in a dictionary and wondered why he, or his countrymen, should have to risk dying for it because foreign powers told them they should.

I wasn't sure if I was being respectful of Tristan's leadership or if silence was easier. But, as a pungent whiff of our baking meal wafted up from its pit in the earth, I allowed for the possibility that it was a bit of both.

When Tristan excused himself to talk with the other guests, Hank wandered over, and two of the Manhattan women joined us, telling us about a luxury river cruise in the Peruvian Amazon they'd enjoyed the previous week.

Soon after, we were called to dinner.

• • •

"Hank tells me you're writing a book about your travels. How's it coming?" Ana Maria asked. She was seated to my right at a long dining table near the fireplace.

I squirmed in my chair as the food arrived.

"Um, well, it's still very much a work in progress," I replied, fumbling for a simple answer to what had become a complicated question.

"What does that mean?" she said.

I flashed back to the moment all those months ago in Ajijic when the idea of a book had come unbidden into my mind and how it had taken me by surprise.

"Writing doesn't come easy," I confessed to Ana Maria. "I've written and published articles for my work, yet writing is by far the most challenging part of my professional life. Over time, as I gained skill, there was less turmoil around writing, but I never wanted to write a book."

I stopped here.

It didn't feel like Ana Maria was feigning polite interest, but I didn't want to be *that guest*, the narcissistic bore who talks nonstop about themselves.

"But you are doing it, no? You are writing a book?" Ana Maria persisted. I studied her face for boredom. Her eyes burned brightly with what seemed to be genuine interest.

"Yes, but it's not at all the book I set out to write. When I started, we'd barely begun the journey. The book I'd envisioned then portrayed a lighthearted romp across Latin America in search of a new home, with photographs and vignettes of the places we lived. But as the journey progressed, it became apparent that wasn't our reality."

"What do you mean?" she asked.

Ana Maria listened as I walked her through the story: The unexpected sale of the New Mexico house. The spontaneous decision to wander. The sense that Ajijic was a launching pad to something more meaningful. The uncertainty and discomfort around our time in Granada. The false longing in Cuenca. Our recent arrival in Cusco.

It had been fifteen months and a lifetime.

It felt good to be talking to Ana Maria and to connect the dots of our journey in ways I hadn't previously articulated. Everything in the restaurant went silent for a moment, and for the first time, the book felt real. I felt a mounting excitement, too fledgling to admit out loud.

"I think this book is going to change you in ways you never imagined," she said, keeping her eyes firmly on mine.

"Do you think so?"

"I know it." She said this with such certainty that I believed it.

Ana Maria had verbalized something I'd sensed for months: that subconsciously, in telling my story, I must believe that I will be changed by it. I got the sudden feeling that nothing about this adventure was what I thought it was. That maybe this nomadic experiment was little more than a scenic detour on the way to our real destination—that perhaps everything is.

After the meal, we were summoned back to the veranda. A local theater company staged an elaborate Andean Gods production on the restaurant grounds, dramatically showcasing the indigenous Quechua culture's legends, traditions, and legacy. Fireworks exploded. Dancers twirled. Music thundered. Cameras flashed. It was close to midnight when we slid the keycard into the bungalow door. Minutes later, we were asleep.

The remaining days were a blur of luxurious exclusivity: A sunset champagne toast at Intipunku (Sun Gate), the stone portal entry point of the Inca Trail. A private tour of the Machu Picchu citadel. An elegant, after-hours catered dinner in an exhibition room of Museo del Arto Pre-Colombino, one of Cusco's finest museums.

I marveled at it all. But being on the trail trumped everything: the Andes' raw, rugged grandeur. The earthy aromas of eucalyptus and wild mint that drifted in the air. The sunshine. The physicality of the hike.

Mother Earth held me. She would always hold me.

19

The Glimmer of Possibility

Two weeks later, I sat baking beneath a fierce Andean sun on a plastic chair in the central plaza of Ollantaytambo, a small village of stone streets and mud-brick homes about an hour's drive from Cusco. Before me, a dozen colorfully costumed dancers stomped and twirled in celebration of El Señor de Choquekillka, the town's patron saint. Hundreds of dancers flock to the annual festival for four days each May, a manic swirl of tassels and trumpets, tambourines and masks, fueled by tradition and chicha, the home-brewed corn beer of the Andes. The ethereal tones of flutes, the pounding of drums, and the jingle of ankle bells filled the thin air. Towering in the distance were terraced mountains and the ruins of the ancient fortress of Ollantaytambo, once the royal estate of an Inca Emperor.

Earlier that morning, I'd climbed into the passenger seat of Ana Maria's SUV in Cusco to discover the car was already occupied. Ana Maria made brief introductions.

"Ellen, meet Holly, Dante, and my sister, Paty."

The atmosphere in the car was friendly and welcoming.

A blonde-haired woman who looked to be about my age smiled

widely and introduced herself in American English.

"I'm Holly, and this is Dante," she said, gesturing to a Peruvian boy seated beside her as she communicated something in sign language.

"*Buenos dias*," Paty said, smiling warmly.

"*Buenos dias*," I replied as Dante rapped the back of Ana Maria's seat. His desire to get going was made clear without a word.

Ana Maria shifted the car into gear, drove along the short side street where we lived, turned up the hill that climbed out of town, and headed toward the Sacred Valley.

During the winding drive to Ollantaytambo, I learned that Ana Maria and Holly had been friends for decades. Dante was Holly's eleven-year-old godson from a remote Q'eros community in the high Andes where Holly had once lived as part of a Ph.D. dissertation project in ethnomusicology.

"Dante attends a boarding school for the deaf in Cusco," Ana Maria explained. "He frequently tags along on these sorts of adventures."

I watched Dante signing with Holly in the backseat, his face lively and open, hands flying fast, and I saw great affection between them. The quiet laughter of their silent conversations felt familiar and comforting in the way that pure love does.

I saw Paty watching them, too, a tender smile on her face, before she returned her attention to the passing landscape outside the open window.

I'd been thrilled when Ana Maria had called to invite us to join her for the weekend in Ollantaytambo. I'd suspected that the crowds and chaos wouldn't be Hank's scene, and I wasn't surprised when he opted out. I'd eagerly accepted, though, excited as much by the opportunity to spend time with Ana Maria as the event itself. But it was Holly who brought the dances to life. A popular lecturer for National Geographic, the Center for World Music, and various academic and travel organizations, Holly revealed the historical stories and traditions behind the dances with the compelling narrative of a skilled storyteller.

When a troupe of black-masked dancers with chains around their waists entered the square, Holly explained they represented the black workers of the sugar plantations during the Colonial Era. When dancers fell to the ground in violent convulsions and were treated by costumed doctors and nurses, Holly said the dance told the story of laborers who went to the tropical valleys and jungle regions in search of work only to return home sick with malaria and yellow fever.

"Every dance is a story," she explained.

Once she said this, I could see it was true and wondered if life, too, is like that: a dazzling performance of costumes, choreography, and past events. It is only when we look behind the spectacle that the story is revealed. The thought filled me with a curious sensation, a feeling of solace, and something new—the glimmer of possibility.

20

Cusco Connections

In the ensuing months, Hank and I settled into an unspoken Cusco routine.

In the mornings, we escaped the cold apartment to the cozy warmth of Jack's Café, an Aussie-owned favorite where we lingered over clay cups of strong coffee, fresh juices with mint or ginger, and a breakfast of eggs heaped with bacon, potatoes, and roasted tomatoes. We justified the daily calories and Western-style comfort food with the steep uphill climb back to an unheated fourth-floor walk-up apartment. More than anything, I think, we returned for the smile and hug we received each morning from Fania, the manager, a short, bright-eyed Peruvian, who made everyone who ate at Jack's feel special and welcome.

We enjoyed afternoons on the apartment roof, immersed in sunlight and a world of words that affected how I viewed the world and how I fit in it. I downloaded and devoured books by the dozens, reading Emerson and Einstein, Huxley and Whitman, Mary Oliver and E.E. Cummings, Thoreau and Lao Tzu, Maya Angelou and Barbara Kingsolver, writers who got me thinking about what it means to be human. In their books, I discovered a sensibility for connection as something profound, magical, and worthy. As the days warmed and we gradually peeled away the layers of alpaca sweaters and Patagonia down jackets that had become our Cusco uniform, who could have ever guessed that a similar molting was taking place inside me?

At night, we drowned out the unabated din of barking dogs, fireworks, and the toot of the nightwatchman's whistle with the soothing sound of ocean waves from a white-noise app.

It was a welcomed respite with time to think, feel, be, and dwell in a private and precious existence.

It surprised me how quickly we'd become accustomed to Cusco's peculiar vibe and tourist tribe: the throngs of foreigners dressed in their Indiana Jones and New Age travel costumes. The self-described shamen from Germany, Australia, and the U.S. pitching hallucinogenic ayahuasca retreats on street corners. The Quechua women and children with cuddly lambs and fluffy llamas who earned money posing for selfies with strangers.

We were part of it, of course, the cliché foreigners living a bohemian existence. Yet, I'd found a sense of community and belonging in Cusco that felt unexpectedly like a home.

Meeting people came easily thanks to excursions with Ana Maria, daily yoga at the Healing House, a weekly writing group, and the South American Explorers Club.

One day I trailed into the upstairs library of the Explorers Club. I met Leona, a middle-aged Canadian volunteer who'd set herself the task of creating a digital database of regional NGO projects and organizations. She was slim with thick auburn hair and a no-nonsense manner.

"Are you here to work?" she asked, nodding to the laptop bag hanging from my shoulder.

"I am."

Without another word, she tidied the piles of paper and notebooks splayed across the wooden table to make room for me. We sat in comfortable silence for much of the afternoon, tapping away on our laptops while I wrote and she compiled her data.

After a while, she packed her things and rose to leave.

"I'm meeting a friend tonight for falafel and kebabs," she said casually. "Would you like to join us?"

I'd learned to perceive this type of spontaneous invitation as the generous gift it was—something people have extended to me all my life: reaching out with kindness and opportunity—and readily accepted.

We exchanged phone numbers and personal details and agreed to walk to the restaurant together from Leona's place when we discovered she lived only a few buildings from our apartment on the same street.

Later that night, Leona's friend Ingrid, a white-haired German living in Cusco via Tampa, Florida, joined us at a Middle Eastern restaurant just off Plaza de Armas. I liked her immediately and even more once I'd learned her story.

I'd discovered by now that everyone has a story. Ingrid's unfolded over shared plates of hummus, falafel, tabbouleh, grilled lamb, and fried eggplant, each dish deliciously spiced and served with heaping baskets of crispy pita bread.

"I came to Cusco on a consulting contract with a boutique hotel," Ingrid explained. "I'd had to reinvent myself after my husband died unexpectedly of a heart attack on a business trip. One day I was a comfortable housewife; the next, a pensionless widow."

I drank my wine and swallowed a rising panic.

I worried about Hank's death even when I was unaware I was worrying or unwilling to admit it.

"How did you get from that to this?" I asked, hopeful she'd reveal a magic formula for pensionless widows, a reality that, on any given day, could be my own.

"It wasn't easy," she said. "I took in boarders, found work, and learned to exist differently. That was seven years ago. I never could've imagined then that I'd end up living in Peru. A lot has changed. I have changed," she added after a pause.

I was about to inquire more when I noticed Leona had suddenly gone pale and sweaty. Ingrid's gaze followed mine.

"Leona, what's wrong?" Ingrid said just as Leona fainted and crumpled to the floor.

A small Peruvian woman rushed to the table with unmistakable concern as Ingrid and I positioned Leona on her back, quickly checking for injuries and breath, but Leona was already regaining consciousness.

The Peruvian woman dipped a cloth napkin in water and handed it to Leona, motioning for her to put it on her forehead.

"Low blood sugar," Leona said weakly. "It's okay. It's happened before. I know what to do."

After Leona felt well enough to be helped back to her seat, we sat and drank the coca tea that the Peruvian woman had organized and spent a few minutes making jokes in the awkward way one does after such an incident.

Ingrid called a taxi while I settled the bill, and soon we were back at Leona's apartment, where her roommate, a French-Canadian ESL teacher, assured us that Leona would be looked after.

Soon afterward, Ingrid and I parted on the sidewalk outside the apartment building where we stayed.

"Will you be okay walking alone?" I said after she'd declined my offer to wait with her for a taxi.

"No need," Ingrid said. "I live just over there," she said, gesturing toward a residential area at the bottom of the staircase across the street. Then she turned and walked away.

I hoped to see her again. I wanted to know more about her

transformation from an unprepared widow to the content and secure woman before me.

21

Inti Raymi

It was a biting cold, late June morning, winter solstice in the Southern Hemisphere and the annual celebration of Inti Raymi (Festival of the Sun), an ancient tribute to the Sun God Inti that retells the origin of the Inca. Cusco prepared all year for this day and the hundreds of thousands of tourists that descended on the Andean city for its most famous festival.

A few days earlier, I'd run into Leona at the Explorer's Club, and she'd mentioned the upcoming festival.

"A group of us plan to meet at Qorikancha at seven a.m.," she'd said. "It's best to get there early to beat the crowds and secure a place with a good view. You and Hank are welcome to join us."

There was a part of me, the fear-of-missing-out part of me, that wanted to say: Sure, count me in.

But there was another part of me, a newly emerging part of me, that whispered, *Are you crazy? You loathe mornings. You hate crowds.*

Before I'd answered, Leona relayed all she'd seen at the fiesta the year before. The colorful costumes, ancient rituals, rhythmic drumming, Andean flutes, swirling dancers, historical re-creations, and the Sun King carried on a golden throne.

"It's pageantry on an epic scale," she swooned.

"Imagine," she said, "hundreds of re-enactors in an elaborate, highly choreographed, roving all-day performance from Qorikancha, to Plaza de Armas and Sacsayhuaman."

I was convinced. I knew I wouldn't miss it.

But I also knew I'd find a way to see it after seven a.m.

"It sounds awesome. Thanks so much for thinking to include us. I'm not sure about Hank, but I will definitely want to see it, probably later in the morning. Would it be okay to check in with you by text?"

"Absolutely," she said. "But be forewarned. The city will be packed with people. The entire city center is closed to traffic. Even by Cusco standards, it's crazy."

With Leona's advice in mind, I'd decided to avoid the throngs and seek out a comfortable perch from which to watch the festivities. I found it at Limo, a high-end restaurant on the second level of a colonial building in the northeast corner of the Plaza de Armas. The terrace dining tables with spectacular views of the square were all occupied, but I could easily see the plaza from the bar through the large terrace windows. Better yet, the restaurant offered a special Inti Raymi brunch and complimentary pisco sours.

When I phoned Leona to invite her to join me, she declined, opting instead for the vibrancy of the streets. But Ingrid, who was with her, eagerly accepted.

"I'll be there in a few minutes," she said. "I just need to plow through the crowds across the plaza. And, yes, please go ahead and order me the special. Especially the pisco. It's insane down here!"

I was thrilled at the turn of events. Not only had I been hoping for more time with Ingrid, but her apparent enthusiasm for food and comfort confirmed what I'd suspected about her; that she was a kindred spirit.

A short time later, she arrived at the door, her distinct voice, a boisterous mashup of Spanglish with a heavy German accent, carried across the room. She wore a long floral skirt, a lime green alpaca sweater, and an elegant purple pashmina.

"You can't believe how good it is to be here," she said, taking an eager swig of the awaiting pisco cocktail as she settled onto the barstool beside me.

I followed her gaze to the spectacle outside the terrace windows: stone streets blanketed in yellow flower petals, dancers leaping and stomping and swirling, Inti, the Inca Sun God, carried on a golden litter by his loyal subjects dressed in regal red and gold.

"How did you ever manage to get a reservation?" she asked, turning her attention to the fully occupied restaurant.

"I didn't," I confessed with a grin. "I simply showed up and couldn't believe my luck when they welcomed me in."

"Well, I'm glad you didn't keep it a secret. This ceviche is incredible. What's for dessert?"

Between bites of elderberry cheesecake, we watched the festivities from our cozy perch until the final dancers had exited the plaza en route to the ancient Inca fortress of Sacsayhuamán in the hills above Cusco for the final climax of the celebrations.

High on sugar and pisco and the good fortune of finding such an agreeable way to experience Cusco's most famous celebration, we asked for the check and made plans to follow the festival up the hill.

Instead, we spent the afternoon in the police station.

When the bartender went to total the bill, Ingrid reached for her wallet to pay, but her wallet wasn't there.

"I had it earlier," she said, hysteria building as she emptied the contents of her purse onto the bar. "I bought bottled water from a street vendor on Avenida El Sol and paid for it from my wallet. I'm certain I put it back in my purse," she said.

"Pickpockets," the bartender said quietly. "Unfortunately, they thrive on festival days."

"Robbed? Really? But I had everything in my wallet," she said. "Credit cards. Cash. My Peruvian residency card. I should have known better. I should never have carried everything with me. Damnit."

The playfulness of the morning disappeared.

We sat there while she digested the idea.

"You should file a report with the police," the bartender gently recommended.

Ingrid closed her eyes as if it was too much to contemplate.

"What good would it do?" she finally said, defeat heavy in her voice.

"It will be helpful when you apply for replacement documents," the bartender said in a tone that suggested he had run into trouble along these lines before.

"I'd better get going then," Ingrid said, with more muster than I suspected she felt.

"WE had better get going," I countered.

She looked at me surprised and then broke out in a huge smile and laughed.

"Okay then. Let's do this." Her eyes actually twinkled.

The rest of the afternoon was a blur. One police station to another. One form after another. It was dark when we picked up a pizza and texted Hank to let him know we were headed home.

Since I'd seen Ingrid last, she'd moved from Cusco to a country house in the hills outside of Urubamba in the Sacred Valley. So she asked to stay with us for a day or two while she applied for replacement identification documents and bank cards.

"Thank you so much for all your help with the police, paying for breakfast and dinner, letting me stay over, and lending me money until I get a new ATM card." She dabbed under her eyes with a napkin, the emotions of the day's events finally catching up.

"It's nothing," I said. It felt good to be able to help.

Ingrid was an ideal houseguest. She filled the apartment with laughter and the aroma of baking bread. And though she repeatedly thanked us for our hospitality, I was secretly pleased to have the time together. My wish to know her better had been granted.

22

Jungle Lessons

Soon afterward, Hank and I flew to Puerto Maldonado in southeastern Peru on a story assignment to make a six-and-a-half-hour boat ride deep into one of Peru's remotest territories, the 700,000-hectare Tambopata National Reserve.

The voyage passed in companionable silence as a tropical landscape glided past towering kapok trees, fluttering butterflies, sandy beaches, and fluffy white clouds against a fierce blue sky.

Along the way, we nibbled on snacks of Amazon bananas, oranges, and Brazil nuts and enjoyed a lunch of vegetables and rice wrapped in a bijao leaf tied with a vine. We also spotted capybara (gigantic rodents) and caiman (a relative of the alligator) along the riverbank.

Our destination, the Tambopata Research Center (TRC), was founded in 1989 and began hosting eco-tourists alongside scientists and researchers in 1992 to help fund the fieldwork and educate adventurous visitors. Less than twenty percent of visitors make the trip to TRC. The adventurous few who come to stay at the remote eighteen-room lodge were there, like us, to see the boisterous flocks of spectacularly colorful macaw parrots and raucous monkey troops that inhabit the area.

Much of our four-day stay at TRC was spent peering up towering ironwood, kapok, and strangler fig trees for elusive wildlife and sloshing along muddy trails in rubber boots as we learned about medicinal plants and animal behavior.

We spotted toucans and monkeys and spied on the secret lives of smelly peccaries (wild pigs) and gigantic tarantulas by flashlight on night walks. And for those who slowed down long enough to notice, an exquisite macro world existed of fungi, ants, and butterflies.

The truth is, I'm not entirely at ease in the jungle. There are mosquitoes and mud, heat and humidity, not to mention lethal plants, insects, and animals to contend with. But there are also long, lazy naps in the hammock, thunderous rainstorms, and the sweet smell of Mother Earth.

It was during one such reprieve from death-by-jungle that I met Hannelie. She was in Peru on vacation with her adult son and his girlfriend. One afternoon, she revealed her story in bits and pieces as we waited out a thunderstorm slumped in side-by-side hammocks.

Born in South Africa and living in the United States, Hannelie was a beautiful woman with flowing auburn hair who looked much younger than her age of sixty.

"I came to America in my twenties," she said when I asked about her life. "And until a few years ago, I would have described myself as incredibly fortunate. I had it all: a flourishing business, a beautiful home, a loving marriage, and a fulfilling family life."

"What happened a few years ago?" I asked.

"Without warning, it all came crashing down," she said. "The business was bankrupt. Our mortgage was delinquent, and my husband had drained our savings and falsified documents to hide the truth and stave off the inevitable."

I was afraid of what she might be feeling, the depth of his betrayal, the extent of her loss, but I sensed that much of Hannelie's hurt and confusion was in the past.

"I should have known," she continued.

Tears shimmered in her eyes. I detected regret but also resilience.

"It wasn't just the shocking loss that devastated me," she said after a long pause. "It was the deception—his lack of trust."

We lay there in silence, letting the destruction of Hannelie's story ebb away into the steamy jungle.

"What did you do?" I asked eventually.

"I rebuilt my life," she said. "The kids were grown. The marriage was over. I wanted back what I'd given away: independence, self-esteem, freedom."

Every fearful instinct in me came alive. I thought of Ingrid and wondered how I would cope if Hank suddenly died or secretly bankrupted us. Suddenly I was engulfed by vulnerability, fear, love, and a few other emotions I didn't have words for yet.

"How?" I asked. "How did you rebuild?"

I wanted to know. I needed to know.

"First, a neighbor offered me their vacant mother-in-law apartment," she said calmly. "Then, I got a postgraduate scholarship, returned to school, and found work I enjoyed. Eventually, I relocated to a different city, creating a fulfilling and meaningful life there. I'm still a work in progress," she added quietly.

"This trip with my son, for example, is an important part of reclaiming dreams that had gotten lost when I forfeited my life to other people's plans and priorities."

The rain had stopped while we talked, and suddenly a brilliant rainbow transformed the dark sky behind Hannelie. I looked over at this brave, beautiful woman and considered the complex circumstances that had brought me to this moment, this woman, this story.

Not only had Hannelie survived a personal crisis that could have destroyed her, but she'd found a way to thrive. And for the first time,

I found myself believing, not without a tinge of surprise, that I could too.

II

Part Two

Letting Go

23

The Shock of Re-Entry

United States of America

In September 2012, one year, eight months, and fifteen days since the phone call that had sent us wandering, we left Peru to return to the United States.

For a time, we reclaimed our six-year-old Toyota at my parents' house in Delaware and stayed on for a few weeks before heading off on a 3,000-mile road trip to reconnect with family and friends.

Re-entry was difficult. No home. No plan. Money hemorrhaging swiftly. A nagging sense of doubt had also returned. I wondered what we were doing with our lives. Was it all foolishness?

The newfound solace and possibility I'd felt in Cusco only a few weeks earlier didn't feel anything like that anymore.

I knew this transient lifestyle, born out of an idea, was no longer that. There was no going back. Nothing would be the same.

Still, I promised myself we would make it work. To adapt. To not take it all, or myself, too seriously. And it went pretty well until it didn't. A vile argument during a visit with my middle sister left me sad and shaken.

"You're looking at the very darkest side of things," Hank said one evening. "It hasn't been all bad. We got to attend Johanna's wedding, and the time in Florida with my brother was easy and relaxing."

It was true. I thought of how happy and radiant Johanna, a German friend from Mexico, had been at her wedding in North Carolina. And how good it was to see her starting a new life in a new country with a kind and gentle man. I thought too of the day we'd gone boating with Hank's brother and sister-in-law, how we'd tossed an anchor and fishing line into the glistening bay, none of us too concerned with catching anything, and smiled at the memory.

"You're right. I'll do better," I promised.

And yet, I missed the privacy and autonomy of the past year. I missed solitary afternoons reading Emerson and Einstein. I missed Fania's hugs at Jack's. I missed the uncomplicated ease of Hank and me alone together. And, oddly enough, I missed Spanish.

On the streets of Mexico, Nicaragua, Ecuador, and Peru, I listened to the Spanish spoken around me the same way I often listened to music, enjoying the beat and melody without giving much attention to the words. As a consequence, the opinions and influence of other people were blissfully muted.

In the U.S., I could understand everything spoken around me again, and it was almost physically painful in its tragedy. Who suffered from cancer or chronic back pain. Who was miserable at work but didn't dare leave because of the health insurance. Who'd lost their job in the latest corporate restructuring. The latest mass shooting. On and on.

Despite my best intentions, disquiet spread through me like wildfire. I yearned for the incomprehension of a foreign language.

By mid-November, driven by a mounting sense of displacement, we returned to New Mexico. We rented the house of a friend-of-a-friend who had gone to Palm Springs for the winter, and we rejoined the mountain community that had been our home for thirteen years.

Would we stay and rebuild a life here? Did we even want to?

I had no idea.

• • •

Don and Corinna's property was next door. As we followed the familiar road to their construction site and the dilapidated sixteen-foot camper they still inhabited, nostalgia rose up within me. Everything was the same, and yet nothing was.

We parked beside a mud-slicked backhoe and walked to the edge of the driveway, where a fifteen-foot-high retaining wall formed a level terrace against the steep mountainside just as Don and Corinna emerged from the trailer.

Don strode over to us as we got out of the car as Corinna shrieked with happiness and ran out to hug us with their dog Hershey leading the way.

We were soon talking over one another in greeting. Hershey caught up in the excitement, circled our legs. Sunshine flooded the landscape. The moment felt welcomed and familiar. As if no time at all had passed.

"What did you miss the most?" Corinna asked when we'd finally settled down enough to step back to admire the view, her tone now contemplative and her blue eyes alive and interested.

I wasn't sure whether she meant what we missed from New Mexico or our travels abroad. Still, as I looked across a vast swath of evergreen forest to the white peak of Sierra Blanca, the 12,000-foot mountain that towered over the landscape thick with juniper and Ponderosa pine, it occurred to me that of all the marvelous things we'd experienced in our travels, it was this, being in nature—no honking horns or marching bands or clanging church bells—that I missed.

I took it all in. The vivid blue sky. The crisp chill of the mountain air. The way the light filtered through the trees. The billowing white clouds casting a patchwork of dark shadows across the forest canopy. The intoxicating scent of piñon, juniper, and sage. Hershey sat leaning against my leg as we talked, ears up and attentive for a long time until finally, he lay down with his head in his paws. For the first time since our return to the U.S., I felt a sense of belonging and peace.

"It's a special place, isn't it?" Corinna said, guessing at my thoughts.

"It is," I agreed. "I can't wait to see your house perched here and you two enjoying this view from your veranda."

"Tell me about it," she said with a laugh and a roll of her eyes.

Don wanted to know every detail about our time away. Questions spilled out of him, one after another. "What was your favorite place? How's your Spanish? Were you lonely? How did you find places to rent?"

After months of secretly longing for someone to express more than a cursory interest in our experiences, I fell uncharacteristically quiet. It suddenly seemed impossible to extract all that had transpired into a few short, digestible soundbites.

"Look at that," Hank said, putting an arm around my shoulders. "She's at a loss for words. I didn't think it was possible."

We all burst out laughing.

It was good to be back.

24

What Next?

We awakened to a winter landscape. A foot of snow had fallen overnight, and the pine trees were bent heavy with it. Outside, snow was still falling, huge wet flakes twisting in the wind, flinging themselves at the picture windows that fronted the house. It was late November and early snow for southern New Mexico, though not unheard of in the high-altitude climate where weather fluctuations come fierce and fast.

I followed the unmistakable aroma of fragrant Peruvian coffee to the open-plan kitchen. I found Hank sitting quietly in the living room, watching the softly falling snow over the rim of his coffee, holding the warm mug between his hands.

It was an inviting room, warm and bright, with southwestern-style rugs scattered about and a large sofa facing a wall of glass windows, a large stone hearth in the corner, and two soft leather armchairs on either side. Magazines and books piled atop side tables.

We'd been fortunate. Don and Corinna had persuaded the owner, a friend and neighbor, to rent us the house for a few months at a price we could afford. Like many summer homes in the mountain community, it normally sat vacant for half the year while the homeowner wintered somewhere warmer.

I poured myself a coffee and walked over to join Hank on the sofa.

"It looks like we won't be going anywhere today," he said, nodding to the weather outside. "It's too bad the Corolla doesn't have all-wheel drive. We could use it."

Before we'd gone traveling, we'd sold a second-hand, thirteen-year-old Audi with all-wheel-drive and more than 200,000 miles on the odometer, agreeing that it made sense to keep the Corolla, with fewer than 25,000 miles on it, for our return.

"Yeah, I miss the Audi," I said, though there was nowhere we needed to go. "I'm glad we shopped yesterday. If the snow continues, we have enough food and necessities to last at least a week."

"But no Internet," Hank reminded me. "I figured we'd head to the coffee house for WiFi and conversation. Oh well."

Secretly, I was pleased by the weather-imposed seclusion. During our time abroad, I'd launched a new blog series, The Internal Traveler, and was excited to get back to it without distractions. Unlike much of my professional travel writing, the series wasn't about taking vacations. It was about discovery. And what I discovered still surprised me.

How often had I concluded from a daily barrage of gloom-and-doom news headlines that life stinks, people are rotten, and the world outside the door is unsafe? And instead, I ventured out to find a world where kindness is the rule—not the exception.

We'd been forced by the financial weight of a materialistic American Dream that no longer fit to make deep, radical changes to our professional and personal paths. And yet, we'd been given a gift—the opportunity to step out of one way of life and into a freer existence. I'd come to agree with Martin Buber that all journeys have secret destinations of which the traveler is unaware.

To soften our transition, I'd created a soothing mantra for myself, a phrase I silently repeated over and over in my mind each time I felt insecure. *If not this, then something better.*

And it helped. It helped me to let go of the leased New Mexico house. It helped when we left one place for another. It helped when we said goodbye to cherished friends. How often had I repeated it? *If not this, then something better.* Imagining the unknown. Willing something better.

Once, when we were in Cusco, I'd gone with Ana Maria to her weekend house in the Sacred Valley. We were seated side-by-side on a garden swing, the sun cresting over the top of Apus Pitusiray and Sawasiray, the sacred Andean peaks that tower overhead when Ana Maria spoke.

"You and Hank should stay. You don't have to go, right? You could stay, and we could always be together like this."

She'd put words to the emotions that flooded my heart at that moment, and I could barely respond. I didn't want Ana Maria to leave my life. I didn't want to say goodbye and leave behind the feeling of belonging I'd come to associate with Cusco. But then I thought of all the goodbyes it had taken to get me to that verdant patch of garden in a valley considered sacred since the time of the Inca, and something heavy and tight in my chest released.

"*Amiga,*" I'd said after a long pause, "if we'd stayed in the last place we loved, I wouldn't be here with you today. Our friendship would never have been possible."

I thought about this as we settled into yet another temporary home in a place we'd once loved. I looked outside at the forest draped in snowy white and imagined Ana Maria on the Inca Trail, introducing travelers to her magical part of the planet. Arlen, with her Spanish students in Nicaragua, Ute transforming Mexican village life into colorful canvases, and Ingrid thriving in the brave and independent life she'd created for herself out of tragedy. I looked at Hank beside me, and my heart soared. Life was far from unfortunate. But neither was it certain.

I sipped my coffee and turned my face to Hank.

"What's next for us?" I asked. "Do you want to find another house here, get our stuff out of storage, and settle in again? Or keep going? Keep exploring?"

Hank said nothing for a while, his gaze fixed on something outside the window. Finally, he spoke.

"Keep going," he replied. "What about you? What do you want?"

"I'm not sure," I said. But in my heart, I knew it wasn't true. If I wanted to work independently, I had to accept that re-creating our past wasn't the answer.

When we'd decided to leave, there had been, for me, an element of guilt. Of failure. I told myself we were searching for a new home, a place where we'd ship our belongings, settle down, and build a life as we'd done before. Somewhere with a life-work balance that afforded the creative lifestyle we'd come to value. The more we discovered new places and made new friends, the less certain we'd become that we wanted to stay permanently in any one place. We'd always been travelers, but this was something else—a deeper vein.

E.L. Doctorow once said, "Writing a novel is like driving a car at night. You can see only as far as your headlights, but you can make the whole trip that way." Was it possible, I wondered, to live a whole life this way? With few plans beyond the present moment?

"It doesn't matter," Hank said, pulling me out of my musings. "We don't have to decide now. Let's see how we feel in a month or two."

25

Deja Vu

As November passed into December, and then January, we were content to set aside the question of What Next for the time. It sounded funny to say, but I was pleased not to have any trips on the horizon for the first time in more than a decade of professional travel. The retainer contracts I had to write monthly articles for small group adventure travel companies and the group travel blog I co-founded and published were enough to keep me earning and engaged with time for personal pursuits. Hank was immersed in a new novel, and the homeowner wasn't due until spring. Temporary life was good.

Then, one afternoon, a friend from Ajijic emailed.

Hey, you two, Elena María and David are moving again and giving up a great apartment just off the plaza, he wrote. *If you're interested in coming back, you should contact them. I think you'd like the place.*

That evening Don and Corinna arrived with a pizza. Shaking the snow off their coats, they hung them on the rack by the door and took off their boots. As had become their habit, they'd walked over through the forest from their property and had Hershey with them.

Corinna headed straight for the fireplace with Hershey at her heels.

Don held out a thermos containing warm spiced cider. "See what you think of this," he said before sitting across from Hank in one of the cozy armchairs.

"It smells delicious," I said, unscrewing the thermos top and carrying it into the kitchen, pouring a mug for each of us. The drink was sweet and spicy, infused with layers of cloves and anise and cinnamon and hints of citrus and vanilla—a delicious Corinna concoction.

We ate pizza with our fingers from paper plates and drank the mulled cider while Hershey slept curled beneath the table, and Don and Corinna treated us to tales from the building site.

"I solved a problem today that had been bugging me," Don said as he reached for another slice of pizza. "I created a wood form for a curved cement ramp to connect the garage to the house. Steps would've been more straightforward," he continued. "But I wanted to be able to push a wheeled dolly up a ramp for moving anything bulky or heavy. I had to curve it to make it fit the space, which was difficult, but I'm really pleased with how it turned out."

"You should come over and see it. It's beautiful," Corinna said. There was obvious pride in her tone laced with affection.

They had dozens and dozens of stories like this, and I was reminded how resourceful they were and how very much I liked these two. There wasn't anything conventional about them, and I preferred that, admired it. They were creators, making something real and lasting in a disposable world.

When a full moon had risen into the sky, and we'd finished the gingersnap cookies I'd baked earlier that afternoon, we said good night. They layered up, scarves wrapped around their necks, hats pulled down over their ears, for the walk back to their camper trailer.

It was well past ten when we opened the door to the frigid night.

"You're welcome to stay over," I offered.

"Thank you, but no. Look how beautiful it is," Corinna said, gesturing to the clear, crisp night sky.

We were silent for several minutes, gazing up at the stars. I patted Hershey's head as he leaned against my leg.

"You could stay, you know. You don't have to go, right?" Don suddenly said, mimicking Ana Maria's words almost exactly.

I glanced at Hank, who gave me a smile of warmth, promise, and equanimity.

"It would be so easy to say yes," I answered, with Hank's unspoken agreement. "Before we left, this is the life I wanted: a comfortable home, good friends, nature on our doorstep in a place we love."

"But?" Corinna said perceptively.

"We had an email from a friend in Ajijic today with a lead on a rental there."

"Oh? Well, of course. It's like home for you there, too," Don said agreeably.

Was it? I wasn't so sure anymore.

"I think we should call about the apartment," Hank said over breakfast. "I like the idea of living in the village, close to the plaza, close to coffee and cafés, close to everything. Where it's sunny and warm," he added, his tone energetic and hopeful.

I closed my eyes, face turned to the low winter sunlight flooding the room, and said nothing for a moment.

I'd grown comfortable living a quiet rural life again, miles from town and people. There'd been weeks in the past months when, except for long solitary walks in the forest, we'd barely left the house. Together, a hermit's life suited us in the way it balanced solitude with intimacy and enough space for creativity.

But I knew what he meant.

In Latin America, we'd become accustomed to stepping out the door and into a community. Mom-and-pop stores. Bustling markets. Roving dogs and vendors. Neighborhood cafés and restaurants spilled out onto plazas and sidewalks. Our life there allowed for an independence and spontaneity I found exciting.

I could feel Hank's gaze on me as I sorted through my thoughts, but there was no impatience in it. He understood silence. Was comfortable with it.

A part of me envied the roots Don and Corinna were putting down. They were sacrificing to build a future for themselves, a home of their own, and I wished for the thousandth time that I had that in me. But I didn't. Not yet. Perhaps never.

I had a feeling that if I asked Hank to stay, he would. And in that moment, I felt the slightest stirring to do so. But I kept coming back to the price we'd have to pay: the loss of flexibility and freedom, exposure to different ways of life, cultivating resilience, and connection with people from different backgrounds.

We'd been happy abroad. Living in rented homes. Walking instead of driving. Traveling somewhere new every few months. It was a risky way to live, I knew. But with much to gain as well.

"Absolutely," I finally said. "Let's call to find out when the apartment becomes available."

Through a series of phone calls and emails, everything was settled by the day's end. The apartment sounded perfect. The location, the price, and the fact that Ute's house was just around the corner. It was ours for the asking.

I couldn't wait to get there.

26

Poco a Poco

Mexico

"Are you telling lies in that book of yours?" Hank asked me one morning after we'd been back in Ajijic for a few weeks. We were seated on a plaza bench, watching a funeral procession make its way from the church to the cemetery. A peppy brass band leading a parade of somber men and women, scampering children, and scruffy dogs.

I laughed and shook my head.

"Only about you," I teased. But I was intrigued. "Why? What made you ask?"

"I don't know. Maybe it's because you seem to be getting somewhere with it for a change."

I couldn't help but smile when I thought back to the two earlier book drafts I'd already scrapped before starting anew—again.

I watched the little village plaza and the bustling life that it contained. I saw local merchants greeting passersby and neighbors leaving their homes and red-faced snowbirds going across the plaza headed to a café for breakfast and coffee. I watched as our landlord, Mario, opened the door to his store, a small shop that carried a bit of everything. His wife, Isabelle, placed colorfully costumed manikins on the sidewalk in front of her dress shop across the street. A warm breeze moved the fallen bougainvillea petals at our feet.

"It's true," I said, bringing my attention back to the conversation with Hank.

I'd been writing again and was surprised to find that I was not feeling frustrated or panicky, my usual emotional response when faced with a blank computer screen. What I felt instead was potential—a fledgling sense that I had something to say. Large parts of our life had fallen away, leaving my mind free to relax and my defenses to drop. No one was watching or keeping score. The freedom was empowering.

"It feels like I've finally found my voice," I said after a long while.

That made him chuckle.

"Oh? I hadn't realized you'd ever lost it."

"Very funny." I gave him a look, the kind of look that suggested he was lucky that I loved him. I tried to play it cool, to inhabit the confident mettle of a real writer, though inwardly, I was still too susceptible.

"Go on, then," he said. "Tell me about this voice of yours."

His tone was playful. And yet, there was something in his eyes that, alongside the teasing, mocking, and familiarity, told of love and trust and safety.

Instead of answering, I removed my sunglasses and let my gaze settle. A rainbow of sunlight glanced off the balloons of a passing vendor—red, orange, yellow, green, blue, indigo, and violet—then it was gone. A flamboyant tree, framed against a blue sky, was so laden with brilliant orange flowers that it looked as if it had caught fire.

"It sounds odd, but I'm not thinking about the story. I'm living it. And therefore, I feel it more. The doubts. The discoveries. The places and people. Everything is experience waiting to be transformed into words."

"Hmm. You've worked all that out, have you?"

I felt myself flush.

"I know, crazy, right?"

"No more than usual," he smiled.

It had become a thing between us. A joke, but not really. We'd both discovered we quite liked the idea of a little crazy in ourselves.

At that moment, a group of little girls, brightly clad in sundresses and hair ribbons, squawked and raced across the plaza, their cries ricocheting off the cobblestones.

Hank rose from the bench.

"Honestly," he said, reaching for my hand. "It sounds like you're onto something. *Poco a poco, mi amor.*" Little by little, my love.

• • •

Poco a poco had become a familiar phrase. I heard it often in Ajijic, usually after I'd misspoken something, again, in Spanish.

No te preocupes, señora. Do not worry, missus. *Poco a poco.* Little by little.

I couldn't help but sense that the sentiment was as much a testament to the graciousness of the people of Ajijic as it was a metaphor for my life just then.

Little by little.

I've always enjoyed learning, especially on my own, but spending my days in a classroom memorizing verb conjugations did not suit my rebel soul. Just knowing that I *should* enroll in Spanish lessons meant, I suspected, that I was innately predisposed not to. I had always been like that— naturally inclined to do the exact opposite of what was expected. I don't know where it came from, this stubborn urge to resist.

Fortunately, it turns out that I am a decent mimic. I can parrot common phrases, imitate pronunciation, and, somehow, much to my delight, almost speak Spanish.

¿Qué tal? What's up?

Ni modo. It is what it is.

Que le vaya bien. I hope all will go well for you.

¿Cómo está tu familia? How is your family?

I didn't have a clue about the grammar behind what I said, nor did I know what many of the words looked like written out, but I was talking. This also meant that I was connecting and communicating and taking myself less seriously. I think this is how we're supposed to be in the world, and Ajijic was a place that made it easy.

I had hoped to practice Spanish with Ute, who'd mastered it with German precision and discipline. But when we'd telephoned to let her know of our plans to return, I was dismayed to learn she had recently relocated to Puerto Vallarta, a fifty-minute flight or four-and-a-half-hour drive away.

"We still have the Ajijic house," she'd said. "But Carsten finally convinced me to give the coast a try. He can fly direct between Vancouver and Puerto Vallarta, which he couldn't do to Guadalajara, and the gallery that represents me here is suddenly selling. To be honest," she continued. "I'm really enjoying it. We're very much living a bohemian life again. A loft-style apartment with a light-filled studio. New scenes to paint. Sunset drinks on the beach. It feels good."

There was a new vitality and excitement in Ute's voice, and though I would miss her, I was excited for my friend. She deserved it. All of it. More time with her husband. The artistic success. The happiness.

Fifteen years her junior, I saw Ute as a mentor. Someone who already inhabited the deepest desires and beliefs behind the life I aspired to—independent, creative, brave, and self-sufficient. And for some reason, she'd lent this vitality to me over the years.

When we'd first met more than a decade ago, Ute had been in a challenging and uncertain phase of life. Middle-aged, she'd followed sunshine and art to Mexico, risking love and security. It took courage and grit and seeing things anew to rewrite her story. And that she'd moved on, once again, to another role, another chapter, and was thriving only seemed to confirm the hope that sparked and flared inside me when I wasn't worried about finances and death and doing life all wrong.

One morning a year from now, I might catch myself feeling ashamed of writing a midlife memoir or panicking about my lack of a career path. But this won't convince me to give up and sell real estate or become a pharmaceutical sales rep. Instead, I'll think of our precarious life and remind myself to view the turbulence as temporary, the way I would in an airplane or a Latin American taxi.

27

Language for Lent

Over the month of February, Ajijic kicked into Carnaval mode with high-spirited revelry and daily mayhem.

The village blazed, night and day, with noisy firecrackers, marching bands, drag queen beauty contests, and parties at the waterfront malécon. Stepping out the door risked stepping into mock battles involving cross-dressing characters, the mischievous masked Zayacas who looped through the streets chasing the bands of children that taunted them and pelting everyone in sight with fistfuls of flour and confetti, a tradition unique to the village whose origin was the stuff of local lore.

On Ash Wednesday, though, the village's excess of noise and hijinks disappeared. Walking to breakfast that morning, we passed somber villagers in the streets with ash on their foreheads and the look of guilty relief. Did they welcome the next six weeks of fasting, abstinence, and penitence?

"Maybe we should give something up for Lent," I told Hank as we passed the church. "When in Rome and all that," I added playfully.

"Or not," he shrugged.

I glanced up briefly and saw he was unimpressed.

"Commit to something then?" I persisted.

"What do you have in mind?" His tone was cautious in a way that suggested he'd been down similar roads with me before and wasn't exactly certain how he felt about it.

"Spanish," I said, surprising myself. "I want to commit to Spanish."

I wasn't sure, but he might have groaned.

• • •

He needn't have worried about teaching me because a solution soon appeared in the form of a young Ajijic woman named Alma.

Alma is the wife of Javier, the owner and cook of a small café we frequented, and when she wasn't busy with their three young children, she helped wait tables at the restaurant. She was twenty-nine, reserved, and strikingly beautiful with a model's figure and face. We ate breakfast at their restaurant most days, and since they lived upstairs, we'd gotten to know their beautiful black-haired children, who sometimes raced through the café, giggling and chasing one another.

Hank and I have an inherent affection for the small, family-run restaurants of the world and felt at home in their café. So, we were crushed when Alma informed us that morning that the restaurant had been struggling financially and that Javier had accepted a chef's job in Seattle to support his family better. We could only imagine the emotional distress that such a decision would mean to the young family.

"It's only for a little while," Alma told us, her eyes moistening with emotion. "Maybe a year. Two at the most."

"Javier went to culinary school in the States," she explained. "And though his dream had always been to own a restaurant here, with his family, he can earn much more there."

"And you?" we asked gently.

"I'm not sure," she confessed, looking terribly sad. "It's not possible to go with Javier as a family, and though I'd like to keep the restaurant open, it will be difficult with the children. We've talked about changes that could help, like cutting back the restaurant's hours and simplifying the menu. But hiring someone to replace Javier will be an additional expense." She hesitated then as if she'd revealed too much.

I searched for words of comfort. In the end, I didn't need any.

"You and Javier know what's best for your family. I am confident you'll manage," Hank said, instinctively knowing how to support and acknowledge Alma's brave spirit. "If you keep the restaurant open, we'll be your best customers. But if you seek more flexible work, Ellen is looking to hire a tutor to help her with conversational Spanish."

I loved my husband so much at that moment, and when our eyes met, he gave me a sly smile.

"I've decided to take up Spanish for Lent," I explained lightheartedly, and Alma's face brightened into a huge smile.

We started lessons the following week, committing to two hours each Monday, Wednesday, and Friday afternoon for the remaining weeks of Lent. After Easter, we agreed to reassess the arrangement and decide whether to continue.

As I suspected after observing Alma with her children, she was a natural teacher, genuinely enthusiastic and patient. Whatever questions I asked her, she was always willing to attempt or find an answer.

With Alma, I wasn't learning Spanish out of shame or guilt but for pure enjoyment. To practice a new skill with a new friend, and I was even getting pretty good at trilling my Rs. Sure, I'd somehow scammed Lent, a time to sacrifice pleasure, but it provided Alma with a distraction and an independent income during a difficult time. And though I didn't know it then, our arrangement would last more than a year.

28

Casa Azul

"The good thing about being nomadic," I told Hank one afternoon, "is that you discover how adaptable you are. The bad thing is that you're forever forced to adapt."

Adaptation was just one of the various attributes of our wanderings that I'd come to appreciate, some of which just couldn't be helped: How you never know what's going to happen next. The way you wake up and everything changes. Unpredictable, exciting, maddening.

Like one morning when Hank woke me with what I took to be good news.

"I think we should stay on," he'd said. "Ask to extend the rental beyond three months." There was more about Ajijic's perfect climate and the apartment's convenient access to everything, but I'd stopped listening after *stay on*. I wanted it too. No, it was more than just wanting. Something other than that, deeper, maybe. It sometimes surprised me the way contentment hummed through me here.

It had been an ideal March morning. Sunshine flooded the bedroom. The temperature would reach seventy-five degrees by noon, but the breeze that slipped through the open window was still cool. I shivered in my bare feet on the tile floor as we padded out to the small, covered patio just off the bedroom. Beyond the giant clusters of purple bougainvillea that spilled over the wall, we could see the shimmering blue expanse of Lake Chapala and mountains rising in the distance. Bright-yellow warblers, red-headed finches, and boisterous kiskadees darted in and out of swaying palm trees. There was a quality to the morning light and cheerful birdsong that made anything seem possible. I immediately texted Mario, the apartment owner, asking if we could extend our stay.

Later that afternoon, I returned home from a lesson with Alma to find Hank and Mario on the patio. Hank told me the bad news. The apartment was already rented with new tenants due to arrive at the end of next month.

Mario must've seen the disappointment on my face.

"I'm so sorry, *señora Elena*. I didn't know. You and *señor Enrique* said only three months."

"Yes, of course. There's nothing to be sorry about," I replied. "We didn't know then how happy we'd be here."

If not this, then something better.

A warm wind kicked up from the south and brought sounds and smells from the waterfront promenade: the shrieks of children, barking dogs, a mariachi band, and a whiff of grilled pork.

Mario leaned against the patio railing and gestured toward the back wall of the property. It's too bad, he said with a sigh. "We're planning to build two new duplexes out there. Two bedrooms. Modern kitchens. Construction will start soon. But they won't be ready in time for you. I'm so very sorry."

Instant relief flooded over me. I caught Hank's eye and knew he felt it too.

It was times like this that kept us happy to be rootless. Saved from the dust, disturbance, and relentless blare of construction hammers and radios, we assured Mario we would be fine.

The next morning, we stopped by the office of a real estate agent from whom we'd rented in the past— most recently, two years ago at the start of our wanderings.

"You're in luck," she told us. "There's a house in Upper Ajijic, near where you've rented before, that I think you'll like. It was just listed today. When did you say you want to move in? We'll need a few days to turn it around, but, as you know, houses in that area rent quickly. Would you like to take a look?"

By noon, we'd agreed to a six-month lease starting the next week at Casa Azul, a funky two-story adobe house perched a few blocks above the town with lake and mountain views.

Mario, it turned out, wanted to add a guest suite to the apartment and was eager to release us early from our agreement to begin the renovation.

Life changes quickly, waves of calm and upset. Change kept rising to the surface with each passing day, week, month, and year, pitching us forward.

• • •

Casa Azul intrigued us. It was neither blue, as its name implied, nor conventional like many of the surrounding homes in the upscale neighborhood where it was located. The entire second floor consisted of a huge ensuite bedroom and sitting room, with three walls of casement windows through which came uninterrupted views of trees and clouds and lake and the honeyed scent of jasmine and roses. But it was also a bit worn out, with an overgrown garden and a grimy patina of neglect.

"Many thanks for agreeing to help us at Casa Azul," Hank told Rosa as we discussed the move with her over an iced cup of *agua de jamaica,* the slightly sweet hibiscus flower tea popular in Mexico.

Rosa is the cousin of Mario's wife, and she came to clean the apartment every Wednesday. A perfectionist, she scrubbed behind the refrigerator and stove, washed windows until they gleamed, and was as reliable and genuine as she was pleasant and caring. We'd grown fond of Rosa during our two months at the apartment and were happy when she'd agreed to include Casa Azul in her weekly cleaning schedule.

My phone rang just then, and I was surprised to see the call was from Ingrid. I flashed the screen with her name and photograph displayed so that Hank could see it and then picked up.

"Ingrid! How are you?" I asked as I stood to leave the room, mouthing silent apologies to Hank and Rosa.

"You're in Florida? You want to stop here on your way back to Peru? Really? How lovely. Yes, of course. But when exactly? Oh, I see—just a minute while I check with Hank."

With the microphone muted, I explained that Ingrid wanted to pass through Ajijic en route from Florida to Peru and to stay with us over the weekend.

I could see Hank's concerns pass across his face. First, the apartment didn't have a guest room— a sort of *Where will she sleep?* Then, some calculations about the date of her arrival and our move to Casa Azul. And finally, acceptance, a look that said, *"Oh, what the heck, Ingrid is good company, and it would be fun to see her."*

"She can sleep on the couch," I said. "Or, she could stay next door at Casa Mis Amores, the hotel where my sister and her husband stayed the last time they visited."

"Whatever you decide," he said agreeably. "Tell her she's welcome, but let her know the situation."

"We'd love to see you," I said into the telephone. "But would you mind sleeping on the couch? Unfortunately, we won't have guest quarters until next week when we move to a bigger place. Or we could recommend a hotel."

"Not a problem for me," Ingrid said. "But if it's too much for you."

"Not at all," I assured her. "We're excited to see you. What a wonderful surprise. Thank you so much for wanting to include time with us."

I felt a surge of excitement at the thought of our Peru and Mexico lives overlapping, a merger I hadn't even known I wanted.

We gave Ingrid the address and explained about taxis from the Guadalajara airport, and I told her a little about Casa Azul, which excited her, since Ingrid loved little more than to transform a house into a home.

In bed that night, long after Hank had fallen asleep, I lay awake watching the moonlight stretch across the room and pondered the possibility of giving up our vagabond ways. I hadn't sought travel assignments in more than a year, though opportunities and the retainer work continued to flow in. Beyond my book, I didn't see a future that resembled the past. I could feel Ajijic reaching out to pull us in.

We could, I imagined, negotiate an affordable long-term lease for Caza Azul and do home exchanges for travel. *Why now?* I wondered. Maybe just comfort, a wish to extend a pleasant time. Maybe something else. We liked Ajijic, right?

29

A Place to Nest

While I dreamed about the possibility of making Casa Azul a home, Ingrid got right to it. No sooner had the taxi driver deposited Ingrid's suitcase in the apartment foyer when she asked: "When do we go see the new house?"

We managed to slow her down long enough to enjoy a platter of fish tacos and a mango margarita at a plaza café, but not for long.

"I'm only here for the weekend," she reminded us. "Let's get at it!"

We laughed when she pulled a pair of gardening shears from her purse.

"I think I'll leave that to the two of you," Hank said, wisely opting to retreat to the apartment as Ingrid and I headed up the hill to Casa Azul.

While I rearranged furniture inside, moving antique armchairs around and unearthing a set of vintage red-clay cooking pots from an enormous kitchen pantry, Ingrid tamed the lush courtyard garden.

She revived a defunct fountain, rescued a wrought iron café table from the garage, and snipped away with her garden shears until she'd transformed the space from an overgrown tangle into a cheerful haven.

"It's enchanting," I said, stunned by the drastic results of her efforts.

"It is, isn't it?" she exclaimed with unabashed admiration.

"This is an incredible garden," she said. "Poinsettia plants as tall as trees. Climbing vines of jasmine and rose. Bougainvillea in every color. Happy geraniums. And this," she exclaimed, as she lowered herself onto a rustic wooden bench with faded and peeling blue paint. "I would kill for a bench like this," she swooned. "And to think I found it hidden behind a thicket of dense shrubbery. This place is a treasure trove."

It was true. Casa Azul was full of surprises.

I looked at the charming little courtyard, at the newly revealed walls painted in a cheery yellow, at the blue-and-white Talavera pot with coral-hued geraniums on the café table, the rustic bench, and found myself thinking about all the change and uncertainty that had made such good fortune possible.

"Now, what about those heavy drapes upstairs?" Ingrid asked briskly, pulling me out of my musings. "A linen gauze would be so much better. It would diffuse the afternoon sun without hiding the view. The cement banquette in the living room could use a colorful cushion," she continued, "and a new bedspread for the main bedroom. Is there a fabric store nearby? Just imagine how gorgeous this place will look with some Mexican textiles. You're so lucky!"

Before I'd replied, Ingrid had out a measuring tape and made scribbles in a small notebook. Oh, how I adored her in that moment. She is everything I am not: organized, prepared, enterprising.

"Let's do it," I said, energized by her vitality. "I know the perfect shop. It's not far, and it's on our way back to the apartment."

I suddenly wondered why it was that I, who had become as migratory as the soaring white pelicans that fly 2,500 miles south to Lake Chapala each winter, was now eager to order curtains and cushions and dreaming about long-term leases before we'd slept a night in Casa Azul.

30

Great Highs

The months in Casa Azul were good in many ways. We talked, read, ate, laughed, and met up with friends at the plaza, including Alma, who continued to tutor me in Spanish. At night, cozy in bed, we watched the spectacle of the monsoon thunderstorms, which raged outside the windows and lit up the night sky with dramatic eruptions of lightning that illuminated layered mountain ridgelines and wind-bent Cyprus and palm trees. By morning, Ajijic's red roof tiles, garden flowers, and cobblestone streets shimmered fresh and clean in the sunshine. A newly washed canvas on which to begin again.

There were the rainy-season troubles of an old, neglected vacation rental, too, with water leaks, power outages, and makeshift repairs. Still, it was a perfectly contented time, better than any vacation could be, filled with pleasure and promise and books.

Day after day, we got lost in reading, sometimes consuming entire books in a sitting. Novels and memoirs, poets and master-thinkers. There was Inspector Gamache, Nuala O'Faolain, Rilke, and Epictetus. On other days, I'd put in my earbuds and head for the cheerful garden courtyard, where I would listen and move to the beats of Marley and

Fela Kuti, Alanis Morissette, Aretha Franklin, Stevie Wonder, Santana, and the Chicks (previously the Dixie Chicks).

Casa Azul was where we welcomed Hank's seventy-seventh year over a dinner of wild-caught shrimp from the Gulf of Mexico, pan-seared in butter, lemon juice, cayenne, and paprika, enjoyed with friends around a large, leather-topped Mexican Equipale dining table. It was a house where we drank coffee, chatted in the mornings, and spoke easily and intimately about things that mattered. It was a house flooded with light and lightness. During the months in Casa Azul, I'd shed years of weight, literally and metaphorically, and was healthy and happy in a new and exciting way.

Then, in a kind of retrospective loss, the bubble burst—Casa Azul was put up for sale. Events, again and again not occurring as expected.

There would be no long-term lease. No settling down in Casa Azul.

An urgent liquidation of assets for an elderly owner, it was explained. Perhaps we were interested in purchasing? Cash only. A bargain at $300,000 U.S. dollars.

So there we were again with no real money, no real plans, a lot of beautiful memories, and a lot of fun times in what was ultimately a charming but entirely impractical house. And yet somehow, out of all that, Ajijic had managed to offer a solid base of warmth and belonging that, for a while, felt a great deal like home. Much of what I wanted was here: comfort, community, and Hank.

It was mid-October, and the timing wasn't right to leave Ajijic entirely. I had to travel soon for a work trip—an adventure travel gathering in Namibia with a follow-up assignment in Botswana—and Hank was still nursing tender ribs from a nasty stumble on the cobblestones. So, for the third time in the nine months since our arrival, we set about the task of finding another rental.

If not this, then something better.

A house soon surfaced. A sublet down the street from Casa Azul: a lovely three-bedroom, comfortably furnished with grapefruit, orange, and lemon trees in the backyard and neighbors we already knew.

Rosa agreed to keep us in her weekly cleaning schedule.

Alma would check on Hank and cook daily meals during my absence.

We agreed to move house at the end of November.

• • •

"Are you going to sell the linen curtains you had made for Casa Azul?" my friend Nina, a Canadian expat, asked me one afternoon.

"I hadn't thought about it. But you can have them if you like," I said, suddenly seeing how well-suited the fabric was for Nina's natural and minimalistic decor.

"Oh, yes. I'd love that. They would be perfect in the living room."

We were celebrating, sipping champagne poolside on the back terrace of Nina's newly purchased house. She had moved in a few days earlier and was busy putting it together in eager preparation for the arrival of Edward, her longtime partner.

At seventy-two (Nina) and eighty-four (Edward), this was the beginning of a much-anticipated new chapter, living together permanently in Ajijic after more than a decade as wintering snowbirds. While Edward was still finalizing things in Toronto, Nina had already sold everything in Montreal.

"I think this pool will do wonders for Edward's arthritis," Nina said as she rose from the chaise to slip off her sandals and dangle her feet in a large lap pool elegantly surrounded by Talavera pots of trailing bougainvillea and decorative palms.

"It's so warm," I said after joining her at the water's edge, my jeans rolled up and bare feet submerged.

"I had a new solar heater installed for Edward. I hope the warm water and perpetual sunshine will help his arthritis. He never complains, but I hate knowing that he suffers."

Her tone was tender and affectionate as she spoke of Edward, and it was obvious, from the heated swimming pool to the side-by-side chairs I'd spotted in a cozy sitting room off the main bedroom suite, how much thought and attention she'd given to transforming the house into a home for the two of them.

I'd never met Edward and had only gotten to know Nina well during these recent months in Ajijic, though we'd both attended a women's writing group one winter years ago. She was writing a novel back then that she'd recently self-published. I'd purchased a copy at a signing party hosted at a local café, and she'd surprised me by offering to be an early reader for my book after learning I had one in progress. From there, an unexpected friendship had taken root over drinks, dinners, long conversations about books and words, and authors and artists. I welcomed the time together as it helped to soothe the creative ache of Ute's absence.

• • •

A week later, I arrived in Namibia from Mexico jetlagged and exhausted from the two days and four flights it had taken to get there. My body felt stiff and sore. But even jet lag couldn't numb the excitement behind the trip. As one of four participants on a photo safari, I was headed to Etosha National Park, a vast protected reserve in northern Namibia home to huge herds of big game. For five days, our focus would be the solitary task of photographing Etosha's legendary wildlife—big cats, elephants, black rhinos, and big game in abundance.

Namibia has a powerful story: one of hard-won freedom (it gained independence from South Africa in 1990), innovative conservation initiatives, ancient culture, and extraordinary landscapes. To go to Etosha was a dream. Each morning, we parked at one of the natural springs that serve as a lifeline for the free-range wildlife inhabiting the arid Etosha salt pan. In a single day, we would visit waterholes teeming with more animal species than I could hope to see in a lifetime.

Once, we watched more than a hundred zebra drink and bathe beside herds of elephants, giraffes, eland, kudu, and impala in a raucous dance choreographed by Mother Earth. In another instance, a mother cheetah nursed four fluffy cubs only a few yards from the safari vehicle. On our final afternoon, a leopard stealthily approached to drink just behind where we'd parked, granting us a rare glimpse of the elusive cat in the wild.

Later, however, whenever I talked about these amazing encounters, it wasn't the experience of photographing the prolific wildlife that I recounted. It was how fully alive and in sync with the natural world the animals were. I'd recall how instinct guided the herds to Etosha's life-supporting water and how the cheetah cubs had displayed basic hunting behaviors like stalking and pouncing in their play—a powerful reminder that our true nature wasn't something we needed to learn. We were born with it.

• • •

November began with my fiftieth birthday. An African celebration of song, drums, and cake rich with brandy and candied fruits at a Botswana safari camp. There were six of us. All women. Each in the travel business. Aged from twenty-six to sixty-six. A few of us were longtime friends. Others were traveling solo. Some of us had husbands at home. One was engaged to be married. Another was single by choice and reveling in her independence. We got along brilliantly, laughing and bonding as only travelers can do.

For three blissful weeks, we viewed leopards, lions, and zebras instead of television. We napped in the afternoon sun beside a private plunge pool and dined al fresco beneath a dazzling night sky in the convivial company of new friends. Each night we fell asleep cocooned in tented comfort, listening to the orchestral sounds of insects and animal calls in one of the richest natural habitats on Earth.

With the ease of chartered flights, the trip hopped from camp to camp, habitat to habitat. Each morning, steaming thermoses of coffee and tea and freshly baked pastries were delivered to the tent in place of a wake-up call. There were massage therapists to ease away any kinks that bouncing around in safari vehicles might incur—gourmet meals paired with impeccable South African wines. Fireside aperitifs were standard perks, as was the private safari guide who greeted the plane at each camp, accompanied every game drive and revealed the secrets of the landscapes with infectious passion and knowledge.

In the arid Kalahari Desert, we walked with native San people as they introduced us to their ancient hunter-gatherer culture through demonstration, song, and dance using the extraordinary tonal clicks of the San language.

On the eastern tongue of the Okavango Delta, we tracked hyenas and wild dogs. We swam in a riverside pool where a pod of snorting hippos, including a rambunctious baby calf, cooled off in the muddy shallow water just beyond us.

In the heart of the Okavango Delta, we explored shallow waterways afloat in a mokoro canoe. As a boatman silently push-poled us through delicate water lilies and grassy reeds where hippos napped, I missed Hank. I took comfort in knowing he was not alone, that he was among friends. But, oh, how he would've loved this trip.

The final morning was at Savute Elephant Camp in Chobe National Park, a landscape famous for its large herds of elephants and Cape buffalo. During our two days at Savute, we'd had elephants lumber by the safari vehicle so close, so uncomfortably close, that I'd held my breath. We watched giraffes amble across the dry Savute Marsh, a dusty relic of a once vast lake and felt the ground tremor beneath the rumble of a massive buffalo herd. We'd seen kudu, impala, and warthogs and awakened to a pack of wild dogs yipping and playing over their morning breakfast not far from the tent.

Then there was the leopard.

The leopard that had climbed effortlessly onto a tree branch overhanging the tent's deck.

The leopard that locked eyes with me as I took its photograph.

The leopard that suddenly leaped from the tree straight toward me as I stood frozen, not because I'd been instructed to do so, though I may have been, but rather because I was frozen with fear.

One second, the leopard was in the tree. The next, he was on the ground in front of me, a few feet away. Seconds later, he'd made the life-saving decision to escape beneath the deck.

Time stopped. Awareness disappeared. I don't know how long it was before I'd noticed my friend Susan's hand on my elbow as she pulled me into the tent.

Then, slowly, conscious of my breath, my trembling hands and weak knees returned. Susan and I giggled in waves of nervous laughter, the lingering aftershocks of shock and awe.

Witnesses from neighboring tents soon appeared and chattered like sports commentators with play-by-play reconstructions of the encounter.

As the fog of fear lifted, a clearer picture of the incident took shape: The wild dogs that had treed the big cat. The camp guests who had startled him. The warning growl. The choice of the panicked animal to flee.

Like a million other times, Mother Earth astonished me.

• • •

Over the years, I'd learned to pay attention to my conversations after returning from travel. To listen for the insights and observations, I exhaled as naturally as my breath—the stories that had become so much a part of me that I barely noticed. Within each story, I now understood, lay hidden a nugget of self-awareness.

So, at some point, after sharing every detail of the trip with Hank, I realized that I would always associate Botswana with the leopard and Namibia with one specific phrase—*It's a pleasure.* In my memory, almost every Namibian conversation ended with this gracious sentiment.

One morning in Swakupmund, for example, as I'd walked alone on a quiet residential street, an older woman had stopped her car alongside me to ask if I needed a ride. Swaddled in almost every piece of clothing I'd packed, I was ill-equipped for the cold October weather of the coastal town and chilled to the bone. I told the woman I was headed to town to purchase a coat. She said she knew just the place and would take me there. I hopped into the cozy orbit of her car, and when I thanked her for going out of her way to deliver me to the store, she waved it off, saying it was a pleasure.

I can still feel the surge of gratitude and awe I'd felt standing there watching her silver sedan pull away. In that instant, I became acutely aware of how much I wanted to be a person who is intimate with the pleasure of kindness.

In the days that followed, with my ears tuned for it, I heard *it's a pleasure* everywhere.

When our safari guide thanked a colleague who'd stopped to help change a punctured tire, he hopped into his Land Cruiser and shouted a cheery *it's a pleasure* over the noise of the diesel engine.

It was in the bits and pieces of conversation between drivers and dispatchers that crackled across taxi radios and at the airport in Windhoek, where a friendly waitress told me it was a pleasure to help me install a local SIM card into my iPhone.

I was inspired by the genuine delight Namibians appeared to take in helping others, and it was contagious. From that point on, the phrase became a daily part of my lexicon, even in Spanish.

Gracias señora.

Es un placer.

31

Where Would You Go?

Where would you go if you only had a few weeks to live? It's a compelling question. Would I drop everything and head off on a thrilling Bucket List adventure? Would I stay right where I was, in a temporary house in Mexico? Would I return *home* to the landscape of my childhood?

Recently, a newly nomadic friend emailed me an op-ed article by *The New York Times* columnist Roger Cohen written around the question.

Seated in the shade of fruit-laden orange trees on the veranda of a rented *casa*, I considered what I would do.

It was an ordinary, sunny Saturday. A lively ranchera beat wafted across a lazy afternoon breeze alongside recurrent strains of chattering songbirds, barking dogs, and the peals of children's laughter. From a rooftop terrace overlooking the backyard, a neighbor yelled down to invite us to dinner for *Pascua* (Easter). The air smelled wonderful, like citrus and roses, like warmth and earth and sweetness.

In such blessed circumstances, it was difficult to contemplate the internal chaos that a fatal diagnosis would surely trigger. Despair as far removed from my current contentment as could be imagined. And yet, the question nagged at me.

The initial, *Would I leave Mexico?* yielded to the deeper inquiry: Would I choose to be anywhere other than where I was?

My gut said no.

For the next few days, as I met Alma for conversation and coffee, as I stopped to buy fresh avocados and mangoes at the corner *frutería*, or sat beside Hank at the glass-topped wooden door that served as a makeshift writing desk, I experienced the euphoria of being alive and content in a way that felt raw and pure and recently familiar.

After a while, the elation faded, and I could feel anxiety tugging at me as feelings of doubt and uncertainty vied for my attention and led to more questions: *Can looseness and connection co-exist? Can we be itinerant and transitory yet still feel rooted?*

In his *NY Times* article, Cohen, who spent his infancy in South Africa, grew up and was educated in England, and then, after an unsettled life as a foreign correspondent, made a home in New York, refers to this type of elective roving as contemporary homelessness. Out of it, he wrote, often, comes anxiety ... anxiety about belonging: displacement anguish.

The anguish, confusion, and isolation of *outsider-dom,* as British literary critic James Wood once named it, had been ever-present, if not acknowledged or understood, for much of my life. The journey of these past years had been coming to terms with that ambivalence. And as my skin grew brown, my hair lightened, and the excess weight I'd carried for years melted away in the Latin American sunshine, I began feeling sturdy satisfaction in the simple pleasures of our itinerant existence.

Amid Mexico's chaos, noise, and color, I finally got that outsider-dom is more feeling than fact. Because I was so actively living a life—for the first time—with no sense of performance or expectation, I was free to let the veil of separation drop.

It was now early April, and after fifteen months in Ajijic, we were making plans for our departure. We mentioned the pending transition to friends at Café Grano, the Ajijic roastery where we met for coffee most Saturday mornings, and it triggered a flurry of ideas and recommendations.

"Remember Roger? He moved to Chiang Mai and loves it," one said.

"Howard and I are headed to Bali for two months. I think you'd like Ubud," another suggested.

"I'm curious about Colombia," I said.

Something in the impromptu conversation brought my thoughts back to the unanswered question of where I would go if I only had a few weeks to live.

Would I want to head for Chiang Mai, Bali, or Colombia? Would I feel compelled to return to the United States?

I suddenly realized, with great clarity, that I wouldn't go anywhere. I would stay put. Wherever Hank and I are together is enough. The fierceness of my conviction was unexpected. I was surprised by the tears that rolled down my cheeks, and I quickly wiped them away.

Hank leaned in to whisper in my ear, "You okay?"

There was confusion and concern in his eyes. I nodded yes and excused myself to the restroom.

When I returned, Hank reached over to cover my hand with his. We sat like this for some time, engulfed in the convivial company of friends.

We walked back a short while later to our temporary house in relaxed silence, navigating the uneven sidewalks and stone streets with familiar ease as we dodged telephone poles, protruding electric meters, and the dog droppings of the town's many free-roaming pets. We often separated, stepping into the street to yield the sidewalk to children and *ancianos* (elders), rejoining after they'd passed.

The steep foothills of the Sierra Madre mountains that tower above the village had turned brown and brittle until the summer monsoons arrived again to turn them emerald green and send torrents of water gushing down the slopes and streets to the awaiting Laguna de Chapala at the town's edge.

"You're my favorite wife, you know," Hank said into the silence, pulling me back into the present moment. A smile settled across his face. His eyes creased with mischief.

I laughed, even as I blinked back tears behind my sunglasses.

Typical Hank, letting me know it's going to be okay. That I will be okay.

32

Deep Lows

Months earlier, I'd been invited to present a session on storytelling and travel at an upcoming travel conference in the States. The event planners wanted me to talk about why story matters, how to become better storytellers, and how narrative deepens and enriches the travel experience.

I was delighted. It was a subject close to my heart. Travel had not only transformed the way we lived, but storytelling also fueled how I worked and viewed the world.

In preparation, I dove deep into research, data collection, and a study of the intricacies and characteristics of the world's best storytellers. I dissected my favorite books, surfed the Web for how-to articles, and watched TED talks by gifted raconteurs like author Isabelle Allende, Pixar filmmaker Andrew Stanton, Nigerian novelist Chimamanda Adichie, and others.

I got lost in other people's stories, and a period of excitement followed, leading me to believe that I, too, could tell stories that would inspire and inform.

And then the time came. I boarded the plane, checked into the hotel, collected my blue presenter's name badge, and fell immediately ill with a malaise of uncertainty whose main symptom was self-sabotage.

My days at the conference were tainted with toxic habits. I could hardly believe how quickly I abandoned myself. I skipped meals to spend extra time in preparation, gobbled potato chips and chocolate bars from the minibar, and stayed up late, sacrificing sleep to practice the presentation.

Fear had me in a vice grip. I was sick with anxiety. I saw the insanity of my behavior but couldn't stop myself.

By the time I had to teach, I was exhausted and wired and stammered my way through a presentation I should've been proud of. The audience and my colleagues were attentive and generous, but I hated letting fear get the best of me. I hated that I'd lacked the poise and confidence to relax and let my innate storyteller shine. And I knew better than to take myself so damn seriously.

I knew there was a lesson to be learned, and my job was to dig for the deeper meaning and find growth in the experience. So I decided to return home, talk it through with Hank, nourish myself, catch up on sleep, and then ask myself the questions that haunted me: *Why had I chosen to sabotage my potential, and how could I do better in the future?*

Instead, I arrived to the tragic news that my friend Nina and her partner, Edward, had been murdered in a violent home invasion. In the awful moment I learned the grizzly details of the bludgeoning and stabbing that had ended their vibrant lives, my petty fears and disappointments disappeared. In their place was a searing sorrow.

Over the next few days, I ignored the emails in my bulging inbox, escaped into afternoon movies, sat in the sunshine, slept late, and went to bed early. I was grief-stricken that a friend's future had been taken away and experienced ferocious surges of love for Hank. I Googled fatal stomach knife wounds in an attempt to determine if death had come quickly. I got sadder.

And then I got to thinking about life and death and priorities, how death is real, and how it can come without warning. I felt a stab of panic at the thought of losing Hank, but I also thought about how Nina and I had laughed and shared and talked about art and creativity and the way they could change the world. And this made me happy.

I asked myself how I could honor my friend's life and concluded the best answer was to honor my own. To listen to the voice of intuition when it whispers my life purpose. To not let insecurities hold me back. To fail and get back up. To cultivate and trust my natural abilities and walk boldly through doors of opportunity. To remember that life is bigger than fear and death. To live until I die.

33

Family

United States of America

It was June 2014, sixteen months after our arrival, when Hank and I finally said goodbye to Ajijic.

We were healthy, homeloose, and headed, first, to Pennsylvania for the wedding of Hank's granddaughter. Then, to visit family and friends. Beyond that, we had no plans.

Once again, re-entry proved tricky.

Greeting us in baggage claim at Philly International was a tickertape of tragedy spelled out in CAPS across the bottom edge of a large-screen television as a news anchor reported the world's worst events at a volume impossible to ignore:

Border confrontations flared between Russia and Ukraine, while heightened tensions led to an exchange of rocket fire in the Gaza Strip.

Suspected Boko Haram militants launched an attack in a village near the northeastern Nigerian city of Maiduguri, killing approximately 45 people.

Four people are shot, with one dead, and three injured, during a shooting on the campus of Seattle Pacific University.

At least 52 people are dead following a series of bombings in Baghdad.

In Syria, the terror group ISIS takes brutality to a new level with graphic video beheadings and the brutal takeover of entire towns.

In Moncton, New Brunswick, Canada, a gunman shoots five RCMP officers, killing three.

It was enough condensed sorrow and violence to bring you to your knees before reaching the baggage claim carousel.

I know that beauty and terror coexist. I know there is kindness and laughter, brutality and injustice in this world. I know that news headlines do not tell the whole story. I want to be well-informed. And yet, there are moments such as this one when I desperately wanted to dial down the awfulness.

• • •

A wedding, it turned out, was the perfect antidote. All kisses and smiles, hope and promise, champagne toasts, and a free pass to dance wild and terrible while the ancient ones smiled from the sidelines, too prim or arthritic to join in but radiant nevertheless from the proximity to such unfettered optimism.

The knowledge that it could all blow up in divorce, tears, and broken hearts a few years or decades later is the beauty of it. The magic in it. That two people are willing to take the risk, to say *I Do* and give love their best shot no matter what, that's worth celebrating.

"You're enjoying yourself more than I'd expect from someone who eloped to avoid her own wedding," Hank said as I came off the dance floor and dropped, sweating and panting, into the chair beside him.

He was right, of course. I'd never wanted a wedding or all the planning and pettiness I associated with it. But wedding guest: that I could do with honest celebration and warmest wishes. No problem.

"You know me," I told Hank. "I'm a sucker for love. And free bubbly,"

I added with a playful kiss.

"Who are you, and what have you done with my wife?" he said with a wry smile.

He was relieved, I could tell, to see me smiling and enjoying myself again after the sorrow and confusion that had overtaken me after Nina's murder.

Though Ajijic had been our go-to place for sunshine and ease for years, I was conflicted about the complicated relationship between the Mexican residents and the foreigners who flock there. I believe in open borders and global communities. I believe that we should not judge what we don't understand. I believe in chosen nationalities and shared cultures, but I'm also aware of the challenges —economically and culturally— behind such commingling. How much did outsiderdom play in Nina and Edward's murders? Was it random or targeted? I often wondered as I struggled to make sense of a senseless tragedy.

On this day, though, this day of celebration, I lost myself and forgot. I laughed and danced, ate the salmon dinner, and drank my share of wine. The future felt wide open, full of possibility.

The next morning, I exchanged the perennial black travel dress and wedding heels for everyday jeans and Birkenstocks. After five easy and enjoyable days with Hank's two adult daughters, we headed to Delaware for a week with my parents.

• • •

Returning to my childhood home was complicated. It wasn't a place of carefree memories. Rather, it was one of inescapable anxiety. Not always. But often. And yet, I was optimistic. After all, I was no longer a child. I had built a life of love and humor with Hank. My parents were older, wiser, no longer overwhelmed by the responsibilities of rearing and supporting four children. The last few visits had gone well, I reassured myself, and I'd left grateful for the opportunity to experience a different kind of relationship with my parents.

So, I wasn't entirely prepared for what greeted us.

My octogenarian parents were in the midst of a turf war, and suddenly, so were we.

"Your father doesn't understand," Mom said. "He wants nothing to change. But I'm tired. Tired of cooking and cleaning. Tired of worrying that he'll fall and break his neck again or that I will. Tired of driving and grocery shopping and maintaining a five-bedroom house."

"Your mother can't seem to grasp the economics of aging," Dad countered. "She wants to sell a comfortable and spacious home that we own outright to live in a resort with three meals a day and maid service. She has made up her mind that we're moving to Meadow Haven, a nearby retirement community where we have friends. But that takes money. At their rates, we could be broke in a few years. Then what? A lifetime of working and saving, gone."

Though their emotional distress was painfully raw, it was a well-hashed argument with no apparent resolution. She was moving forward no matter what. He was convinced it would be the death of them.

The tension was toxic and taking a toll on their health. They'd visibly aged since we last saw them, and Mom had stopped preparing meals in protest. They couldn't go on like this, and there was no way, as I saw it, that we could leave in a week as planned.

I didn't know what to do. Part of me understood how overwhelmed they were and wanted to do whatever I could to help, and part of me felt powerless against such ingrained ways of relating. I wanted to stay. I wanted to flee.

Night after night, they rehashed the same argument.

"Where there's a will there's a way," Mom would say blithely. "I don't believe we're as destitute as your father makes out. I find that things usually work out in the end."

"That's the problem," Dad would counter, frustrated and seething. "She's always gotten her way. But this time I can't do it. I can't pull a rabbit out of the hat to make this magically happen."

"Your parents have other options," Hank pointed out to me late one night when I was at my wit's end, exhausted and emotionally spent. "They could hire more help, for instance. With the entire upstairs no longer used, there's certainly enough space to accommodate a live-in caregiver if or when it becomes necessary." But when he suggested this to Mom and Dad, they shut him down immediately.

"No way. I would never have a stranger living in our home," Dad said. "It's bad enough with the help we have now. David helps me with the yard work and maintenance since your mother won't allow me to do it myself anymore. And Ana and Paula come once a week to help clean and change the bed linens. No matter how helpful they are, it's still a nuisance."

"It does nothing to solve the problem of aging in a three-story house," Mom said. "I'm worried sick that one of us will fall on the stairs. Also, if we want a social life, we have to drive at night or in winter weather. At Meadow Haven, we'd have on-site friends and activities and help in an emergency. No," she said firmly, "staying here is no longer an option."

"I'm not sure what to do," Dad admitted to me one night as we sat side by side at the oak desk in his study, poring over ledgers and budget calculations. He was teary-eyed, as defeated and vulnerable as I'd ever seen him, and it broke my heart.

I assured him that he was not alone, that he didn't have to figure this out on his own, and that he had help. But his engineer's mind craved a mathematical path forward, and without hard numbers to guide him, he was paralyzed—unable to make choices he didn't want to make about a future he couldn't imagine.

I suggested that we stick to the facts.

First, I called Meadow Haven to determine the actual expenses. Applicants, I was told, needed to provide documentation proving their income and assets were sufficient to meet the monthly fees, ranging from $3,000 to $5,000 for an independent living apartment or cottage, with inflationary increases of about three to three-and-a-half percent a year. Meal plans, health care, and home care expenses were extra, with pay-as-you-go rates from $160 to $248 per day for assisted or nursing care as needed. There was also a $300,000 entrance fee—an upfront deposit to be kept as a financial reserve for potential future care if they ran out of money.

Seriously?

I was beginning to understand what Dad was up against.

"These might help," Dad said one night, gesturing to a towering stack of promotional packets from various retirement communities on the corner of his desk. "I sent for these once the house went on the market, and I realized your mother was dead set on moving. But it's all marketing hype. Plans and packages without much real information about costs. Maybe you can make some sense of it."

He was right. There was scant information about rates and fees in the packets. So, with the help of my out-of-state siblings, we started making inquiries.

I created a Google spreadsheet to record and compare the data in a format that spoke to Dad's analytical mind, and a clearer financial picture soon emerged. Dad's relief was palpable. For the first time, he had concrete figures to compare with his current expenses and budget.

The previous summer, Mom and Dad had toured potential retirement communities. Some, like Meadow Haven, were local or just over the border in Pennsylvania. Others were in Salt Lake City, Utah, where my younger brother Rob and his family had relocated a few years earlier.

Of all us kids, Rob, with middle-school-aged twin daughters, was deemed the one least likely to move anytime soon. He was also actively encouraging Mom and Dad to choose a retirement community nearby.

A month later, a decision had been made that short-circuited the war, at least for a time. After the house sale, Mom and Dad would move to a Salt Lake City retirement community located only four miles from Rob's house.

"It's the right choice," Mom explained. "There's no entrance fee, and restaurant-style dining, on-site entertainment and activities, and weekly cleaning are all included in a monthly fee close to our current expenses. Plus, no more home maintenance costs or property taxes, and, best of all, Rob and his family are only minutes away. I'll miss my friends," she added, "though many of them have already moved away to be closer to their kids. It's that time of life."

"I resisted for too long," Dad confessed. "Our health isn't what it was even a year ago. Change is necessary to remove the burden of responsibility from you kids in the event of a health crisis. We can't keep up with such a big property anymore. I see that now. And the prices near Rob are much more reasonable than here. It's the right choice."

I understood the logic and admired their fortitude. It wasn't a future that Hank and I saw for ourselves, but Mom and Dad were in sync for the first time since we'd arrived, and as we listened to them talk, it became clear that, after so much anxiety and heartache, they were relieved to have made a decision.

• • •

We would leave soon afterward, though only after Mom and I had found a professional moving consultant, a kindly middle-aged woman, to help with the complex logistics of relocating. Together we tackled a lifetime of belongings, going through their home of forty-five years room-by-room to divide and package it into three categories: To giveaway. To sell at auction. To take to Utah.

The consultant also arranged for a charity and auction house to collect any items not destined for family or Utah and for a cleaning crew to come in after the house was vacated.

Dad mostly kept his distance from the preparations, making it clear that he would choose and pack his things. Mom reluctantly agreed to the arrangement, perhaps as a concession to the meal delivery service Dad had agreed to until the move.

The battle was over. Solutions were in play. Mom and Dad were back on track.

34

Not-So-Scenic Detours

In the weeks before we left Ajijic, I'd created an online profile on a housesitters website. I'd done it spontaneously, with no real expectations, thinking it might open up future travel opportunities. Then, caught up in the maelstrom at my parents, I hadn't given it any thought until the day an email containing an invitation to housesit appeared in my inbox. The homeowners, a retired couple in Las Cruces, New Mexico, with two elderly dogs, had spotted our profile and thought we might be a fit for two months while they traveled in a motorcoach.

The combination of emotional exhaustion, no real plans for the immediate future, and photographs of a luxurious home had me tempted. Hank, not so much.

"Are you serious?" he asked after reading the email. "Las Cruces in August heat? Elderly dogs? It would help with finances," he admitted after a pause.

It seemed silly to perceive the housesitting offer as fate, but it felt that way. From the ether of cyberspace, we'd been handed a place to plan our next move in a comfortable home with the goodness of dogs and time and space to regroup.

"I know, I get it," I said. "It's not ideal, but it could be a place to catch our breath, a refuge after all this, while we figure out what's next. I'd like to learn more."

The sun had long gone down, and we were reading in bed. It had been a good day after a run of difficult ones. Mom and Dad had found obvious consolation in their decision and had the insight to realize that an end to the war was in their best interest. The fear wasn't gone, though they did their best to hide it. It was there, simmering in the cauldron of an unknown future in Salt Lake City.

Adrift for three years now, Hank and I knew first-hand the challenges of an uprooted life and the trauma of giving up a home, community, security, and an identity. Moving away is an act that upends everything familiar. The life you knew is over. The future is vague and uncertain, though time and again, in these past few years, I've come to see that standing still, wishing that nothing would change, is not a viable life plan and that there is much to be gained in forward motion.

And yet, I understood that in a world where more than 100 million people have been forced by war, persecution, and disaster to flee their homes and countries, it would be beyond callous to compare our experiences, or my parents, to theirs. No matter the angst, our displacement was chosen. In places where Hank and I had been welcomed, many desperate and deserving were denied entry, put into camps, and informed they were unwanted, unworthy, and illegal—if such a designation for a human being can be made. Was it possible to know this and still see our story as valid?

Part of me understood how fortunate Hank and I are to have a passport and circumstances that allow us to move about the world with relative ease and freedom. Part of me perceived how random and unjust that is and how quickly our fate could change. Another part of me clung to the belief that, somehow, somewhere within that paradox, was this journey's meaning, purpose, and hope.

Unfortunately, I am almost as good at failing to see trouble ahead as I am at fooling myself that all is well when it obviously isn't. The red flags were there for the housesitting gig: The homeowners' certainty that we were the perfect (only?) choice for the job. The way, at the last minute, two senior dogs suddenly became three.

"Sadie's a recent rescue with a few issues that don't make her ideal for the motorcoach. Don't worry," they said, "she's a real sweetie since the anti-anxiety meds."

By this time, I frequently communicated by telephone and email with Samantha, the homeowner who'd written to invite us, and I'd become fond of her. So when she mentioned that they needed to leave Sadie behind but would still be traveling with their two other dogs, I was almost grateful. I reasoned unreasonably that three animals to care for were better than five.

"But we love dogs," I said to Hank when he suggested this might not be a good idea.

A month later, I swallowed back tears at the vet's office while Baxter, the sweetest little old dog, died in my arms, and I loved Hank even more for letting me sob against his chest instead of telling me he'd told me so.

Who knew that Sadie the Devil Dog would be bipolar? Who knew a friend's elderly father would live alone in an assisted living community a mile from the Las Cruces house with his only daughter and every friend he had, a two-hour drive away? Who knew he'd take to phoning us in the middle of the night to ask for a glass of water or how to use the television remote? And who knew he'd end up in the hospital twice during our stay, delirious with pneumonia and infection and no one but us nearby?

I thought of the time with my parents and how I'd imagined Las Cruces as a refuge. I thought of the shaman's ceremony in Peru when

I'd hoped that what I needed to learn would be revealed and of Hank's warning about how brutal those lessons can be. I thought about how wrong decisions can seem like the right ones and that if I cared enough to make a meaningful life, if I cared enough to not always get it right, then I needed to care enough to experience heartache alongside fortune again and again.

35

This Is Starting to Feel Familiar

Most people have a plan for the next month, the next vacation, the next five years. At least, that's what I believed about people with houses, career goals, an IRA, and six months of living expenses in their savings account. The fiscally savvy with a mastery of frequent flyer points, cash-back credit cards, and corporate loyalty programs. People. Not. Like. Us.

We'd had two months in Las Cruces to plan our next step. And yet, we hadn't.

Fortunately, meaningful coincidences continued to occur. In between caring for the dogs and our friend's elderly father, work continued to flow in. Word had spread within the travel and tourism community about our nomadic wanderings, and people were curious. We are neither twenty-something gap-year backpackers nor retired expats putting down roots overseas, and an untethered life at our ages was unusual enough to warrant curiosity. Even more so at a time before Airbnb and remote working became mainstream.

One travel editor commissioned an article outlining the pros and cons of a nomad's lifestyle, and a follow-up piece about freelancing abroad after the first article attracted interest. An expat magazine published a Q&A interview with us about the nuts and bolts of being "homeloose," a term I'd adopted to describe our version of homelessness. And, like the Internal Traveler blog posts that I continued to write and publish, the articles provided a chance to reflect and articulate all that we'd experienced. The unexpected change in circumstances. The perils and pleasures of learning to live a different way of life. The slow surrender of control.

If not this, then something better.

One evening, we were reading on the back patio of the Las Cruces house when the phone rang. The dogs were sleeping at our feet. A fiery New Mexico sunset lit up the sky. Our friends Don and Corinna were on the other end. We put them on speakerphone and listened to the exciting news that they had moved into their dream home.

"We did it! We finished the house!" Corinna exclaimed with all the excitement one would expect after nine years of living in a dilapidated camper trailer while they'd built a house they'd first imagined, then sketched, then made into a blueprint. For the better part of a decade, they'd cleared land, built a road, dug drainage ditches, built retaining walls, and, eventually, built the house they now inhabited.

"Wow! Congratulations," we said with genuine awe.

We listened as they explained how precarious the final push had been. How low their funds were. How worried they'd been that they wouldn't finish before winter. In the end, they'd had to borrow money to hire contractors to complete it.

"It was worth it, though," Corinna said. "The house is amazing. Just as we'd imagined. The view, the windows, the under-floor heating, the rainwater system, the greenhouse, the kitchen— it's incredible. Check your email. I sent pictures."

"And the best news," Don added generously, "is that the guest house is ready for you. Will you come? We'd love it if you did. You can stay as long as you like."

"It's pretty bare-bones compared to what you might be used to," Corinna warned. "There's a new mattress with a box spring on the floor and a small but well-equipped kitchen. We can give you a couple of folding chairs, and I'm still tiling the shower, but it has a fantastic view. Well, you know. You remember."

So much had transpired since that February morning some four-and-a-half years earlier when Don and Corinna had joined us for breakfast when the idea of wandering had first taken root.

I recalled the times when we'd cooked together in the gourmet kitchen in the leased house on the hill when they didn't have a home. I thought back to the previous winter when we'd rented their neighbor's house, and they'd tramped through the woods on snowy evenings to share pizza and central heating.

I turned to look at Hank. He smiled and nodded his acceptance, which mirrored my feelings. Renting their guest house would help all of us.

This wasn't about comfort. I wanted to explain to Corinna but I didn't yet have the words for it. Something more subtle governed our decisions now. A feeling I was only beginning to recognize as freedom and friendship.

"Thank you," I said. "Yes! We'd love to come."

One minute, we had no plan. The next minute, everything had fallen into place—again.

This was starting to feel familiar.

• • •

We made the two-hour drive to Don and Corinna's a few weeks later. The compact, one-room guest house was as sparsely furnished as they'd described: a solitary, double bed, two low-slung folding chairs, like the kind you might take to the beach or a picnic, and a partially tiled shower. Light poured in from large, undraped windows with deep, unfinished windowsills and a sliding patio door. The galley kitchen had open shelving inside a small, recessed pantry that looked as if it would one day have a door. The countertop was handcrafted from a thick plank of dark cherry wood. There were bare terra-cotta tile floors, champagne-colored walls, and a European-style wood stove that divided the sleeping alcove from the living area. The overall effect was simple and stylishly minimalistic.

The spacious and sprawling main house attached to the guest house by an oversized garage and workshop had a similarly unassuming and open plan. A curved wall of narrow, floor-to-ceiling windows framed a vast forest and mountain view. Twins of the two guest house camp chairs faced the view in an otherwise empty dining alcove. There was no television. No furniture. No artwork on the walls. No comfortable reading chairs, though I spotted open boxes of books stacked against a wall in the corner of the kitchen.

"That will be the office," Don said, following my gaze. "Those books have traveled with me from Colorado to Alaska, New Zealand and the Pacific Northwest. I plan to build bookshelves and a wrap-around desk with plenty of space to write. I wrote in bed every morning in the trailer," he said, quickly turning away.

I sensed complicated emotions behind the words and wondered briefly: *Could he miss the trailer? Is he discouraged by all the work still to be done?*

"How's your book coming?" I asked, knowing that, like me, Don had a book in progress.

"I haven't had much time to work on it these last few months with the building crews here daily," he said. "But I'm eager to get back to it, especially this winter, now that we're in the house."

While Don described radiant heat zones and the UV filtration system to Hank, Corinna took me through the kitchen, explaining in detail the carefully selected appliances and cabinetry choices inspired by years of preparing meals on a one-burner hotplate and toaster oven in the trailer.

This was a well-equipped, well-imagined kitchen, from the sleek German oven to the deep, self-closing drawers and water-saver dishwasher. High on function. Zero pretentiousness.

I noted how the island unit was optimally positioned for an uninterrupted mountain view. The way it was the exact height for Corinna and how the backsplash wasn't yet tiled.

"I'm going to create a mosaic there, like the one in your shower," Corinna explained, showing me some small ceramic pieces she planned to use.

As the sun set, we sat together on the front terrace in the camp chairs and ate lentil soup from mismatched bowls on our laps. As the sky turned yellow and red and then navy blue before turning black and starry, I gazed upward and felt full of contentment. I thought about how much I adored and admired what they'd created. From the winding tree-lined driveway to the pale alder-wood doors, the sweeping ten-foot windows, and the pottery studio in the garage. This was an artist's house with no sign of a desire—or urgency—to fill it with stuff.

That night, as I overturned two empty paint buckets scavenged from the garage and topped them with a leftover floor tile to create makeshift nightstands, I thought of the storage unit located a few miles up the road where we stored our past. How it contained the belongings that had once filled the four-bedroom, three-car garage house on the hill where we'd been happy. I thought about the well-worn reading chairs and the cozy library with overflowing bookshelves. About hand-woven Mexican rugs, a high-tech coffee maker that brewed and ground the beans automatically, a long Tuscan-style dining table, and the Bowflex gym system Hank had used every morning.

That we had so many things seemed obscene. That they remained unused in storage was insane.

"I'm glad that we can inject a little extra money back into their ever-draining cash flow with rent for the guest house," I said to Hank in bed that night. "But we could also offer to let Don and Corinna use whatever they need from the storage unit."

"Yeah. Sure," Hank agreed. "Assuming they can find anything."

We half chuckled, half groaned in remembrance.

When we'd hired movers to pack our belongings, we'd considered the possibility of relocating abroad, so they'd packaged everything into one massive, shrink-wrapped bundle ready to be transferred upon request to a shipping container. This meant that Don and Corinna couldn't just walk into the unit to pick and choose what they wanted. But if they were interested, we'd figure out a way.

"Oh! I remember those custom counter-height chairs you had from Santa Fe," Corinna said with unexpected excitement when we brought up the idea the next morning. "You know, the ones you had at your kitchen island? They might be perfect for ours."

Hank and I smiled. We loved those barstools too. And, as was true for so many things that had once furnished our homes, they had a story. Purchased in 1994 during the summer vacation when we'd spontaneously married in Santa Fe, they'd been shipped to our home in Pennsylvania, where we lived then. Four years later, they were loaded onto a moving van and transported back to New Mexico when we relocated there.

I loved that Corinna had singled out the barstools and was excited by the idea of them being enjoyed in this beautiful new home.

The conversation continued this way with increasing eagerness as different items were remembered and mentioned: "What about those leather library chairs? Or floor lamps? We could use a couple."

Enthusiasm quickly fizzled, however, once we explained the huge, shrink-wrapped bundle that was the current state of our belongings.

"Oh, I don't think we want to tackle that," Don said, looking slightly alarmed.

"The emptiness actually feels refreshing after the clutter of the cramped trailer," Corinna added, quickly backtracking.

"I can't blame them," I said to Hank once we were alone. "I'm certainly not keen to have a go at it during the couple of months we might be here."

"Glad to hear it," Hank said, looking at me with amusement. "I was wondering how I'd talk you out of it. Though I'm not wild about these camp chairs," he added with a moan as he lowered himself almost to the floor to sit down.

III

Part Three

Moving Forward

36

Synchronicity

We were quickly settled in at Don and Corinna's, with an easy intimacy flowing between the connected households when a rental listing for Guanajuato, Mexico, appeared in my inbox.

A year or so earlier, an American friend living in San Miguel de Allende (about an hour's drive from Guanajuato) added my email address to an expat Yahoo Group that served the two communities. I received sporadic notifications about events and opportunities. Usually, I clicked delete after a cursory glance. But on this day, a Guanajuato rental caught my eye.

Maybe it was because the mid-September nights were already dropping to near freezing, and snow would soon be coming. Maybe it was that I could still remember the healing effects of our last Mexico winter. Or that we'd been stateside too long. But, it somehow felt significant that I'd spotted the rental. When I shared the listing with Hank and asked if he thought we should follow up, he told me to go for it without hesitation.

We never did receive a reply to my initial inquiry. But because the message had been visible to the entire group, another member reached out about a different rental:

Dear Ellen,

I saw your interest in renting in Guanajuato starting in November. I have a three-bedroom, fully furnished, and equipped house in the Historic Center, just two blocks from the main plaza and all the museums, galleries, restaurants, language schools, etc., in the Historic Center. You can walk everywhere. No need for taxis or buses, although they are plentiful at all hours. My house, on a pedestrian-only street, is a small three-story townhouse with a roof terrace and city views. The house has all amenities: telephone, Internet, washing machine, and a fully equipped kitchen. It is available at the end of October, and the rent is 6,000 pesos per month plus utilities. Photos are available of the house and neighborhood.

Grace Hamilton

We clicked on the provided gallery link and found photographs of a cozy house with a terrace view of steep, narrow lanes, rainbow-colored buildings, red tile rooftops, and cathedral spires. It looked glorious. I could barely contain my excitement.

And yet, I didn't want to influence Hank's reaction as I had regretfully done with the Las Cruces offer. So I played it cool.

"What do you think?" I asked.

"Looks good," he said. "Do you know the dollar equivalent of 6,000 pesos? "

I entered the amount into a currency app on my phone and reported, in a monotone that concealed an escalating eagerness, that today's conversion was approximately $425.

"Really?" Hank said, pleasantly surprised. "That's a good deal. I think we should grab it before someone else does if you're interested."

"Absolutely! I was hoping you'd say that." I felt thrilled in the way I do before a new adventure. "The timing is perfect," I continued, unable to rein in my excitement. "And I've always wanted to go to Guanajuato. It's on my wander list."

"Is there any place that's not on your wander list?"Hank asked, bemused.

I wasn't fooled. I knew he had it in him too. Hank has seized opportunities his entire life. This was the man who, at age fifteen, fast-talked his way into a summer job as a cowboy on a Montana ranch when a friend for whom the position was intended couldn't go at the last minute. The Pennsylvania boy who had then traveled alone on a fifty-two-hour bus journey to work with the rugged ranchers who nicknamed him Hank, not Hal, for Henry, as his family called him. Who set off for California in a vintage Plymouth with his best friend on the night of their high school graduation. And who hasn't stopped adventuring since.

When we wrote back to say we were interested, we learned that the woman we'd be subletting the house from, Grace Hamilton, also lived part-time in Ajijic.

Dear Ellen,

I live in Ajijic and rent a house in Guanajuato (GTO) and have a place in Puerto Vallarta. What I consider "home" is Ajijic, but I spend winters in PV and autumns in GTO. Each place is unique in its ways, and I enjoy the changes. I am a bit of a gypsy and have always enjoyed living in different cultures. GTO is an exceptional place. It is a university town with students of all ages and backgrounds. Its cultural offerings are extraordinary and inexpensive. If you have never visited GTO, make it a must on your bucket list. It is the most beautiful and colorful city in Mexico.

Grace

PS: I enjoy your blog! It reflects many of my feelings.

That Grace was in her eighties and living her dream life—and possibly ours—sealed the deal. The next day, we purchased one-way airline tickets for a November first arrival.

We were beginning to tune into the rhythm of synchronicity.

How many nights had we gone to bed under one set of circumstances and awakened to another? How many times had opportunity surfaced when we weren't looking? How often had we turned our hearts toward an inner wisdom and borrowed its power?

I was born into a life ruled by anxiety and fear, but perhaps that didn't matter much. Experience was teaching me another way.

37

Getting Back My Groove

Mexico

Disoriented and breathless after a long travel day and wheeling our suitcases up the steep stone *Callejón* (narrow alleyway), we knocked on the rustic wood door of the Guanajuato rental house and hoped the housekeeper would be there to greet us as planned.

I felt at home in Mexico, and I hadn't realized how much I missed it until a woman with a kindhearted smile and a cheerful yellow apron opened the door, and a wave of relief flooded through me. The intensity of the emotion startled me.

"*Bienvenidos*. I'm Viviana. Come in. Let me help you," she said with the hospitable warmth I've come to associate with Latin America.

Viviana looked to be in her forties and had an exuberant, singsong voice that reverberated through the narrow, three-story house that seemed to match the cheerful mood of its yellow, orange, and green walls.

I marveled at her good-natured ease as Viviana settled us into the house—showing us the hot water heater on the terrace, where the gas tanks were, how to operate the washing machine, and where to find extra light bulbs—and was touched by how quickly she made us feel welcome.

It was our first time in Guanajuato. The beauty of its tree-lined plazas immediately enchanted me. The brightly painted houses that tumble down steep mountainsides and the elegant mansions with wrought-iron balconies and pots of geraniums I'd glimpsed as the airport taxi navigated its way through a maze of subterranean roadways to deliver us to Plaza Cantarranas, the leafy square at the base of the hill that climbs to our newest temporary home.

Our arrival on the first of November coincided with *Dia de Los Muertos* (Day of the Dead), one of Mexico's most celebrated holidays, a festival of remembrance in a culture that savors and honors the memory of its deceased. We unpacked our few belongings and headed to town to check it out.

Following a labyrinth of narrow alleys and stairways, we made our way down to the Jardín de la Unión, Guanajuato's main square, and communal living room. The sun shone. A brass band played in the gazebo. Families filled the plaza's cafés, benches, and walkways with the casual intimacy of generations and an uninhibited affection that I admired and envied. Seeing the children as they chased pigeons and imagination, secure in the visceral tenderness of family and community, I understood how seductive those bonds could be, how connected they can make you feel, and the satisfaction one could derive from feeling so rooted.

"You're unusually quiet," Hank said with a warm smile as he took my hand. "I thought you'd already be campaigning to move here."

A great gust of gratitude for my husband and his special ability to make me laugh brought me back to the music, the joy, and the colorful flower petals that carpeted the streets.

Three weeks later, through the most ordinary activities, buying fresh papaya at the market, lingering over coffee with Hank, or writing at the simple pine desk at the top of the third-floor stairs that had become my office, life was once again transformed.

Between the sunshine, the color, the snug comfort of Hank's love, and the mischievous influence of Mexico, Guanajuato had unfurled my soul, and I couldn't have been more grateful.

There was another factor fueling the rediscovery of my creative groove.

Shortly before we left New Mexico, I'd helped my friend Kerry build a new website for her marketing agency. We locked ourselves in her office over a weekend, ordered takeout, guzzled iced tea and coffee, and hunkered down in front of her super-sleek, super-sized Apple pro-display to transform the working pieces of her company into a snazzy new website. We wrote copy text. Studied other sites. Selected imagery. Strategized content and navigation structure. And while I understand that none of that may sound exciting, we had a blast.

Kerry seemed to love the collaborative process—and the result—as much as I did. Enough that she sent me off to Mexico with a contract to do web design and development for her agency.

I didn't know it then, but a long-term partnership and a new career path were born from that collaboration. And what I would come to understand in the years that followed is that web design ticked many of the boxes of my innate interests and learned skills.

The technical part satisfies the mathematician in me.

The visual aesthetics utilize my photographer's eye.

And copywriting requires me to tell a story.

More significantly, it returned travel and photography to the personal realm. I no longer carried the heavy lenses and multiple camera bodies necessary for professional photography. I traveled lighter and lighter, with only an iPhone now. There was freedom and playfulness in photography again. That was because I was creating simply for the joy of it—with Guanajuato as the perfect muse.

The transition to the new work became another step in finding my creative footing and provided me with a portable career that suited my introverted temperament. Exactly what I'd wished for those many months ago in Peru and the partnership predicted by the tarot card reading in Ecuador.

Meanwhile, I may not have been actively working on my book, but it continued in bits and pieces. A fleeting inspiration here, a sudden burst of an idea there, a piece of a conversation, or something I read would come to me as I carried on with work and building a temporary life in a new place.

Even still, I'd started to miss the professional travel tribe I'd left behind and struggled with regrets. One minute, the independence and solitude would feel empowering, and the next, I'd feel nostalgic for our old life—one that was neither financially sustainable nor temperamentally well-suited. It was confusing. It was perfect. It was disorienting again.

Then, just as I'd be on the verge of self-recrimination and regret, I'd remember all the things I loved about this life. The stimulation of exploring different places and making new friends. The autonomy of independent work in a place and pace of my choosing. The pleasure of slowly settling into a new culture and living in a way that supports the soul.

And still, that knowing was at odds with a powerful urge deep within me: the desire to have it all—freedom and security, flexibility and belonging, love and community.

38

New Tribes

We knew one person in Guanajuato when we arrived: Louisa Rogers.

I'd met Louisa more than a decade earlier on a Pacific Coast beach in the small town of La Manzanilla, Mexico.

Hank and I had rented the hilltop casita of a friend-of-a-friend in La Manzanilla that winter when I'd passed Louisa walking on the beach. I'd stopped to ask her if she'd purchased her swimsuit locally. She told me she hadn't. We struck up a conversation and walked together long enough for me to learn that she was an American with a home in Northern California and that she and her British husband traveled extensively. Then, we parted ways after exchanging contact details.

We'd remained in touch sporadically over the years, so I knew that Louisa had purchased and renovated a home in Guanajuato where she and her husband, Barry, lived part-time.

They were in town for a few months when we arrived, and Louisa agreed to meet up to reconnect and help us get acclimated. She joined us at Café Italia, a European-style coffee house tucked into a narrow alley beside the Basílica Colegiata de Nuestra Señora de Guanajuato. The café had fast become our go-to morning destination, mainly because it was the only coffee house nearby that opened early.

As Louisa filled us in on where she bought groceries, banked, took Pilates classes and Spanish lessons, a steady flow of life passed by the open window. There were giggling clusters of uniformed school children, university students with bulging backpacks, sun-wrinkled older men and women, and a few tourists.

I was already smitten with Guanajuato. A large part of its appeal was its complex mix of bustling university-town vitality, laid-back café culture, and a level of prosperity that came from being a UNESCO World Heritage site.

Not yet an expat hotspot, in place of the gray-haired retirees that filled the coffee houses and bars of Ajijic and San Miguel de Allende, Guanajuato's cafés were enjoyed by local professors and students, legislators and lawyers, multigenerational families, Mexican tourists, and a small community of foreign residents.

Part of that small community, Louisa revealed, was Tim Leffel, a mutual acquaintance and professional colleague from travel and tourism who lived in Guanajuato.

Through Tim, we met his wife, Donna, whom I would later work with for personal fitness training, and Kate, a travel journalist and guidebook author who lived just a few houses away from our rental.

Like Louisa, Donna (American) and Kate (Australian) had fiery, adventurous spirits and were busy living vibrant multicultural lives.

When I first met Donna, she had a feisty directness that made me immediately recognize that she would kick my butt in training. Just what I needed. She also brought energy, laughter, and hilarity into our lives, which was as beneficial as the workouts.

Every Tuesday and Thursday afternoon for six months, Donna exploded through the front door of the rental house and into the kitchen for pre-workout water and a chat. Then, she'd regale us with the latest teenage-daughter-drama in her family life or a list of upcoming cultural events we'd probably never learn about otherwise.

Hank and I both looked forward to her visits.

Kate, I adored from our first hello. She oozed creativity, from the red-framed eyeglasses she wore to the way she'd retained the charm and character of her modest little Mexican house while infusing it with large, colorful canvases of Australian aboriginal art and Mexican textiles. She spoke with real zeal and conviction about the various countries—Mexico, Greece, Portugal, South Africa, and Australia—she covered for Lonely Planet. Her energy, enthusiasm, and ease with languages inspired me so much that I instantly hoped we'd become friends.

Kate ended up guiding me through Guanajuato as she did in her guidebooks, with detail, insider intel, and insights into the place and people.

It was Kate who introduced me to a delightful afternoon addiction: the *beso negro* ("black kiss"), an ultraconcentrated hot chocolate at Café Tal, a hip student hangout with the glorious aroma of coffee roasting on the premises.

It was Kate who generously provided the key to their house so that Hank and I could retreat to the sanctuary of their home office to write during the periods when she and her husband, Chris, were away.

And Kate who entrusted me to get her twenty-something goddaughter to a doctor when she'd arrived from Ecuador feverish with a raging sinus infection a few days in advance of Kate and Chris's return.

One day, I answered a knock at the door and met Mara, an expat from New York who was renovating a townhouse up the street. She'd heard we'd moved in, stopped to introduce herself, and soon proved to be a light-hearted companion open to adventure.

In these women, I was finding my way back to a tribe and a powerful reminder: that women can be strong and silly, that women can be independent and in loving relationships, and that women can be a lifeline for other women. They woke me up to my desire to live a vibrant and connected life and the deep value of the bond between women.

One night, Louisa invited us to a meet-up at their house with the regional Mexican chapter of Couch Surfing, a global organization that connects travelers with local hosts and a place to stay.

"It'll be a chance for me to host a gathering entirely in Spanish," Louisa said when she called me on the telephone about the event. "And good for you, too, to meet more locals and converse in the language," she added as an incentive.

She was right.

I didn't understand much of the rapid-fire Spanish spoken around me, but the members were warm and welcoming and instinctively slowed their speech when speaking directly to me or if they perceived I was being excluded. Once again, I was experiencing firsthand the generosity of community.

By default, I am reluctant to expose my vulnerabilities. But Louisa, Donna, Kate, and Mara were so open, so secure in their lives while being tender with mine, that I had become comfortable enough to peel back the layers and reveal more of myself. They were displaced people, just like us, and they understood well the value of these kinds of connections, these special places where you can let your guard down and be yourself.

I didn't suddenly set aside all my insecurities. That's not the way life works. But the time in Guanajuato gave me a new female tribe and new awareness with which to proceed.

The tribe keeps growing.

The work is still being done.

39

Scheming and Dreaming

Even after Guanajuato introduced me to the rewards of community, I still wasn't sure what it looked like for us. With the income and engagement of creative work, I was blessed with the closest thing to freedom I'd known. Nearly four years had passed since we'd become nomadic, and I'd found unanticipated happiness in our wanderings. There was no reason to be dissatisfied. But I'd never quite broken free of the impulse to nest. I bought pots of bougainvillea and put them out on the little rooftop patio. I filled vases with aromatic lilies; I draped colorful textiles over benches and chairs; I rearranged furniture.

One day, Kate mentioned that a newly renovated house on the plaza near her place was a possibility for a long-term rental or purchase, and I felt the delicious daze of seduction again, the sharp rush of inspiration to rearrange, reprioritize, and reimagine life.

"I could live here," I told Hank over breakfast the next morning with a view of the house framed in the café window.

"Isn't it a bit large?" Hank asked, looking across the little plaza at the stately three-story colonial townhome that, according to Kate, had been built by a wealthy political family.

"Well, yes. I guess it is," I said, ignoring the obvious implication that this was probably not the home for us.

I continued in full scheming-and-dreaming mode. "Kate thinks it could be possible. She says the California couple who renovated it urgently needs to return to the States and might be open to a creative offer."

"Is that what Kate says?" Hank said. He was smiling. His face was relaxed and happy, his eyes crinkling as he looked at me over a morning plate of *huevos a la Mexicana*. I knew he knew I was thoroughly infected with the excitement of imagining *I could live here*.

"I think we should investigate it anyway," I said, undeterred.

"Okay. See what you can learn, but I'm not sure Guanajuato is where I want to stay."

That weekend, I decided to poke around. A knock on the carved wooden door of the house yielded only a friendly housekeeper in a cheerful floral apron who informed me that *No, señora, los dueños no están aquí* (the owners are not there) and no information as to how to contact them.

I asked at the Café-Te-Arte at El Zopilote Mojado, the small hostel on Plaza Mexiamora, where we ate breakfast each morning. Nothing.

I called the telephone number Kate gave me for a real estate agent she thought might know something. It went straight to voicemail.

The following Friday, I came home after writing and deposited my bag beside the front door. Hank was pouring a glass of iced tea in the kitchen and warming up a portion of chicken empanadas. I filled a glass with water and sat at the table to join him.

"Any progress on the house hunt?" Hank asked as he turned off the stovetop and plated his food.

"Nothing," I said. "The owners are still not in residence, and the agent who returned my call knows nothing about it being for rent or sale. The friend who told Kate about it learned it secondhand and hasn't heard anything more."

"Sorry, babe," Hank said. "It sounds like it's not meant to be." His tone was tender and genuine.

"I know, right? If it had come together easily, I'd be thrilled. But in a way, I'm relieved. The future is unknown again."

"You don't want to look for another place?" Hank asked.

"No. I think I only wanted the house on the plaza to have Kate next door. To have our favorite breakfast place only a few steps away. To invite friends to come and stay and have enough space and privacy to hang out for a while and watch them experience Guanajuato's magic. But it might also have meant the end of this adventure, of wandering, of discovering new homes, and making new friends."

I grabbed a fresh, ripe banana from the kitchen table fruit bowl and peeled it back from the skin, releasing a sweet, tropical aroma.

"No," I said. "It's okay. It's working out just the way it's meant to."

Hank sat there and digested this, no sign that my latest crazy zigzag vexed him.

"Okay," he said, picking up the pitcher to refill our glasses. "Where next?"

That's when it struck me.

I was no longer worried about an uncertain future. I was excited by the possibilities.

40

Cusco Revisited

Peru

On a February morning, three years after we left Cusco, we emerged from the arrivals hall of Alejandro Velasco Astete International Airport into Cusco's harsh summer sunshine and thin high-altitude air to find Ana Maria waiting for us. Wonderful Ana Maria! She waved, and her face brightened when our eyes met. It took a few seconds for my eyes to relay the sight of her to my brain and a few seconds longer for my brain to believe we would soon be living in the downstairs flat of her home.

Ana Maria and I kept up a sporadic WhatsApp exchange over the years, and when she told us her rental flat was available, I took it as a sign. Plans were made for us to return, and Ana Maria told us she would pick us up at the airport. She was tiny, with wavy salt-and-pepper hair, mahogany skin, and restless energy barely contained. She looked like a teenager in her thong sandals, hip-hugger jeans, and Andean wool belt. We hugged and together hefted our bulging Patagonia duffels into the hatchback of her SUV.

We asked about her recent travels in South Africa, Botswana, and Zimbabwe with her son and sister and were shocked to learn that she'd only returned yesterday after nine weeks away. Had we known, we protested, we'd never have arrived today. She waved away our apologies, and we repeated our gratitude.

From the car, I looked out over the passing chaos of the city and perceived an overwhelming sense of order at work behind the scenes. If we hadn't been offered that last-minute assignment to hike the Inca Trail in 2012. If Ana Maria hadn't been our guide. If we hadn't stayed in Cusco long enough to spend time together. If she hadn't mentioned in a message that she'd had an unexpected tenant cancellation, and if she'd told us that our arrival was so soon after her travels, we might never have found our way back to Cusco.

We'd been back just three days when Ingrid returned from a trip to Florida to visit her sons. I'd kept up with Ingrid since we left Cusco, and, like Ana Maria, she was a big part of our desire to return. She was still living in the Sacred Valley, and though she was eager to get home, it was an additional hour and a half drive from Cusco. When we invited her to stay overnight with us after her flight, she agreed.

Once Ingrid telephoned from the taxi to say she was only minutes away, I set the table with the Andean salad and pumpkin ravioli I'd purchased that afternoon a Orgánika Cusco, the vegetarian restaurant situated two hundred stone steps down Calle Resbalosa, the steep Inca passage upon which Ana Maria's house is perched. Ana Maria came down from her upstairs apartment to join us, and soon, we talked like old friends, and I felt the jolt of just how precious the moment was.

In bed that night, I asked Hank if it felt that way to him too. Was he glad to be back?

He put down his book. He thought for a minute and said: "Do I love listening to you girls chatter and cackle and never getting a chance to say anything? What man wouldn't?"

And then he smiled.

"No, it was a very enjoyable evening," he said, pulling me close. "The people we meet are the best part of our travels. When I think about how you keep in touch with everyone and the friends you bring into our lives, I know we are better for it. Besides," he said, "I like Cusco as well as most places. I could live here."

We laughed, but I wondered if in saying that Hank had just predicted our future.

Two months later, when Ana Maria's annual contract with a guiding company came due for the flat, we moved into the apartment on Calle Lucrepata where we'd stayed in 2012, and four months after that, when our visas were about to expire, we extended.

• • •

We settled in more easily month after month. The winding labyrinth of narrow Inca passages felt less and less exotic. We'd become such familiar neighborhood faces that the street hawkers nodded hello or ignored us rather than accosting us to purchase their trinkets. Ana Maria insisted it was because we no longer gave off the energy of a tourist, and I had to agree.

I stood by the carved granite jaguars at the entrance to the house on Lucrepata just as I had three years ago and watched the near-daily processions of twirling dancers and brass bands block traffic and make their way down to the Plaza de Armas. They were dressed in the same colorful costumes, feathered headdresses, and barefoot sandals I had seen at the Inti Raymi festival, with saints on pedestals and bells strapped to their ankles. Their confident faces showed the pride and commitment of people dedicated to their traditions.

Every morning we tread the slick cobblestones worn smooth by centuries of footfall on the narrow streets of San Blas as we walked down to Jack's Café, where Fania and her brother Jhedi worked, and were greeted with an affectionate hug. We would have coffee and breakfast, and then, just as we had three years previously, we would regret the generous portions on the steep uphill climb home until the next morning.

My work life had also settled into an agreeable routine. With each new web design project followed a growing need for continued content management and copywriting services, which I now provided under additional retainer contracts along with the design and development agreement. Best of all, I could do this whenever it suited me, a little here and there, leaving me largely free to enjoy life.

I took to overnighting at Ingrid's in Huran or staying with Ana Maria at her country house in Calca several times a month. I started tagging along on short day trips with Fania and Jhedi. Hank was content to be a happy hermit while I was away.

One day, Ana Maria invited Ingrid and me to stay a few days at a crumbling family hacienda. It had been three years since the courts decreed the return of the estate to the family and two years since the death of Ana Maria's mother, who had spent years petitioning for its return after the Peruvian military government expropriated the hacienda under the 1969 Agrarian Reform Law, an act that resulted in the land being farmed but leaving the large house abandoned and neglected. Her mom had lived long enough to live there for her final year. But since her death, Ana Maria and her three sisters had to decide what to do with it.

Two of the sisters wanted to sell. The other two felt obliged to honor their mother's desire for it to remain in the family.

Ana Maria envisioned leasing it to a boutique hotelier who could bring the funds necessary to restore the historic home and transform it into a luxury basecamp for wealthy adventure travelers. Set in a bucolic setting at the southern end of the Urubamba River Valley in a region yet to be discovered by the masses, its rural riverside location made it ideal for activities such as kayaking, cycling, and birding. Then there were the historical and cultural attractions of the area. Ana Maria's plan made sense. But the sisters weren't convinced.

After hearing so much about it, Ingrid and I jumped at the invitation and were eager to see the place.

"You'll be roughing it," Ana Maria warned. "There's electricity and interior plumbing, but barely. I have extra sleeping bags if you need one," she said. "And there's no heat, so bring warm clothes for the nighttime."

She needn't have worried. Ingrid and I were immediately enchanted. Yes, it was rustic and dilapidated. But the once elegant gardens were now overgrown and beautifully wild with old roses and lilacs and nasturtiums. The Andean night sky sparkled overhead, and the river that surged outside the windows lulled us to sleep.

It was magic.

It was complicated.

41

Precious Months

Seven months had passed since our arrival, and we were well into August 2015. The winter days had been warm and sunny with crisp blue Andean skies and endlessly glorious because of it. Festival season and the ubiquitous dances and processions went on forever, it seemed. But the world news headlines were heartbreaking: The death of Michael Brown, an unarmed eighteen-year-old in Ferguson, Missouri, sparked protests, rioting, looting, and violent police response. Actor Robin Williams was found dead of suicide. Malaysia Airlines Flight 370 disappeared with two hundred twenty-seven passengers plus staff on board. Rocket fire from militants in Gaza and Israeli airstrikes were escalating. A deadly outbreak of Ebola spread rapidly into the largest and deadliest in history.

Within Peru, the Shining Path, a guerrilla terrorist organization, was reported to have attacked a natural gas work camp in the Cusco region. Peruvian authorities arrested twenty-four people on charges of Shining Path affiliation, and security forces killed three and injured one Shining Path insurgent during an apartment raid in the Echarate region.

One September morning after breakfast, while we sat soaking up the sunshine on a bench in the Plaza de Armas, I asked Hank a question I struggled with: "How can I concern myself with—and write about—friendship and food and ordinary things when life is at its hardest and most broken for so many?"

"What if you think of it differently?" Hank replied. "As a form of connection, for example."

I was unprepared for his earnestness and razor-sharp perception, though it was one of the qualities I admire most in him.

"Stories," he continued, "are about the things that happen to people and how what happens makes them feel. If you think about it, you're sharing human experiences, and that's what stories do. Good stories make people more human, more aware of things than they might otherwise be. People need that. This screwed-up world needs that. I think that's what you're doing. That's no small thing."

At such moments, I understood how often Hank puts my heart at ease: Never fickle. Never prying, but always knowing how to see things differently.

• • •

"Oh, that looks good," Ingrid said as she poured hibiscus tea, and I put out the slices of tres leches cake I'd brought from Cusco.

As much as I loved living amid the stimulation and chaos of the city, I craved time in the country with Ingrid. Her place was an elixir. Ingrid didn't care about politics or gossip or the weather; she cared about beauty. She created beauty.

"How is it possible?" I said looking around at the hand-woven hammock strung between two eucalyptus trees, the copious geraniums, roses, herbs, and potted succulents, the pink-striped tablecloth clipped to a picnic table, the bulging vegetable garden, cut flowers in assorted vases, and the rustic bench with a weathered patina, purple seat cushion, and a scattering of alpaca wool pillows. "It looks like you've lived here forever, not a year. I can't believe how you've transformed the dirt yard of a rural mud dwelling into this lush oasis."

"I can't not do it. I know it's only a rental, but it's in my DNA," she said lightheartedly.

She went silent for a moment, then added: "I've come to understand that the reason I put so much creative energy into gardens and decorating is because I believe that beauty works its way into the soul, that it is healing regardless of whether you're aware of it or not."

At sixty-five, Ingrid seemed invincible. She hauled boulders down mountains to her garden. She hefted sofas and chairs from downstairs to upstairs. She catered dinner parties for thirty on a whim and traveled alone internationally for months. She was fully engaged in her life in a way that was rare.

Did she know her time here was precious?

Did we know our time here was precious?

•••

One evening, a month or so later, I stopped to use the cash machine kiosk on a corner of the San Blas Plaza because I'd forgotten to stop at the Banco Continental ATM on Avenida El Sol that we normally used.

The next morning, I awakened to three bank transaction notifications on my iPhone. Three? I'd only made one withdrawal. A log in to online banking confirmed three consecutive $200 ATM withdrawals. Bugger.

A call to the bank's fraud department resulted in the prompt reimbursement of the unauthorized transactions but also the inconvenient cancellation of the bank card and problematic news that they would only send a replacement card to the account address in New Mexico.

Double bugger.

"We could ask Don and Corinna to retrieve the new card from our mailbox and FedEx it to us," Hank suggested after I filled him in.

"We could," I agreed, though the one time we had something sent to us in Cusco by international courier, it was held up for weeks in Customs.

"We could fly home for a month or so," Hank offered. "We need to stock up on supplements and things that we can't get here, tend to our responsibilities, and it would be good to give the car a run after so long in storage".

We'd been told when we moved into the apartment that we could stay as long as we liked. We'd settled in and bought a coffee maker, bedding, Andean rugs and alpaca blankets, and lounge chairs for the rooftop terrace. We liked it here. The idea of staying felt good.

"You're okay with that?" I asked Hank.

"Yeah," he agreed. "Why not?"

The plans came together easily. Affordable flights were available. Don and Corinna's guest house was vacant, and they were happy to have us stay. We would fly via Salt Lake City and briefly say hello to my parents, newly installed in their independent living community, and see my brother, sister-in-law, and nieces.

The problem wasn't how the trip would be organized, but what it meant—keeping the apartment, leaving belongings, a commitment to return. Implicit in the idea of roundtrip tickets was the reality that this was a significant decision.

Do you fly from Peru to New Mexico for a replacement bank card? Do you alter your future because you got hacked?

It was starting to look that way.

Over the next few days, we prepared for the trip. We asked the apartment owners for permission to leave it vacant or available to friends during our absence and made arrangements to pay the rent remotely. We told friends about our plans. I went to my favorite stores and picked out presents to bring home. I went to the market and bought Peruvian coffee and *huacatay,* the tangy Peruvian black mint paste that had become a pantry staple. I should have purchased the plane tickets—but I didn't. I was wrestling with a disquiet I couldn't yet articulate.

"What's up?" Hank asked in bed one night.

"It's all so sudden," I said uncertainly. "It's just . . ." Nothing came out after that.

Hank was silent, letting me work it out within myself.

"It's funny," I said after a long pause. "All this time, I was certain we would ultimately make a home again. That the wandering was a transitional phase ending somewhere special like Cusco."

I could feel Hank's gaze on me in the dark.

I tried to explain what I was feeling. I told him I'd grown to enjoy not having plans, to appreciate not knowing what was next. That I liked having the flexibility to respond quickly and easily to serendipitous opportunities. How gradually and quietly freedom had transcended stability. How I wasn't ready to give that up, which is what it felt like we were doing.

"You don't have to," Hank said. He squeezed my hand beneath the bedding. "Whether we stay or go doesn't matter as long as I'm with you. I'm okay with whatever you want to do."

"I think we should go," I said, grateful for Hank's generosity. "But let's not keep the apartment, not be obligated to return."

The words surprised me, but they felt right. Everything felt right again.

On our last morning, we ate breakfast at Jack's, and Fania joined us at the table. She told us we'd be missed, and she hoped we'd be back. She had a gift for me, a pair of earrings I'd admired once when we shopped together. She told us how lovely it had been that we'd come back and stayed so long and that she hoped we'd return again. We hugged her and said that she was welcome to stay with us wherever we were in the world and genuinely hoped that she would. She said she would love to.

Saying goodbye is too painful, too heartbreaking. I soothe myself with the idea that we will be reunited. So, later that afternoon, when Ana Maria pulled up outside the apartment to take us to the airport—I knew it wasn't goodbye.

42

Oaxaca

Mexico

We'd been back in New Mexico for four months when a Facebook post caught my eye.

A small-group tour operator in Oaxaca (wah-hah-kah), Mexico, had posted an opening for a rental property on his farm, Las Zanjas, situated in the Etla Valley, about twenty miles from Oaxaca City.

The company's Oaxaca art and culture tours had been on my travel wishlist for more than a decade, and our paths had occasionally crossed professionally, so I knew enough to suspect that something they had a hand in would be special. Posted with the rental announcement were appealing photographs of a small cluster of low-slung adobe buildings set within a bamboo thicket and an alluring description of a cozy, ecological country cottage with beautiful light and patio doors opening onto shaded verandas porches with meadow and mountain views and an outdoor shower in a sun-dappled banana grove.

Perhaps the seed of desire had been planted at Ingrid and Ana

Maria's country houses in Peru. But from the moment I read even a few sentences, Carrizo House took potent hold of my imagination.

That evening as Hank and I sat out on the patio before sunset, I showed him the Facebook listing, the photographs, and a Google Map of a twenty-eight-hour, 1,872-mile driving journey across southern New Mexico to the Texas border and then the entire north-south width of Mexico to Oaxaca.

The town of Etla is about a mile away. You can get fresh produce here daily and all sorts of delicious prepared local foods. Go on Wednesday, and the whole center of town has turned into a bustling market. A bit closer is the unexcavated archeological site, ancient church, and pilgrimage destination (5th Friday of Lent) called Las Peñitas. The movie Nacho Libre with Jack Black was filmed here. Twenty minutes up the hill in San Agustin is CASA, an Arts Center that hosts art workshops, exhibitions, movies, and events year-round.

I was almost irrepressible with excitement as I read the description. I kept taking the iPhone out of Hank's hands to open new browser tabs to show him Oaxaca photography galleries and Wikipedia pages about the Etla Valley until Hank asked: "Wait, how do you know this company again?"

I told him about the travel and tourism connection, meeting the owner of the tour company at an Adventure Travel conference in Chiapas, Mexico. I told him all the signs were there: That the personal connection might help because we weren't complete unknowns. That we were available to go because we'd chosen not to return to Cusco. That the remote location necessitated a car, and because we were back in the States with access to our car, we could drive there.

Neither of us was cut out for sameness or routine, but this wasn't anything like the café culture and urban lifestyle we'd grown comfortable with abroad.

There was a brief silence. And then, to my surprise and delight, Hank agreed: agreed to the ecological country cottage, agreed to the Mexican road trip, agreed to the outdoor shower.

For that, for his sense of adventure, for his uncomplicated ease, for his unconditional, irrational love, I adored him.

We finalized the details two days later and committed to staying for four months. I marveled at the way it came together. I saw a post on Facebook that I rarely logged into anymore, and because we could, we would soon be journeying deep into Mexico.

You will be here between two seasons, the owner wrote in an email. *April and May, the depth and end of the dry season, then June and July, the often-exciting onset of the rainy season. It's a beautiful time to be here, especially as the rains set in. But April and May are wonderfully warm, even sometimes balmy, and I love that time in the country. I'm traveling and won't be around, but a friend, Mila, will be there to receive you and will be living in another house on the property for at least part of your stay, but most certainly to welcome you and get you settled in. We will set up a weekly housekeeper for you, and I will always be at the other end of an email, skype, or phone call should there be an issue or if you want ideas about places to explore.*

• • •

"When, exactly, did you know that composting toilet meant outhouse?" Hank said as he returned from the pit latrine that was the bathroom at Casa Carrizo. He had to shout to be heard over the birds, the cicadas, the frogs.

"Oh, Hank. Don't make me laugh. I'll have to go to the bathroom!"

I said, explaining that I hadn't had a clue that the house was without an indoor toilet until Mila had given us a tour of the property.

"You understand that we probably should have asked more questions, right?" Hank said.

"Yes, that's what normal people would do," I agreed, and we laughed at our absurdity.

What had been an idea—renting a country house in rural Oaxaca—was now a fact. We'd arrived the previous afternoon exhausted and relieved from navigating a nearly 2,000-mile journey and the final stretch across the dirt farm roads that led past oxen-tilled fields and into the deep bush to Las Zanjas. After a brief welcome and tour of the property, we'd fallen asleep to the hustle and hum of a million small insects and distant heat lightning in the Sierra Madre mountains.

43

Fire and Magic

When we came to Oaxaca, we knew of its longstanding political struggles. A decade earlier, in 2006, I'd had to cancel a travel assignment due to a social uprising that had taken control of Oaxaca City for six months and ended with brutal repression by the federal government.

Ten years later, and one month after our arrival, Oaxacan protestors had once again seized control of the capital city, this time against an educational reform passed by the Mexican national government, but all kinds of civil collectives, from public health workers to students, cab drivers and freight haulers, agricultural associations and local merchants had also taken to the streets to express their grievances.

We soon discovered that decades of complex conflict and civil disobedience were part of daily life across much of the state, with regular road closures, blockades, work strikes, protests, and marches. Little by little, we found ourselves immersed in a surreal story of overlapping realities—normalcy and turmoil.

At Las Zanjas, we could sling a hammock between two ash trees, close our eyes and listen to the breeze squeezing through the leaves or step beneath the cool stream of the outdoor shower during the heat of the afternoon sun and think that there wasn't a finer place on Earth to be.

Every Wednesday, Mila and I headed down the dirt roads into Etla for the market day when the streets were filled with vendors and overflowing with fresh produce harvested from the small farms scattered across the lush valley. We'd stroll down the lanes of stalls that sold stringy *quesillo* cheese, deep-fried *chapulines* (grasshoppers), palm-leaf baskets, traditionally baked bread, and delicious *mole negro* laced with chile and chocolate and spiced with cloves, cinnamon, and cumin.

By June, protests escalated from blocked roads and work stoppages to throwing rocks and Molotov cocktails and setting vehicles ablaze. In the municipality of Nochixtlan, a ten-minute drive from Casa Carrizo, police response to yet another roadblock had escalated into gunfire and the tragic death of eight protestors.

And yet strangely, our lives ran the way they always did, reading, writing, working, going for long walks, and doing our daily routines, only with the addition of a growing fondness for Mila.

On the evening of the summer solstice, just as the sun dropped into the horizon, I glanced out a kitchen window and saw that the skyline was ablaze with fire. Alarmed, I rushed out of the house, ran across the small wood-plank bridge that spanned the water canal, and into the grassy meadow to find Mila standing alone dwarfed by a mountainous and burning brush pile of cut tree limbs and garden debris. I spotted a fuel can and a water tank on the ground beside her and tried to calm the primitive part of my brain that screamed FIRE inside my head. Mila nodded a greeting, her eyes glistening in the firelight, but she said nothing.

I stood silently beside her, watching the flames and steadying my breath until, finally, I stepped back and sat down in the damp grass where the farm dogs lay sprawled out sleeping. Mila joined me. The fire crackled and hissed. Above us, a milky trail of stars glimmered while the night insects seethed away in surround sound.

We'd been quiet for a long time before Mila spoke. "The ancient ones," she said without looking away from the blaze, "used fire to purify, to cleanse, and release what is no longer serving you."

I sensed sadness in Mila but also a strong inner compass.

"Is that what you're doing?" I asked.

"Yes," she said, staring into the fire. "I'm not sure if the owner told you, but we lived here together as a couple for the past two years. It's complicated, but when he left, it was the end of our relationship. We agreed that I would stay as a property manager while he's in the States for the summer and finish constructing a second rental bungalow while I figure out what's next. But it wasn't my decision. Letting go—of this place, rejection, and lost love—has been painful."

"I'm sorry," I said. "What a difficult situation. I appreciate your sharing. We didn't know."

I felt a surge of affection for Mila and thought of the harrowing dance of love and loss and how there are things we find only at our lowest depths. I thought of how, through the alchemy of suffering, trust, clarity, and true integrity often emerged. But I said nothing of it. Let the fire do its magic.

44

Coming and Going

"I agree with Hank," Kate said. "Anyone would be crazy to leave Mila."

We received an email from Kate earlier that week. She would be flying from Guanajuato to Oaxaca for a book project. She had a busy work schedule, but could she visit us at the farm? Yes, please!

We sat on the veranda catching up while a cat slept in Kate's lap. Mila had joined us briefly but long enough for Kate to see what we saw—an intense and extraordinary woman in her early thirties with a natural beauty and quiet dignity.

"She's one of the good ones," Kate said after we were alone again. "How lucky you are. This place is enchanted. Well, for the lack of an indoor toilet," she teased.

It felt good to be with Kate again. Like Hank, she possessed a straightforwardness, candid humor, and perceptive intelligence that I envied and adored.

I breathed in the earthy smell of the *carrizo* grasses, the tall cane that grew along the *zanja* (canal) and watched as the day's colors slowly dissolved into gray, and in the distance, the mountains, how the rows upon rows of closely packed, rounded hills, grew soft. The sight of it filled me with contentment. I thought back to earlier in the day, to the valley farms we'd passed by on the backroads home from the airport, many of them small-scale and oxen-tilled and hand-seeded for generations with squat, low-slung houses like Casa Carrizo made of baked mud. Warm air wafted across the breeze along with the distant ding-a-ding of a passing bicycle and donkeys braying. The longer we stayed in the valley, the more remarkable it seemed, and the longer I wanted to stay.

And the longer I wanted Kate to stay.

"I could stay here forever," Kate said as if reading my mind. But she was gone by breakfast. Work called.

As it turned out, people visited us at Las Zanjas more than we would have thought. Mara from Guanajuato had come and stayed a week. Our Ajijic friends, Emma and Harrison, had stayed for ten days. Even a couple we knew from a Cusco writing group staying in Puerto Escondido on the Oaxaca coast had come for a visit.

"I think we've had more house guests out here in the middle of nowhere with a sleeping loft and outhouse than anywhere else," Hank commented after Kate left.

We laughed at the thought of it, though we understood the draw. Life at Las Zanjas was idyllic.

We had our routine: Awake. Dress. Have coffee, a bowl of fruit, or eggs and beans. Then, outside, to read or talk, to share a passage of writing, or sit comfortably in silence in the chairs on the front porch and look at the land. Mainly, we just hung out, being ourselves together.

Most days, I worked at the laptop in the studio or wrote on the veranda, pen in hand, notebooks overflowing with words. After lunch, Mila and I took the dogs for long walks down empty dirt roads, returning well before the threatening late afternoon storms.

The summer rains began in late May when the warm, moist air

from the Gulfs of California and Mexico met over the Sierra Madre mountains and amassed into clouds heavy with the daily deluge that soaked and transformed valley cornfields and native grasses into a sea of green as startling as a van Gogh canvas.

By late afternoon as rain drummed on the roof and electricity and the Internet waned, Hank and I would retreat to the bedroom until the rain let up, the sun returned, and everything glistened and buzzed with insects.

At sunset, we sat on the veranda, the farm dogs and cats sprawled out around us, listening to the crickets and frogs until the sky turned thick with stars, flashing and flickering, or clouds thinly veiled the light of a silver moon.

One day, we extended our stay from four months to five.

• • •

It was late August 2016, a year since our Cusco departure, and we'd driven to Oaxaca City as we did most weeks to get our urban fix and drink dark Oaxacan coffee in the courtyard at Café Brújula. It was our favorite ritual, drinking coffee together, a daily habit of twenty-six years, both ordinary and sacred. A time each day when we reunited like old friends and affection and laughter flowed like an elixir in the ink-black drink. For me, love and coffee and Hank are invariably linked.

"Are you ready to leave?" Hank asked as the waiter arrived to clear the table.

"As in, leave the café or leave Oaxaca?" I replied.

"Oaxaca. It's our final week," he said.

Through the café door, I saw people walking past a wall of political street art. My thoughts drifted to the roiling conflict and the pall of social injustice and civil disobedience that continued across the city and state. Oaxaca was an enigma—alluring and alive, complicated and cruel.

"I might be tempted to stay if Mila wasn't leaving," I replied. "But without her, it wouldn't be the same."

"Yeah, I agree," Hank said.

I studied his face and saw sadness there. Mila represented the best of Oaxaca, coupling immense power with quiet kindness. She also knew the heartache of loving a place and leaving it.

Later, as we drove out of the city, I took in the familiar sights. The faded grandeur and vibrant colors, the roving vendors piled high with baskets and blankets, the little girls in their frilly sundresses and braided black hair, the political graffiti. Could this be the last time we passed this way? Would we return? I didn't know.

Life, I understood, can change in an instant.

45

Following Hope

Colombia

I started to think about Medellín as our next temporary home on the return drive to New Mexico from Oaxaca. Over the years, I'd followed nearly every phase of Medellín and Colombia's metamorphosis: Medellín as the world's most dangerous city (Pablo Escobar, gangs, guns); Colombia as the epicenter of the drug wars (kidnapping, forced displacement, indiscriminate violence); Colombia as failed peace agreement (1984, 1991, 1999); Medellín as a radical experiment in urban planning and social projects (gondolas as free public transport, award-winning architecture as a public library in the slums); Colombia as historic peace agreement (ceasefire, decommissioning of weapons, security guarantees, Nobel Peace Prize); and, finally, its latest iteration, Medellín as a cultural hub (Museo de Arte Moderno, the bronze Rubenesque statues of Fernando Botero, single-origin coffee trendsetter).

"What do you think of an extended stay in Medellín, Colombia?" I asked Hank one day in the car. We were driving the final leg in

Mexico from Saltillo to Del Rio, Texas. We were in the early days of the transition between what was and what's next, and when we are often irritable and exhausted from long travel days. But the day's drive had been glorious, the sort of journey we loved. Riding along back roads through a wide-open landscape framed by a vast blue sky without traffic to distract from the view. The purple bloom of the desert sagebrush glistened in the late afternoon light. I felt myself smile. It felt good to be on the road.

"I don't want to burst your bubble," Hank said after careful thought. "I'm all for the idea of urban conveniences like indoor toilets, but isn't Medellín a city of several million people?"

"Yeah. About three million," I confirmed. "And at any other time, I might be content to continue exploring small UNESCO World Heritage cities and towns. But thanks to five months on the farm living amid the upheavals of social revolution, I think I'm ready for a modern urban success story. I'm ready to follow hope."

Hank said he was game for investigating the idea further once we'd caught our breath in New Mexico. I agreed. I wasn't convinced Medellín was a fit for us yet, but the legacy of Oaxaca nagged at me. Maybe by moving into a story of hope, into a culture that had courageously confronted a complicated past, I would make peace with some demons of my own.

I started researching Medellín as soon as we settled back into Don and Corinna's guest house. The work was easy—nearly every major fashion and travel magazine and website featured articles on the city. *Vogue* called it cool. *Condé Nast* pegged it as the best destination in South America. At some point, I stumbled across a vacation rental website featuring trendy studio lofts in the Envigado neighborhood of Medellín for under fifty dollars a night. The serviced studios were small, about four hundred square feet. Still, the ceilings were high, and I was seduced by the design details: the metal and leather bar stools, the ceramic pendant lamps, the sleek minimalist kitchen, the bamboo floors, the exposed brick wall, and the organic linen duvet set. Modern. New. Not a whiff of nostalgia for the past. Not an outdoor toilet in sight.

The results of my research didn't surprise me half as much as how I felt about it: the unexpected excitement that came from imagining big city living after five months of rural solitude, the relief of finding a short-term apartment to serve as a temporary launchpad, and, strangest of all, an eagerness to hear Spanish again. What was that about? Where did this quick stab of affinity for Spanish come from? I shook it off and showed Hank the loft apartment listing.

"I don't think we'd be comfortable with a studio long-term," Hank said, "especially because we like to have a guest room for visitors. But it looks like a good option while we look around for something bigger once we're on the ground."

I wondered when we'd gone from investigating the idea to being on the ground and waited for him to say more, but nothing came.

"Maybe you want me to look for something in the Poblado or Laureles neighborhoods?"

Envigado wasn't one of the trendy central districts popular with foreigners, and I was worried that I was pushing it and that later he would be disappointed. I said as much, and he told me that I was nuts, that off-the-beaten-expat-path was his preference.

In the end, we booked the Envigado studio for ten days and a one-way flight for mid-October 2016, with vague plans to stay for three to six months.

• • •

Furnished rentals in Medellín were in high demand, especially those we could afford. The Envigado loft was continuously booked after our ten-day stay, as were all the building's other units. So, our first few days in Medellín were occupied with finding a rental apartment. A fifteen-minute taxi ride north from Envigado to the city center along Avenida Poblado deposited us at the property management firm that managed the loft apartments.

There we met Jack, the twenty-something booking agent who would help us in our search. We were seated in front of his desk in modern ergonomic chairs in an airy open-plan office while Jack showed us possible listings on a large Apple monitor display. He spoke to his colleagues in rapid-fire Spanish, but with us, Jack switched effortlessly to English with an accent that sounded vaguely like Joe Pesci. He laughed when we asked about it and told us that he'd repatriated with his family to Colombia from New Jersey three years earlier.

Each morning, I got up early to get work out of the way, then we checked with Jack to learn what new rental listings were available. Jack would give us a brief description and scheduled viewing time over the phone and a text message with a link to the listing. Then, we'd hop on the metro or into a taxi and discover a new part of the city. The company's portfolio was impressive, and Jack seemed determined to find us an apartment.

The first listing was a stylish high-rise two-bedroom unit just seconds away from Parque Poblado and a few minutes walk to Parque Lleras with a small balcony and fast 20 Mbps internet.

"It's located in the heart of Poblado's top restaurants and bars with a lot of nightlife activity," Jack cautioned. "It's also at the top of your budget, so keep that in mind."

The next place was set among the trees in a prime Laureles location.

"This budget-friendly one-bedroom doesn't have the guest quarters you wanted," Jack said, "but it's in a quiet four-floor apartment building with valley views and a private balcony. Residents also have access to the rooftop social area with a jacuzzi."

Units went fast. Both apartments were taken before we'd returned to Envigado.

Then there was the premium location only a few blocks from Parque Lleras in the Provenza neighborhood.

"It's the best of Medellín on your doorstep," Jack said, "with some of the best bars, cafés, and restaurants within a few blocks."

Jack called to cancel the viewing while we were en route. It was booked.

The apartments all started to blend together. The redbrick high rises, the leafy neighborhoods, the Ikea decor. What did stand out was how at ease we'd begun to feel in Envigado.

Andrés of Andrés Bakery, a tasty bistro across the street from the apartment building, greeted us by name now that we were addicted to his crab quiche. The neon-vested traffic cops who congregated on the street corner nodded hello with familiarity when we walked past on the way to Antonio's Gelato for a creamy Stracciatella. Even the ladies in the hair salon smiled and waved like old friends since I'd stopped in twice for a wash and dry.

The Envigado loft was smack dab in the middle of Jardines, a leafy restaurant district of artisanal sidewalk cafés and bars, on the street called La Calle de la Buena Mesa, the street of the good table. There was a dash of extravagance to the district: the valet parking, the beautiful Colombian bodies in tight designer jeans, and the strings of twinkling café lights. It felt like a scene out of a film.

One evening, over a chicken bowl with organic kale, baked chickpeas, asparagus, avocado, cherry tomatoes, sesame, stracciatella cheese, and a Moroccan lemon vinaigrette, I asked Hank if he liked any of the other neighborhoods as much as Envigado. Like me, he was convinced an apartment on La Calle de la Buena Mesa would be just about perfect.

Before bed that night, I dashed off a quick email to Jack inquiring again about apartments in the area. You never know, I said wistfully to Hank as I clicked send.

In two days, we had to be out of the loft, and we were no closer to finding a place to live than when we'd arrived.

Jack had an apartment in the Sabaneta neighborhood for us to look at, but for the first time since our arrival, it felt like things might not work out. I knew landing in a foreign city without a plan was a gamble, a leap of faith. It made me anxious, but it also made me feel intrepid.

The Sabaneta apartment was available immediately but only for a month, putting us looking again in thirty days at the height of the holiday season. So we took a pass, reserved a hotel room for the next week, and began exploring other possibilities.

With one day left, Hank and I were bent over our laptops, surfing the Web for information about Cali and Cartagena, two Colombian cities that also interested us. Our computer screens were plastered with images of swaying palm trees, colorful murals, traditional colonial buildings, and beautiful people dancing salsa when a text message from Jack pinged my iPhone.

"Call me! I might have found you an Envigado apartment."

After a brief moment of tamping down my excitement, I showed Hank the message. He didn't tell me to make the call because I was already itching to, and Hank knew it.

I tapped the mobile to dial and put it on speakerphone when Jack picked up.

When we turned out the light that night, I felt myself buzzing with happiness: After days of dead-ends, we had an affordable six-month lease agreement on an apartment in our favorite neighborhood. Jack had worked miracles on our behalf. He'd juggled bookings to make long-term availability an option. He'd also negotiated a lower rent. We wouldn't see the apartment until we moved in, but we weren't worried. We'd viewed the two-bedroom, two-bath, open-plan apartment online, which looked like the kind you'd see in a magazine. It was under Jack's management, so we knew we were in good hands, and with it coming available at the very last moment on the last day of the studio rental, it felt like kismet—like we were never meant to stay anywhere else.

On the day of the move, Jack sent a staff member over to help us with our bags, and it wasn't until we stood on the apartment balcony that I realized I was looking into the classroom windows of a Spanish language school. A teacher stood at a chalkboard. A small cluster of students was seated at a round table. In English, the words "El Dorado Spanish School. Get Started Today" were advertised on a vinyl banner strung across the second story of the building. Below it was Andrés Bakery. How had I not noticed before?

After so many days suspended, I was purely in the here and now again with the emergent hope of an unimagined future ahead of us.

46

The Unthinkable

More than two months into our tenancy on La Calle de la Buena Mesa, each week still brought a delicious new set of discoveries and flavors: Fresh-baked sourdough bread and almond croissants from the European-style Eduardo Madrid Panadería. Trout tartare at Andrés Bakery. Artisanal pizza with buffalo mozzarella, serrano ham, organic arugula, and salsa Napolitano at Pizzeria Olivia. Seafood paella with saffron rice, jumbo shrimp, mussels, and calamari at El Barral. Grass-fed Argentine beef medallions, wild rice, and homemade chimichurri at Black Pepper Steakhouse, the restaurant we lived above.

Living above a restaurant in a Zona Gastronomica had its advantages. With a quick phone call, we could slip in, hand the hostess a container from home, and within minutes enjoy a sumptuous meal and a pitcher of house-made sangria or basil-infused lemon water in the comfort of the apartment. It was a nice way to live.

Then, one Tuesday morning, I awoke to an email from my brother in Utah: Dad had fallen and broken his left hip and hand.

He provided a few additional details; the hospital name, floor, and room number. The cardiologist cleared Dad for immediate hip surgery, and from there, things escalated—and deteriorated—quickly.

Thirty-nine hours and forty-six minutes after reading my brother's email, the text of Dad's passing pinged my phone in Medellín at 1:41 a.m.

In that moment, I understood what it means to have a heavy heart, as my chest constricted in grief and loss and a bone-deep sadness for my mother, for the days, weeks, and months ahead of her that no one is ever prepared for. But there was also something more complicated going on, something about absence and choices.

It's the traveler's great dilemma: to go or stay. The what-ifs loom large. What if the unthinkable happens while we are away? What if we can't get home in time? What if we're not there?

And yet, we go.

We go because we know that staying does not stave off the unthinkable.

We go because we know that proximity doesn't guarantee anything.

We go knowing we might not be there.

And, if we're fortunate, we go with the blessings of those who love us.

Though Hank and I had chosen to alter or postpone our travel plans several times over the last few years when it was helpful or necessary, our wanderings had become a source of unexpected connection for Dad and me.

He was curious about our adventures in a manner that hadn't previously been a part of our relationship. He asked detailed questions and listened to the answers, often replying with more questions.

"Tell me more about the underground network of roads and tunnels in Guanajuato. How does it work?" he'd asked when I mentioned how pleasant it was to live in a city where much of its traffic was diverted beneath it.

He wanted to know if the tunnels had once been part of the silver mines for which the region was famous. What about ventilation and stability? Access to homes and businesses? His engineer's mind latched onto practical details that made me stop and think about our everyday existence abroad in ways that no one else did.

It surprised me, this curiosity about my life. As the youngest of three daughters, there were times growing up when it seemed he didn't even know my name. I recall him absentmindedly rattling off our names as if covering all possibilities before issuing some mundane missive: "Kathy, Cheryl, Ellen, empty the dishwasher for your mother."

Looking back now, from an age when there are days that I barely remember my own name, I can only imagine how he managed under the numerous and persistent demands of work and marriage, and family.

And the truth, if I admit it, is that I was the one lacking in curiosity. Did I ask my dad about his work? His life? His past? His dreams? His fears? No. Those weren't conversations we shared for much of my life.

Maybe I'm slow or a late bloomer, as I prefer to think of it, but it wasn't until these last few precious years that I finally felt compelled to know my dad not only as a father but as an individual—a desire I am fortunate to have had the time and opportunity to pursue.

The night my father died, I tried to make sense of it all: how the distance of a traveler's life had brought us closer; how, through the shared experiences of crisis, we'd finally been able to see one another beyond the roles of father and daughter; and how when death came, continents separated us.

And though I wasn't there in the end, my grief was softened not only by the fact that he didn't have to endure a long and painful passing but also by the intimacy and connection we'd shared in his final years.

Perhaps the traveler's great dilemma isn't whether to go or stay, but rather in going or staying, whether or not we make time to nurture and cultivate relationships that matter.

Travelers know well the risks and rewards of pushing beyond comfort zones, stepping outside routines, roles, and responsibilities long enough to connect with what is real. We can do this in places foreign and familiar, with strangers and our families, and within ourselves.

My dad left me with many memories, but the one that sticks with me and will guide me moving forward, is to be curious about the people we love and who love us. To ask and listen and then ask some more.

47

Connection

"Do you think it's possible to live this way, arriving and departing, staying as long as a tourist visa allows, and still be connected?" I asked Hank. We were sitting in Cocolatte, a coffee house located exactly thirty-two footsteps from the apartment, where we stopped by at least once most days for a locally grown organic coffee or chai tea frappe. It was a January afternoon. A lashing rain had blown in, so we were waiting it out with an eggplant panini and spinach empanadas. The café front was open to a small sidewalk patio, and we were seated just inside on a small sofa, a few inches beyond the spray from the enormous raindrops coming down outside.

"I'm as connected as I want to be," Hank said. He was looking at the trees and lush greenery outside getting pummeled.

"Seriously," he continued. "I think our bonds are broader, deeper, as a result of living this way."

Hank slurped through the paper straw of his frappe and smiled. "Is this what goes on inside that mind of yours? Deep thoughts about interconnectedness? Or is it just the rain that makes you introspective?"

"Perhaps after nearly three months of Spanish lessons, I've acquired the poetic mindset of a Latin American," I said and pointed to the Spanish phrases painted on the café wall across from us:

Te espero con un café,
Y si vienestrae contigo tu vida entera,
Es que hay tanto por hablar...

"Tell me what it means," Hank said, testing my Spanish as he often did.

I knew it well by now:

I'm waiting for you with a coffee,
And if you come bring with you your entire life,
It's that there is so much to talk about...

Honestly, I relished being immersed in Spanish again, the thrice-weekly lessons at the El Dorado school, the daily situations that forced me to use the language, trying out the local slang in weekly conversation with the neighborhood women at the hair salon, or when the melodious inflections of the regional *Paisa* accent spilled out of my mouth nearly effortlessly. In those moments, I did not have existential doubts. Life felt meaningful just when I wasn't thinking of meaning.

Seated in the cozy café, I found myself rethinking perceptions of home and belonging. In the last few years, I'd come close to defining the nameless intention that had pushed us this far: the freedom to adapt, evolve, learn, earn, connect, and freely move about in the world.

• • •

Envigado had felt familiar from our first arrival, not unlike Ajijic in Mexico, but on a more urbane scale: the way the indoors seamlessly blended with the outdoors, happy families filled the streets, and the echoes of children's laughter filled the air. We experienced a warm welcome everywhere we went. How fortunate we are to live this way—immersed in the stimulation of discovering foreign places, meeting a variety of people, and learning new languages. But since my dad's death, I'd felt the huge distance between our life abroad and the closely-knit families epitomized by Latin America. I hadn't made the friendships here that I'd formed in other places. There was no Arlen, no Ana Maria, no Kate, no Mila. I attributed it to living outside the itinerant traveler communities filled with displaced people like us. In Envigado, the strong family bonds made the need for external friendships nearly nonexistent. A sister, a cousin, or an aunt always filled that role. I laughed at the strangeness of wanting independence from traditional relationships when I so much liked the benefits of a tribe.

But just at the moment I was thinking these thoughts, a WhatsApp notification flashed across the iPhone display. It was from my niece Madeleine. She and her boyfriend Sahil wanted to visit. They'd found discount flights out of NYC, where they lived, direct to Medellín and wanted to know if they should buy them. Absolutely! I texted back. Madeleine and Sahil had visited us in Mexico and were easy houseguests. Hank and I both enjoyed their company. An email from our brother-in-law Greg, Madeleine's dad in Massachusetts, followed the next day:

We had 2-3 inches of snow this morning, and I had to snow blow the driveway before work. I have had enough of winter already and am looking to bail out. I would like to know about the possibility of coming down to Medellín on Saturday, Jan. 14th, and flying back on Wednesday, the 18th. I know Mads and Sahil were also contemplating coming down around then. I could stay at a nearby B&B /hotel for the few nights I am there. If it is too much to have all of us there simultaneously, say so, and I can try to find another time to come down.

Arrangements were quickly sorted. Madeleine and Sahil would stay in the guest room, and Greg booked into the studio loft across the street where we'd first stayed. Suddenly, our immediate future included an abundance of family, and I was looking forward to it.

When Hank's granddaughter Kelsey and her husband Kent emailed asking if they could visit, it was as if our time in Medellín was destined to be about family—those we'd lost and those who were there with us.

Then came the tragic news that Hank's fifty-six-year-old daughter Debbie died, and everything in us waned: My enthusiasm for Spanish classes. Hank's interest in exploring beyond the neighborhood. The frequency of our evening walks for gelato. It wasn't something we spoke about because the layers of bereavement were still too complex and raw, but a significant shift had taken place. Hank withdrew into reading and Netflix. I spent more time alone. There were silences between us, each of us deep in separate internal worlds. Not always, but more than before.

By the time grandkids Kelsey and Kent arrived in early April, a few weeks before our departure, the evening card games, stories of their explorations, day trips into the surrounding countryside, and dining out together each evening at the neighborhood cafés cheered us both.

Grief is a strange thing. Had anyone asked us if we were struggling, we would've said no, but even then, I recognized we were going through something difficult to understand.

48

New Beginnings 2.0

It was a perfect September morning in the Graça district of Lisbon, Portugal, the sky a crisp, vivid blue, and hilltop views of terracotta roofs and the Rio Tejo. We'd spent the summer of 2017 reconnecting with family and friends in the States and planned to spend the fall in Lisbon.

We arrived at a short-term apartment on the city's highest hill three days earlier. Each day, we'd walk the steep and narrow cobblestone streets, passing tiled facades and the 28 elétrico—the city's famous yellow tram—with nine days to find our next temporary home. Once again, being on the threshold of discovery and uncertainty with a new language to decipher filled me with excitement.

I felt certain that Lisbon was the place for us to transition from the melancholy of Medellín that still shadowed us. When I'd telephoned Kate, who'd lived in and written extensively about Portugal, to tell her of our plans, she was enthusiastic, but I also sensed a hesitation.

"Portugal is an excellent choice for you two," she said. "You'll love it. And I can see the Lisbon attraction: nice weather, low prices compared to other European capitals, friendly people, and a cool, creative vibe. I've recently returned from there myself," she told me. "I'll send you links to the travel articles the trip produced for some ideas. But if you decide to look beyond Lisbon," she added gently. "You might like Évora, a beautifully preserved medieval town about seventy miles inland."

I'd jotted down the recommendation in a pocket notebook then but hadn't given it any more thought—until now.

For the last decade, foreign investment and tourists had poured into Portugal—especially Lisbon—and the country had just been titled the World's Best Destination and Europe's Leading Destination. I fantasized about finding a co-working writing space in one of the former textile mills transformed into cutting-edge creative hubs, hanging out in hip cafés and coffee houses occupying eighteenth century buildings and browsing fashion shops, contemporary art galleries, and design ateliers. However, by the end of the first week, after researching, making calls, and going on viewings, it was clear that the city had loads of short-term rentals but relatively few places for long-stay travelers like us.

We'd chosen a September arrival in Lisbon with hopes of fewer crowds, lower accommodation costs, and mild autumn weather for the three months a Schengen visa would allow us to stay. Instead, tourists packed the city, the few rentals were already taken or too expensive, and the weather was agreeable throughout the country.

"What was the name of that place Kate recommended?" Hank asked me one afternoon.

"Évora," I told him, Googling as I spoke.

A few days before this, we'd found ourselves waiting in line with a reservation at the Michelin-star restaurant Belcanto in the trendy Chiado neighborhood, one of six restaurants by Lisbon's celebrity chef Javier Avillez. That same morning, we were unable to find a seat at the Graça coffee house we liked. Lisbon was everything I imagined: music and style and art. The food was incredible, and the architecture gorgeous. But it wasn't our scene. Too crowded. Too much traffic. Too unavailable. We easily agreed to look elsewhere.

Moving on to Évora wasn't a dream destination. It was Plan B. We knew nothing about the place—but it seemed like a good alternative. Mostly, we thought that if Kate figured we'd like it, we probably would. But we loved it from day one: The first century Roman temple set right in the middle of a pretty little square, free for all to enjoy; the Catedral de Évora, Portugal's largest medieval cathedral; the labyrinthine old town; the Èvora University students dressed in flowing black capes; and the quaint cafés tucked away among the UNESCO World Heritage historic buildings. By day three, we'd secured a three-month lease for an elegant serviced apartment in a renovated fifteenth century palace turned "Residence for the Arts, Sciences and Humanities" located in the heart of the historic district. One bedroom at the top of three flights of narrow stairs, but from there, we could observe the streets, watch the sunsets, and become fit from the climb.

For the next three months, our time in Évora was full. On top of my monthly retainer contract, I took on extra agency design projects to compensate for the unfavorable euro-dollar exchange rate. I joined a local yoga ashram and was befriended by Monica (British) and her husband Marcello (Italian), who were renovating an Évora townhouse into a multi-residence rental property. Manuela, the director of training at Casa Morgado Esporão, where we stayed, introduced us to the pleasures of weekly permaculture food delivery, invited us to musical performances at the Garcia de Resende Theater, Thursday wine tastings, and Saturday coffee with an eclectic gathering of friends in the public garden. Hank and I tuned our ears to Portuguese, letting the language penetrate our brains as we went about our Évora lives. We also downloaded the Duolingo language app and practiced with one another, seated side-by-side on a sunny bench in the Jardim Diana after breakfast each morning. *Bom dia/Boa tarde/Boa noite* (Good morning/afternoon/night). *Olá* (Hello). *Tchau* (Bye). *Até logo! ... Até amanhã* (See you soon ... see you tomorrow) *Adeus* (Goodbye). The distance I'd felt between us in Medellín faded away as we surrendered to the warmth and welcome of Évora. The expiration of our visas was on the horizon, and I was determined to savor the time before we had to go.

Over the months, I worried less about what was next and enjoyed the present moment more. I noticed the fork-tailed swallows that swooped overhead against a deep royal blue sky at dusk just before sunset. I noticed the iridescent turquoise, green, and purple in the extravagant tail feathers of the peacocks that roamed the public gardens, the fuchsia bougainvillea that tumbled down white-washed walls, the feel of the sun on my hair, the smell of baking Portuguese egg tarts (*Pastéis de Nata*) wafting across an early morning breeze.

I'd fallen in love with life again. With the world we'd created for ourselves, one we carried with us long after we'd gone.

And then, it was time to leave. To say goodbye once more.

49

Hello Again

New Mexico, USA

Back in New Mexico, local acquaintances—shopkeepers, postal employees, and neighbors—were surprised to see us again so soon. I briefly explained the limitations of the Schengen visa that covers most European countries, including Portugal, and how tourists cannot stay within the Schengen Area for more than ninety days in a six-month period. Most people seemed surprised by this, having assumed, they explained, that places like Europe were within reach of anyone who could afford to go for however long they wanted to stay.

It was December 2017. It had been a year since the former reality TV show star Donald Trump was elected president, surprising most of the world after running an anti-immigrant "America First" campaign. Nearly a year since the firing of acting Attorney General Sally Yates, who refused to defend Trump's travel ban, arguing it was unconstitutional. Sometimes, when someone expressed shock about the Schengen restrictions, I asked if they supported open borders or unrestricted access to this country. Still, I understood that the grocery store checkout line or the post office wasn't necessarily the place for that conversation.

Since our return, I saw New Mexico anew. I had always considered it an exotic outpost, with its multicultural comingling of Native, Hispanic, and Anglo populations and diverse landscapes at its heart. Outsiders, whose image of the state was that of turquoise and silver, cowboys and Indians, and Santa Fe art galleries, were often disbelieving when they arrived to discover ski slopes and sand dunes, to see elk and wild horses, and feel the cold chill of the high altitude nights. With under twenty people per square mile and over 13,000 ranches covering over sixty percent of the nation's fifth largest state, New Mexico's wild, empty vibe had always made my heart sing.

But in the aftermath of the election, in the light of Trump's popularity among the rural ranchers and vacationing Texans who flock here, the place felt different. The cowboys and pickup trucks that had represented the often-romanticized attitudes, ethics, and history of the American West were now co-opted into symbols of anti-immigrants, the National Rifle Association, and bumper sticker vows of allegiance to Trump. Where once there was tolerance for alternative opinions or behavior, there was hostility. Aggression was in the mountain air. I could smell it. Perhaps it had always been there.

I felt a wrenching sense of foreboding. Even the atmosphere at Sacred Grounds, a long-time indie coffee and tea house where hipsters, old hippies, ski bums, and local eccentrics could sit back and let the opinions fly, had changed. For years, it had been a friendly gathering place where the baristas knew you and your usual drink. Now, after expansion and relocation under new ownership, it was a cavernous tourist hotspot with long lines, vibrating pagers, a cocktail bar, and an astonishing staff turnover rate.

One night, I stepped out into the crisp winter air. Wrapped in a baby-alpaca wool blanket brought back from Cusco, I sat in a wooden rocking chair retrieved from storage and breathed in the sweet fragrance of piñon cedar burning in the wood stove. The kind of night that reminded me why I loved New Mexico winters. Beneath a milky trail of stars, my thoughts traveled back to Oaxaca, Medellín, and Évora. Mexico. Colombia. Portugal. North America. South America. Europe. Different, and yet the same, connected by trade, treachery, and travel.

I thought of the compact book of Portuguese history lent to me by Manuela in Évora. Like most world history, it read like a soap opera—full of envy and pride, conspiracy and greed, manipulation and vengefulness. I thought of a friend who had relocated to Catalonia, Spain, and of the recent political and emotional turbulence that had sent her packing after eleven happy years. I thought of all the world's conflict, injustice, and oppression and wondered if this would always be the human story.

Then, I thought back to a conversation with my Spanish tutor in Medellín, who'd told me about a Colombian government peace campaign where mothers wrote letters to sons ensnared in the guerilla movement inviting them home, no questions asked, and of a defense minister who'd hired an ad agency to sell forgiveness instead of war. I thought of the peace and prosperity of modern-day Portugal and was reminded to see the bigger picture: regimes and public sentiment change. The effects of this time would fade, and it would last forever.

Good times and bad. The familiar and the new. The humble and the brash. It resides within every place—within me. Could I learn to hold the ups and downs, the dark and the light? Did I have a mind and a heart big enough and spacious enough to accept it all?

A few weeks later, Hank and I were driving through Lincoln, a nearby town made famous by Billy the Kid, Pat Garrett, and other infamous characters of the Wild West now preserved as a New Mexico

Historic Site. We spotted a sign for Annie's Little Sure Shot Espresso Bar at the Old Lincoln Art Gallery. Smoke chuffed out of the chimney. The promise of hot coffee and a cozy fire was all we needed to inspire a stop on the brisk January morning.

We discovered inside a mad mix of art and colors housed in a small nineteenth century bungalow with a coffee bar tucked into the back room. It felt like we'd stepped into an artist's home. Colorful canvases hung on every bit of wall space, and floor-to-ceiling shelves bulged with ceramic cups, vases, and bowls. Stacks of textiles sat neatly folded atop chairs and benches while metal art dangled from the ceiling. And yet, it managed to feel cheerful rather than claustrophobic. Behind a tall Old West oak bar stood a small woman with a welcoming smile and a long blonde braid, wearing a Lost in Space 1970s TV series tee shirt.

"Annie?" I asked.

"Officially, Annemarie," she said. "I couldn't resist the name Annie's Sure Shot as a nod to Annie Oakley, the sharpshooter who starred in Buffalo Bill's Wild West."

Once comfortably installed in cushioned chairs before a woodstove where flames crackled and danced behind glass, Annemarie joined us after delivering the drinks: a rich Guatemalan black coffee for Hank and the house specialty for me, a *Chimayoca* made from double-shot espresso, Ghirardelli chocolate, and a dusting of the distinctly reddish-orange New Mexico Chimayó chile. It was addictively delicious.

She laughed when I asked about her Chimayó source, knowing that the rare chile was grown only in small batches by a group of Chimayó farmers from heirloom seeds passed down from generation to generation.

"You must be New Mexicans," she said. "Not a lot of people know just how precious that chile is."

We exchanged histories: our arrival to the area in 1998, Annemarie's return to New Mexico after time in California and Colorado, and discovered we shared an affinity for coffee, food, color, and eccentrics.

As the morning passed, customers strolled in and pulled up a chair with an ease and familiarity that signaled they were locals. By the time we left, we'd met most of Lincoln's fifty residents.

On the drive home, as we passed the white-washed buildings of Fort Stanton Historic Site, once a remote military post to protect settlers from the indigenous Apache Indians, I wondered how the Lincolnites had viewed us. Welcome or unwanted outsiders? I hoped it was the former. We'd found a surprising refuge in the quirky little coffee house.

Three months later, as we prepared to leave again, we were regulars.

50

Migrations

Peru

By May 2018, we were back in Cusco, Peru, for our third extended stay in six years. Once again, we rented Ana Maria's apartment at the top of Calle Resbalosa. Cusco views don't get better than her hilltop apartment with its picture window view overlooking the Plaza de Armas. With two bedrooms and open-style living space, the apartment was comfortably well-equipped with all the modern amenities and a light-filled and stylish restoration within the historic district. For two people building an itinerant life, Hank and I were fortunate to cycle back, again and again, like migratory birds, returning to the same cozy nests.

Still, Hank's arthritic hip was causing him pain on the steep stone stair climb up and down from the apartment's perch. He never said a word about it, but it was easy enough to tell it hurt, and we both huffed and puffed, our chests heaving in the thin 11,000-foot air to a degree I hadn't remembered previously.

Nevertheless, we quickly picked up where we'd left off three years ago, beginning with breakfast at Jack's Café, where Fania and her brother Jhedi welcomed us back with the warmth of old friends. But now, when we returned to the apartment, it was by taxi rather than making the two hundred stairs climb up Calle Resbalosa. Taxis are inexpensive and everywhere in Cusco, easy to hail on the street at all hours of the day and night. And yet, even the taxis struggled with the steep climb up to San Cristobal as car tires grappled for traction on ancient granite streets made slick by the traffic of motor vehicles for which they were never intended.

On Tuesdays, Iris, who'd first befriended us at the South American Explorers Club and helped us with weekly housekeeping in 2012 and 2015, arrived to help again. Iris included us like family in her life and that of her young sons, Franklin and Paolo. She helped me with Spanish and Quechua and invited us to soccer games, church ceremonies, and birthday celebrations. The boys greeted us with big hugs and affectionately referred to us as *Madrina y Padrino* (godmother and godfather). We adored them and were happy to have the family back in our lives again.

On Friday mornings, Monika came with fresh flower arrangements for the apartment. Monika arrived in Peru more than a decade ago via Germany and London. She taught floral art at Casa Mantay, a nonprofit organization for teenage mothers and their children. Each week, Monika filled variously sized vases with locally sourced roses, eucalyptus, daisies, and the exotic African lilies that thrive here. She'd arrive with the raw cuttings wrapped in brown paper bundles. I'd brew coffee, and we'd chat about life and mutual friends as Monika expertly clipped and snipped the aromatic cuttings into stunning arrangements before moving on to do the same at a few Cusco hotels. Our cost for the privilege supported the social, medical, and legal assistance provided to the girls and children of Casa Mantay. Ingrid had first introduced us to Monika and Casa Mantay, where Ingrid helped plant and maintain community gardens.

During the three years we'd been away, Ingrid had taken the leap after seven years of renting in Peru and purchased a home and land in the Sacred Valley. She'd texted photos of terraced gardens, mountain views, and a beautiful home with a glassed-wall sunroom, but I was excited to see her and the new property in person. Ingrid was away traveling in Europe when we arrived. And then, upon return, she'd immediately set off for Arequipa with the college-age nieces of a German friend. I thought she'd sounded exhausted when we spoke on the phone afterward, but that was understandable, given her recent travels abroad and explorations in Peru with two twenty-something-year-old women. She briefly mentioned some digestion issues, harbingers of an unseen battle taking place inside of her, then dismissed it as a side-effect of the trips. At sixty-eight, she was still living at full throttle.

"Why don't you and Hank come out and stay a few days?" Ingrid asked. "I'm keen for you to see my new place, and you'll have the guest quarters to yourselves. Plus, there's a full moon trance dance at Hacienda Huayoccari on the 29th. It's a magical place not far down the valley. I recently bought a vintage Volkswagen Beetle, and I could drive."

Ingrid's eagerness was evident despite it all.

"Oh, do come! It'll be such fun to catch up. I've missed you two."

• • •

"What, exactly, is a trance dance?" Hank asked with amusement after I'd told him of Ingrid's invitation the following day. We sat on a bench looking out across the San Blas Plaza, waiting for the Meeting Place Café to open and rejoin the writing group that met there on Thursdays at eleven a.m. in an upstairs room. The plaza bristled with energy, and everywhere there were young hippies and musicians, tourists, and Andean women in layers of bright, colorful clothing selling trinkets and photos with cuddly lambs and llamas. I loved it. We were both peeling off morning layers under a blaze of sunshine when the café doors swung open.

We were happy to see some familiar faces in the writing group. We briefly reconnected with Martin (British), Lisa (American), and Vera (New Zealander) and exchanged introductions with Sara (Belgian), Dani (Mexican American), and Bela (Indian). We inquired after Jason (American), Jonathon (Iranian), and Carlos (Peruvian). We learned that Jason and Jonathon were still in Cusco, though not currently active in the group, and that Carlos had moved to California. Neither Hank nor I brought work to share. Still, it felt good to be back as we listened to the writing—short stories and book chapters, poetry and essays—and the resulting discussions, with English being the shared language among the diverse nationalities.

At the weekend, we headed to Ingrid's with her texted instructions on my phone:

Hello, my friends,

I have a local driver arranged for you on Wednesday, so he can take you back and allow us to be spontaneous about the departure time.

When you order the Cusco taxi or Uber, let the driver know it's a dirt road and a little bumpy.

Call if you get lost!

See you soon, Ingrid.

51

Change Is in the Air

"It might be a parasite I picked up in my travels," Ingrid said in explanation as she excused herself for the third time during dinner. "I'm sorry. I can't seem to keep much in me these days. It was worse on the trip to Arequipa. I was forever searching for a bathroom. An herbalist in Urubamba told me to drink Muña tea, a local medicinal plant that aids digestion and treats intestinal infections. I think it's helping," she said brightly. "I've also scheduled a San Pedro ceremony with a healer in Pisac next week and an appointment with an internist in Cusco. I suspect it will clear up soon."

She gave us a brave smile, though it seemed, to me, that it was as much for herself as it was for us. I saw doubt in her eyes.

We were seated at a simple wood dining table covered in a crisp linen tablecloth in the glass solarium of Ingrid's newest home—the cutlery and glassware glittered in the light of a cut-metal lantern above our heads. Ingrid had prepared a creamy mushroom risotto generously peppered with fresh thyme and parsley and a blanket of grated Parmesan. I'd brought mixed organic greens and local sweet potatoes garnished with rosemary and garlic. But it was apparent, now that we were here, that Ingrid could not enjoy the meal. She'd lost weight, and her hand wasn't quite steady; a little wine spilled onto the tablecloth as she poured. The sudden glimpse of vulnerability—in Ingrid of all people, with her indestructible approach to life—surprised and troubled me. I wanted to ask her if she was all right. Instead, I brought out a housewarming gift—a set of four petite espresso cups handmade in Portugal painted with bold stripes in cheerful colors. She greeted the present with a squeal of delight.

The room was colorful and inviting, just like Ingrid herself, who was in good humor despite the digestion issues. I knew how much she loved to entertain, and it felt good to be together again in her new space. It was more expansive than the texted photos had revealed. Throughout the evening, my gaze kept returning to the view outside. The layers of stone wall terraces overflowing with flowers—fuchsia, geraniums, bougainvillea, poinsettia, begonias, angel's trumpets, daisies—and the large terra-cotta pots of succulents and palms scattered throughout. A serrated mountain ridgeline towered overhead, visible through the glass ceiling. The house was a thick-walled, adobe-and-stone construction, textured over with a mixture of clay, sand, and straw strikingly similar to the adobe homes in New Mexico and Oaxaca. The stone terraces, however, were distinctly Andean.

As the last amber rays of the sun fell across the landscape, the conversation passed from global political instability and climate change to our time in Medellín and Portugal to Ingrid's decision to sell her Florida house and settle permanently in the Sacred Valley. As I cleared the table for dessert and moved into the kitchen, I overheard Ingrid talking to Hank about renovation plans for a new guest wing. How she envisioned hosting painters, writers, and creatives seeking a quiet place for extended stays of the type Hank and I enjoyed abroad.

It was just after nine o'clock and dark outside, with a clear sky and stars above. A large orange cat strolled in through the open patio door and then went skittering off into the kitchen.

"That's King Edward," Ingrid said. "The neighbor's cat who has decided he prefers it here."

I could see why.

As Ingrid explained the new guest wing design, we rounded off the meal with fresh plum strudel with vanilla ice cream. Then espresso, crisp and tart, served in the Portuguese cups. I caught a wafting of fragrance from the night-blooming trumpet flowers outside as Ingrid told us how when she gets old, she wants to have a slow exchange of interesting people of all ages and nationalities come and stay with her.

She explained how the new addition would have a two-story luxury loft apartment on one side and a more dormitory-style space with bunk beds and room for several people on the other.

"I'm working with a young Peruvian engineer to design a floating steel staircase for the loft," she said. "He understands my vision and has the skills to make it happen. I can't wait!"

Ingrid radiated excitement and energy now. She was back in form, the small moment of vulnerability gone, as she retrieved a file folder with magazine clippings of decorative details and described how a cylindrical tower housing a spa-style bathroom would join the two connecting suites.

"There's never an ideal time to pull the roof off," she said with pragmatic brusqueness. "It needs to be done now, during the dry season, or I'll lose the chance for another year."

We learned that contractors were already in place, with construction due to start as soon as possible. Ingrid had hired her friend Paula, a sturdy and sensible Swiss woman in her late thirties and fluent in Spanish, to manage the project.

Over the next few days, Ingrid was very much herself. She and I gardened, sipped champagne, and iced lemongrass tea. We exchanged music and book recommendations, enjoyed long walks up steep mountain trails, rested and read in patio hammocks, and generally caught up with one another. We made plans for another visit and spoke nothing of illness.

Hank was content to read and nap and enjoy alone time. He joined in for meals and conversation in the mornings and evenings and helped with cleanup in the kitchen. On our final night, he waved Ingrid and me off as we departed in high spirits for the full moon trance dance.

It was late May, and the winter night was cold. Glowing lanterns and a flickering bonfire bathed a grassy hilltop lawn in a warm glow as we approached the venue down a dark dirt-track road. Ingrid's Volkswagen rolled up to a large gate where a barrel-chested Peruvian man directed us to a small parking area. Ingrid and I were swaddled in puff jackets with alpaca scarves around our necks to combat the cold, but the local man wore a short-sleeved tee shirt and was barefooted.

When we picked our way up the moonlit hill path to the seventeenth century Hacienda Huayoccari, we paused to find the Southern Cross in the Southern Hemisphere sky. I noticed that I wasn't in the right mood to lose myself in music and dance for a few hours. Then I spotted Ana Maria with Monika and Ingrid's friend Barbara, a German naturopath who worked with Hank and me in Cusco and was the event's organizer, and I reminded myself to let go. Still, I felt uneasy as Barbara outlined the evening's twenty-first century version of the ancient shamanic ritual of dancing to trance-inducing drumming and a specially created electronic music playlist. The smell of change filled the chilly night air.

I glanced over at Ingrid, who was already swaying to the music, her face rapt with contentment. She sensed my gaze and threw me a peculiar smile full of mystery and mischief. Once again, I was reminded of how fond I am of Ingrid—her exuberant style, her appetite for beauty and joy. Which made what was to come all the worse.

The drums began to beat, and as we made our way out onto the grassy lawn under a luminous purple sky, I told myself not to worry. And in the dark, cocooned by the music and its driving rhythms, the uneasiness faded as I lost myself in movement. Such total abandon was out of character for me, but I didn't care. Something told me this was the time for it.

52

Do You Know How Lucky You Are?

"Still no word from Ingrid?" Hank asked as he took off his jacket and hung it over the back of the café chair at Jack's.

"No. But I'm not worried," I replied. "Construction is in full swing. Even with Paula managing the workers, I imagine she is busy cleaning, selecting paint colors, ordering materials, and moving and storing furniture."

The morning was brilliant, crisp and bright; the whitewashed buildings glimmered in the sunshine, the painted doors and window trims bright blue as the sky above. In their matching uniforms and floppy-brimmed hats, schoolchildren raced past hand-in-hand. The tantalizing scent of strong Peruvian coffee, earthy and seductive, drifted in the air when we arrived at the café. A line quickly formed behind us at the door as Fania greeted us with a warm hug and kissed us on both cheeks.

"What would you like?"

"A cappuccino and—"

She held up a hand and gave Hank a big smile. "I know. Chocolate milkshake."

Jack's was an everyday indulgence better avoided was it not for

Fania.

The waitress brought the drinks to the table and took our order. Eggs and bacon for Hank. Fresh fruit and muesli with honey for me.

Hank took a swig of milkshake and said: "I think I'll skip writing group today. I'm not writing anything, and without Jason and Carlos, it's not the same."

I nodded. "The vibe is different," I agreed. "Something I can't quite put my finger on. Less focused, perhaps. Still, I think I'll continue."

As it turned out, I was glad I did.

Ingrid was immersed in the renovation project. And Ana Maria was occupied with the responsibilities of guiding and maintaining three properties—the Cusco triplex, the Calca cottage, and Chuqui, the inherited hacienda that she and her sisters had yet to decide what to do with. We saw little of our two friends in recent weeks.

They're busy with their lives, I told myself. Lives that continue, of course, during the years we are away. It's a small enough price to pay, I knew, to live the life we desired; to do what we want; to go where we want, to have work and friendships and experiences that we carry with us wherever we go.

But I sometimes wondered.

There was an envious, uncertain part of me that felt slightly bereft, though it's absurd.

And yet, somewhere at the back of my mind, I was aware that despite everything—the ache in my heart when we said goodbye, my wavering doubts, and fears—I felt a soaring certainty that this was a life that suited us. One that continuously brings diverse friendships, fresh experiences and nurtures what matters most—people, freedom, connection.

Over the years, I have had to learn to step outside my comfort zone: To let go when I most desperately want to cling; to speak unfamiliar words in unfamiliar languages. And though I tilt overly toward introversion, I got in the habit of seizing moments of connection with people who shine.

• • •

Dani was drinking ginger tea in the upstairs room of The Meeting Place when I arrived at the writing group. Dani of the infectious giggle and soulful poetry. She wore an oversized chunky sweater, black leggings, and thong sandals, her long brown hair tied up in a top-knot, and a broad, irresistible smile. It was a few minutes before eleven on a crisp June morning. The sun poured in through an open balcony door, and we had the room to ourselves.

"Hello," I said. "Do you mind if I join you?"

She smiled and gestured toward the armchair beside her.

In her early twenties, something was compelling about Dani. There was intelligence and beauty, but it went beyond that—an aura of youthful innocence and wisdom beyond her years. Hank had sensed it immediately, and I'd heard it in her writings.

I settled into the chair beside her, and we worked our way through introductions. I learned that Dani and her twin sister had been brought by her mother to Arizona from Mexico as undocumented children at age nine. Dani had come to Peru to travel and learn. But now, due to Trump's anti-immigrant attack on Obama's Deferred Action for Childhood Arrivals (DACA) program, she was at risk of deportation to Mexico should she return to the United States. She told it as a story to tell, not a problem to solve. Still, I felt a surge of anger. Why shouldn't this gracious young woman be allowed to return to her family in a country where she'd grown up, gone to school, gotten a driver's license, worked, and paid tuition and taxes?

Then the room filled with people arriving for the meeting, and we spoke no more about it. When the hour was over, Dani introduced me to Sara of Belgium, a former lawyer, now a yoga instructor. I gave them my mobile phone number and our address with an open invitation to visit.

• • •

"Do you realize how lucky you are? To enjoy this way of life together?" Sara said when she and Dani visited Hank and me a few days later.

My mind cycled back to the Galapagos cruise, to the luxury trek along the Inca Trail, and to those years when I repeatedly asked myself the same question: *Don't you know how lucky you are?*

But back then, the question was tainted by guilt, and there was the suggestion of unsustainable expectations. It was a life that looked good on the outside yet didn't feel entirely true inside. Today, there's a new sense of confirmation, a feeling of confidence, of pride. Sara was right; this life together felt wildly fortunate, and I told her so without hesitation.

• • •

The following week, Hank returned to the writing group seduced by lunch plans with Dani and Sara afterward at Pachapapa, a nearby rustic restaurant specializing in traditional Andean cuisine. We invited Bela of India via Silicon Valley, Denmark, and, most recently, Pisac to join us.

At Pachapapa, we found a dozen people eating at picnic tables and benches in an open-air courtyard, with room for a dozen more. Plumes of herb-scented smoke wafted up from a large clay oven.

We took our seats, and almost at once, a waiter arrived with water and menus. When he returned for the order, Dani, Sara, and Bela each chose a vegetarian option: the Veggie Capchi, a creamy stew of yellow chili with mushrooms, fava beans, and soft paria cheese with steamed quinoa. Hank and I opted for Andean trout baked with wild fennel, tomatoes, potatoes, and roasted vegetables.

Over the meal, the trio revealed bits and pieces of their lives: Sara's university years in Tennessee and then at a law firm in London; Bela's experiences in Denmark as a project manager for high-tech companies and how she was in Peru as part of a multi-year artistic sabbatical; Dani's months in Hawaii with her twin sister before traveling solo to Peru. *What an exciting group.* With Dani, age twenty-one, and Hank, age eighty-one, and nearly every decade represented in between, the conversation was expansive, funny, reflective, and global.

Just like that, we had new friends.

The bonds strengthened during the six months that followed as we enjoyed more and more time together: at writing group; at the lunches afterward, that became a ritual; and at our apartment where Sara came biweekly for yoga sessions; where Dani sought frequent refuge from hostel-life; and where Bela stayed overnight whenever she was in Cusco before heading back to Pisac in the Sacred Valley where she painted and wrote. It worked for Hank too. I could tell it made him happy.

Time with Ingrid and Ana Maria, however, was surprisingly spare, making it all the more precious when it happened. There were a few weekends with Ana Maria at her Calca house. And a spontaneous trip in her SUV high into the backcountry. I was always happy to be with Ana Maria, especially as she and I sang, laughed, and reveled in the magic of fresh air, dirt roads, Andean peaks, and sunshine and sky as vast and blue and bright as an ocean.

• • •

On a sunny late-September morning, I rose early to get to the *Colectivo* terminal at Calle Puputi and caught a shared van out to the Sacred Valley. I was to meet Ingrid at the Viva Peru Café in Huaran. I'd eagerly accepted when she'd telephoned with an unexpected invitation to join her for coffee and homemade apple crumble. I arrived early. So, I ordered a cappuccino at the counter inside and then selected a table in the sprawling garden to sit, sip, and wait for Ingrid. When she arrived a half-hour late with bruises on her face and a blue-black eye, I couldn't hide my alarm.

"I tripped and fell," Ingrid explained. "I was carrying a small boulder down from the mountain for the new guest wing garden when I stumbled. I know," she added with a sheepish grin. "I'm too stubborn and independent for my own good."

The initial sting of alarm was soon softened by affection as Ingrid dropped into the café chair, giving a grateful smile to the barista who'd come out from behind the counter and outside to take her order.

Ingrid was thinner and weaker than two weeks ago when we'd gone shopping together in Cusco for floor tiles. A silhouette of her previous vibrant self, the elegant sky-blue alpaca sweater she wore hung loosely on her diminishing frame. She'd chosen it, I suspected, because it complemented her blue eyes and tangle of curly white hair. Still, nothing, not even the exuberance of her red-framed eyeglasses, could hide the exhaustion.

I suspected that a part of her was as scared as I was about what was happening inside her. But I knew that bombarding my fiercely independent and self-sufficient friend with questions, clichéd positivity, or unsolicited medical advice would not be welcome. Still, it would be just as wounding to ignore what was in front of me.

After the barista had delivered a plate of apple crumble topped with a massive scoop of ice cream and two dessert forks, I asked Ingrid what she'd learned from the appointment with the Cusco internist.

As I watched Ingrid enthusiastically dig into the food, my mind whispered: *Please let the news be promising.*

"Well, the good news is that they don't think it's cancer," Ingrid said.

Think?

That's wonderful, Ingrid," I said as relief surged through me.

It took great restraint not to ask the question that hung over us like a dark cloud: *And the bad news?*

Instead, I savored the contrasting sensations of hot apples and ice cream and provided Ingrid with space to reveal—or not—the remaining news in her own time.

She paused, and I could feel her tracing back through the medical appointment in her memory. Then she shot me a smile and said: "It's ulcers. They found stomach ulcers. Not such bad news, is it?"

I looked across the table at Ingrid and felt an overwhelming sense of relief and joy.

Ulcers explained the digestion problems, the weakness and weight loss, and the vomiting blood she'd confessed to. Ulcers are manageable. People don't die of ulcers, I told myself, though I wasn't sure it was true.

"Oh, yes! Not such bad news at all. Ulcers are manageable," I said brightly and believed it.

Ingrid smiled—a better smile than before, which brought a playful gleam to her eyes.

She nodded and looked at me with no fear in her eyes and said: "That's what I said."

We laughed, and I no longer saw the bruised face, the blackened eye, the skeletal frame. Gone were my earlier dismay and anxiety. I let out a deep breath. It was as if the news had somehow returned my faith in Ingrid's indestructibility.

Then, after the bill had been paid and we'd hugged goodbye, and my heart still soared with hope, Ingrid said: "I knew it wasn't cancer. I knew my body didn't house the deadly stomach cancer that killed my mother."

In that instant, the fear roared back. Fear that the doctors had missed something. Fear that, inside Ingrid, cancer simmered in wait. Fear that one day a new diagnosis would tell her that they'd been wrong, that the ulcers were tumors, and that, in the end, we'd lose Ingrid too early. Fear that she'd never get to host the painters and writers and explorers, she was so eagerly renovating her home to greet.

53

Moving On Is the Hardest Thing

Ana Maria had tickets to a movie premiere and wanted to know if we could join her.

"Some of it was filmed at Chuqui," she said, taking a seat on a kitchen barstool in her rental apartment, now our temporary home.

I poured water into the electric kettle for tea as Ana Maria reminded me they'd been in preparation for filming the last time we were here in 2015.

"You were gone by the time production began," she said. "But I have photos." She tapped the screen of her mobile phone a few times, furiously swiping up and down, then dropped it onto the kitchen counter in frustration.

"I can never find anything on this stupid smartphone," she muttered. "Fico bought it for me and is forever trying to teach me how to use it. But it's useless. Technology hates me," she said before returning her attention to the movie premiere.

"It's sort of a big deal," she continued, all frustration quickly forgotten. "Exclusive showings in Lima and Cusco. After parties. Director's cuts. You know."

It was fun to see Ana Maria so animated and to hear the excitement in her voice. The past months had been harried and stressful for her.

As I prepared for us *mate de coca,* the traditional Andean herbal tea, I realized how few moments like this one we'd had together and how much I missed it.

I handed Ana Maria a mug of tea and watched as she instinctively wrapped both hands around it, soaking in the comforting heat. I took a sip and waited for recognition.

I saw surprise, then pleasure in her eyes as she took in the mug's familiar red clay and Andean iconography. It was from the Urubamba ceramics workshop of Paolo Semintario, a piece from an older collection.

"Do you remember giving these to us as a going-away gift six years ago?" I asked her.

She nodded yes and gave me a quizzical look.

"They're part of our travel kit," I told her, answering the unasked question. "They go where we go."

She shot me a shy smile and said: "It feels good to have them home again—like you, *querida.*"

Home. I used to think it was so simple. Back when I viewed the contentment of home and the thrill of exploration as mutually exclusive. Before the two merged, almost imperceptibly, into one.

It was a clear winter evening. We moved from the kitchen into comfortable armchairs that faced the picture window. Golden light flooded the room as we watched the sun go down over the rooftops. Hank was at his computer in the guest room.

"When is the movie premiere?" I asked.

"Late December."

"Oh, amiga. Thank you for the invitation, but we have decided to go when our visas expire at the end of October. To leave before the rains begin."

I felt a little stab of pain as I said this, realizing that I'd avoided the conversation of our departure. I kept waiting for a surge of *I could live here* desire to overtake the lure of leaving, but it didn't come. I was eager for a warmer climate and new soils and ready for change.

Ana Maria looked at me intently. "Are you sure?"

For a moment, I thought she might say more, her eyes meeting mine, then she shifted her gaze out the window.

I was silent as I gathered my thoughts.

"Do you know what the greatest surprise of this way of life has been?" I finally said, looking at the thousands of city lights that sparkled like stars against the now-dark sky. "It's been the normalcy of impermanence. Waking with an awareness that the things that make the days special are gifts; you coming down from upstairs for a chat and a cup of tea, Thursdays at the writing group, time with Ingrid, passing enormous zigzag stone walls built by the Inca as part of everyday life. There's no illusion of it lasting forever. No taking people for granted. Quite unexpectedly, we've found great pleasure and value in living connected to the pulse of impermanence and change. I like living that way. I don't want to stop feeling that way. To have as many days like that as possible. Does that make sense? When moving on is no longer practical or possible, we'll stop if it ever comes to that. But not yet."

"You might think I don't understand, but I do," Ana Maria said. "I will miss you, and I regret that I've been so unavailable. I hadn't planned it that way, but I know you need to move on."

"Next time!" we say in unison. Then we laugh.

• • •

During the following month, Ana Maria and I spent as much time as possible together. Even if only for a moment in passing on the steps outside the house. Or a quick meal at Las Frescas Salad Bar. Or, better still, a weekend at her Calca house. I offered to help her with the new smartphone, and we spent short training sessions at her kitchen table going deeper into various applications. Email. Camera. Photos. WhatsApp. It was fun. A small way for me to give back, to be together, and, hopefully, to make technology less frustrating.

Then one day, a week before our departure, I got a call from Ingrid. She'd come to Cusco for a doctor's appointment and ended up in the hospital. Could I bring her some overnight clothes and toiletries?

Concerned, I called Ana Maria, who immediately offered to accompany me to the private clinic where Ingrid had been admitted. I was relieved. It seemed important that Ana Maria, a native Cusqueñean, was there. I quickly packed a small duffel bag with pajamas and slippers, my favorite baby alpaca poncho, toiletries, an iPhone charging cable, and a stack of books. At the same time, Ana Maria retrieved her car from a nearby parking space.

We found Ingrid in good spirits when we arrived. She was busy fielding phone calls from friends and cheerfully chatting up nurses for an extra pillow, a warmer blanket. Ana Maria and I sat side by side on the edge of an empty patient bed, and Ingrid filled us in on why she was there.

"They want to do another endoscopy and a series of X-rays, maybe a biopsy. I'm not really sure," she told us. "The goal is to see if the antibiotics and acid blocker treatments have healed the ulcers. I shouldn't be here for more than a day or two," she added optimistically.

Ana Maria and I smiled in agreement and murmured words of encouragement as we tried not to reveal our worry. An IV bag hung above Ingrid, drip-dropping liquids into her emaciated arms. Eventually, Ana Maria went off searching for a doctor and more information while Ingrid filled the silence with a steady stream of chitchat.

In the days that followed, Ingrid had a constant flow of supportive friends visiting her at the hospital. Paula was there with clothes and belongings from Ingrid's house in the valley and status updates about the renovation project. Barbara, the German naturopath and Ingrid's dearest friend, helped with communications among the medical team. Lisa from the writing group and Ingrid's former roommate brought supplemental food and drinks.

When Ana Maria deposited Hank and me at the airport the following week for flights back to the United States, Ingrid was discharged and recuperating at Barbara's Cusco house.

Still, the test results revealed the ulcers had failed to respond to treatment. I didn't know what it meant but feared it wasn't good.

54

Immigration Troubles

Portugal

"Remind me again. How many days before we must leave the country if our visa extension is denied?" Hank said.

We were eating breakfast at The Bakery Lounge in Évora. It was early September 2019, six months since our return to Portugal, and the serviced apartment at the top of three flights of stairs at Casa Morgado Esporão.

"Rita told me they'd probably allow us up to ten days," I said. "However, she didn't think it would come to that."

Rita was the lawyer helping us to petition the Portuguese Immigration and Borders Service (SEF). SEF is the security service described on their website as *"Responsible for carrying out checks on persons at the borders, monitoring aliens inside the national territory, preventing and fighting organized crime involving illegal immigration and trafficking in human beings, deciding upon asylum applications, issuing passports and identification documents to foreign nationals."* In our case, the agency to determine if we could remain in Portugal.

"I hope she's right," Hank said just as Cristina arrived at the table with our meals: scrambled eggs, *presunto* (Portuguese smoked ham), and buttered toast for Hank. An Açaí bowl with homemade granola and fresh strawberries for me.

We'd been pleased to see Cristina again upon our Évora return. She was at work on a master's degree in biology at the University of Évora during our 2017 stay. We thought she might have returned to Ecuador, her homeland, or taken a position elsewhere. But academic jobs weren't forthcoming. So, while she applied for Ph.D. programs and employment in her field, she worked at the bakery. We loved beginning our days with her sweet smile and the thick chocolate milkshakes she made special for Hank.

Cristina placed the food on the table and asked: "Did you enjoy your time in Porto?"

We'd traveled to Porto recently because our friend Johanna had flown in from North Carolina to join her twenty-three-year-old daughter Paulina to walk the Camino de Santiago. We'd first met mother and daughter in 1997 in Ajijic when Johanna was married to Paulina's dad Rodrigo. Johanna and Rodrigo had owned a small natural foods café back then in the courtyard of an art gallery. Paulina would sit on my lap while we ate breakfast each morning that winter when she was only a year old, and Hank and I were on a yearlong travel sabbatical. Over the years, we'd watched Paulina grow into a beautiful, intelligent, multilingual young woman. They'd visited us in New Mexico. We'd seen Johanna happily remarried in North Carolina. After a couple of gap years traveling in Southeast Asia and Australia, Paulina was at University in Germany. We were thrilled when she'd texted us an invitation to join them in Porto before the two set off for a month of hiking.

We told Cristina an abbreviated version of the story and how grateful we were to still be in Portugal while they were here.

"That reminds me," she said. "Any news on your visas?"

We shook our heads no.

"Nothing yet," I said.

"Well, everyone here is rooting for you. David is serious about that employment contract," she smiled before leaving.

I was surprised by the tears that filled my eyes as I recalled the day David, one of two adult sons managing the family-owned bakery, offered to provide me with a work contract for media services. "Whatever it takes to keep you two here, we'll do it," he'd said as his Portuguese mother fiercely nodded in agreement.

The fact that we were still in Évora on this sunny September morning, nearly three months beyond the ninety days permitted by the Schengen visa, was thanks to Rita. In April, she'd petitioned SEF on our behalf for a temporary short-stay visa extension. In August, we received approval.

Still, the process hadn't been straightforward. Our Schengen visas had expired forty days before approval was granted. The overstay was legal because our applications were in the system, but it also meant we couldn't travel freely within the E.U. outside of Portugal. And, now, with a second application in the works, we were just four days shy of the first extension expiring, leaving us uncertain if we might have to go suddenly.

We were fortunate, we knew, to have doubled our time already. And yet, it was all a little unsettling.

We finished breakfast and walked up Rua de Vasco da Gama, the narrow cobblestone street that climbs up to the Roman temple and the Jardim Diana, where we were headed when Hank asked: "If we get approval, will you be permitted to travel to Germany to see Ingrid?"

We chose a garden bench facing the temple to sit in the sun, and it occurred to me, in the quiet moment before I answered, how much I was feeling the visa restrictions. Part of me wanted to book a flight to Germany, knowing that if I left, there was no guarantee I'd be allowed back. The same part of me that wanted to believe that the German doctor's terminal diagnosis of Ingrid's stomach cancer was a big mistake.

Ute and her husband Carsten were visiting us in Évora after seeing family in Norway and Germany. I was riding high on the joy of being with Ute again, exploring, photographing, and catching up over late dinners and Portuguese wine. I'd filled Ute in on Johanna and Paulina as she'd known them too in Ajijic.

Then we learned that Ingrid had traveled to Europe for treatment and that everything was about to change for her.

Cancer. It was the first time I'd said it out loud when I told Hank.

In the despondent aftermath of the tragic news, I had a dream of Ingrid. In the dream, she was in the renovated guest loft of the Sacred Valley house, packing a suitcase. She wore the same floral skirt, lime-green alpaca sweater, purple pashmina, and impish smile she'd worn at the Inti Raymi festival.

The dream felt as real as life, and for just a moment, I forgot.

When I awakened, I succumbed to the tears that welled up.

Time had turned elastic. The past was twisting itself around into the present—the future troublesome and enigmatic.

• • •

At dinner, a month after SEF confirmed an extension through late November but still no travel outside of Portugal, I shared with Hank the newest text message from our friend Robyn about her arrival plans for the following morning. She and her husband Simon were due to fly from New Jersey to Lisbon with an eight a.m. arrival. If everything went to plan, they'd check in at Casa Morgado Esporão just after eleven.

"Does Robyn remember how to get here?" Hank asked. "Are they staying in the next-door apartment again?"

"She does. They are," I answered. The thought of it sent a surge of warmth through me.

I was thrilled that Robyn had decided to return to Èvora. In late May, she'd come alone for five days, staying in the apartment next door. I had rented a car, and we'd driven to Praia Odeceixe, a quiet little beach town that Hank and I discovered during a previous getaway. Monica from yoga class joined us. We'd positioned ourselves beneath a blue-striped beach umbrella on rented lounge chairs and enjoyed a quiet day at the beach. Then, we'd watched the sun go down over the Atlantic Ocean over a feast of seafood salad, sardines, Aljezur sweet potato, dry-cured ham, black pig chorizo, sheep cheese, and olives at Kiosk Agapito, an unassuming and delicious little seafood shack along the cliff. In addition to a delicious menu, they had good music, Gin Sul sundowners, mocktails, and incredible coastal views. On the drive home, we blasted Natalie Prass's layered album "The Future and the Past," grooving to its heartbreaking lyrics and mix of funk, disco, jazz, and '90s pop R&B.

And now Robyn and Simon were coming for fourteen days. I couldn't wait.

• • •

"I still can't believe I'm back," Robyn said.

We were seated at a small café table in the sun at Páteo de São Miguel, the back garden of a thirteenth century royal palace, drinking the local Cartuxa wine. We were on our second glass, Simon and Hank were back at the apartments catching an afternoon nap. We sat there talking about anything that came into our heads, and my mind traveled back to 2011 to the three blissful weeks we'd enjoyed together in Nicaragua at Hotel La Bocona. I could see Robyn in my mind's eye kicking off her sandals, sprawling her tall, willowy body across a short sofa, her toned brown legs and flowered sundress draping over its end as if it was yesterday, not eight years ago. I'm still not sure how I would have gotten through that time in Nicaragua without those weeks together.

When I mentioned this to Robyn, she said: "I remember my confusion when I first met you in Nicaragua. Do you know the feeling when you meet someone and can't figure out how you survived without them this long?"

I smiled at her, my heart clutching in my chest. *Yeah. THAT feeling.* I thought with a gust of recognition and gratitude.

From the beginning, this was what we'd been to each other: Familiar. Transient. We laughed, lifted each other when feeling down, and picked up where we'd last left off, regardless of how long it's been. That hadn't changed. It broke something wide open in me to have Robyn here again, which is why I didn't see what happened next coming.

On a Friday evening, our last before Robyn and Simon were to leave, I was shopping with Robyn at a small Évora clothing boutique I liked. It was one of the stores I'd taken Robyn to early into her stay. She'd purchased several outfits that looked stunning on her statuesque brown body, and she had returned in search of a gift to take home for her son's girlfriend. The saleslady, an older Portuguese woman in her late fifties or early sixties, remembered Robyn and greeted us warmly.

I looked at an earring display while Robyn browsed a belt rack. Vaguely, I heard Robyn mention to the saleswoman that a belt was missing some beads. I wasn't paying close attention to the conversation, so it didn't quite register when the woman said: "It's their way—always looking for a flaw so they can get a discount."

They? Who was she speaking to?

The woman gave a coarse cackle and handed the belt back to Robyn.

I continued browsing, unaware, holding a vivid-print Italian dress in front of a mirror. The saleslady followed, commenting on how the colors suited me. When I looked around for Robyn's opinion, she was gone. I put the dress away and found her standing outside the store.

"Is everything okay?"

Robyn recounted the woman's slur and how her words—and the prejudice behind them—were all too familiar.

I didn't know how to parse through the layers of insult and was embarrassed to have overlooked it. I thought then of the small acts of refusal like this one that people of color have to endure all the time.

"It's okay," Robyn said, stepping into the café next door where we had a dinner reservation.

As we waited for the meals, I was preoccupied, replaying the moment over in my mind. *What could I have said? What should I have said? Why didn't the insult register?*

Though I was pained by what was left unsaid, I didn't want to put Robyn in the position of comforting me. So I followed her gracious lead and let it be.

Still, a few days later, I went back to the store, and in a moment without customers, I said to the saleswoman: "Can I talk with you about something you said that's stayed with me?"

Afterward, she expressed no remorse, claimed I was overly sensitive, said it was just a joke, and told me she'd lived in North Africa and that *They* were always looking for a bargain.

I never returned.

Looking back, I realize that I needed to be better prepared in the future. I needed to exert myself to see a world that wasn't a secret but was well hidden, even in plain sight. And that if I did, if I developed that kind of curiosity, if I had an innate interest in the welfare of my fellow human beings, this life of travel just might have some impact.

55

Final Days

After weeks of sunny warm days and pleasantly cool nights, Évora experienced a rainy, cold snap not long after Robyn and Simon left. The rain outside came down hard, lashing the apartment windows. The daytime highs hovered at a chilly twelve degrees Celsius (52°F) under damp gray skies. It did not bode well for the impending arrivals of Hank's granddaughter Kelsey and her husband Kent, his grandson Kyle and Kyle's girlfriend, Annette. The group had booked a nearby Airbnb and was excited to explore the area. They had purchased tickets to a Benefica professional football club live match in Lisbon. Visits were planned to the Adega do Monte Branco and Reguengos de Monsaraz wineries, producing some of the best Portuguese wines. And a day trip to the wild Comporta coastline with its pristine white beaches was scheduled with reservations for a sunset seafood dinner at the oceanfront Comporta Café, a perfect place to end the day.

"They'll be fine," our friend Andrea, an Alentejo native, assured us when I expressed dismay about the weather. "November weather can indeed be iffy, but with plenty of sunny days too. Plus, the low autumn sun turns everything golden and gorgeous, and the nights are crisp and starry against ink-black skies. They'll love it."

She was right. The weather was glorious. The kids had a great time, and so did we. It soothed the sting, just a little, of not being permitted to travel to Germany.

Andrea owns a Portuguese artisanal store that is my go-to place in Évora to shop for the things that have transformed the hotel apartment into a cozy temporary home: dishes and bowls, blankets and pillows, and gourmet food items. Andrea and I had been friendly in 2017, but now, she was a cherished friend. Andrea stopped in for coffee most mornings at the bakery, so we had that in common. But early on, she had invited me to join her and a small group of local women for yoga class three evenings a week at a university theater department building. That invitation proved to be transformative.

I was happily enrolled at a local yoga ashram for the biweekly morning classes I'd begun in 2017, where Monica and I practiced. The yoga there offered a pure, Indian form with the purpose of a quiet mind and a better connection to the body. We breathed. We moved. We chanted. My body loved it.

The evening group, however, embodied something even more precious, something my soul craved—community. Many of the women had been practicing together for years, some going back more than two decades. The teacher, Esperança, a gentle and kindhearted Portuguese woman in her seventies, united the group with warmth and commitment. For a nominal fee, enough to cover the room rate, Esperança never missed a class and organized class picnics and field trips like the one we'd taken at the summer solstice to Almendres Cromlech, a nearby megalithic standing stones complex.

When Robyn visited, Esperança welcomed her and went out of her way to make her feel comfortable, as she'd done for me in a class conducted entirely in Portuguese. I felt so at home within the group that my usual reticence with the language was unlocked during those evenings before and after class, the words pouring out. The women laughed with me at my broken Portuguese, though strangely, they seemed to understand, even when my guttural, marble-mouthed attempts produced sounds that don't actually exist in Portuguese.

Margarida, a soft-spoken ethics professor at the university, often walked back to Casa Morgado Esporão with me as she lived nearby. I learned she'd once studied in the United States in Washington, D.C.

And now, with our departure looming, Esperança had organized a going-away dinner party after my final class at a nearby restaurant.

It was the walk to and from those evening classes—up the narrow Travessa das Casas Pintadas, past the Jardim Diana, and the Roman temple, along the university paths, then down across the IP2 ring road—that will forever mark the passage of time and season in my memories of Évora.

In March, the sun was just dipping beneath the horizon on the walk to class at seven p.m., the garden trees just beginning to bud. In April and May, it wouldn't be dark for close to an hour after the walk home a little after eight, the garden flower beds in full blossom with bright orange poppies. Margarida and I walked home beneath a sun still burning high in the sky and the evening swallows skimming low over the garden fountains in June and July. By August and September, we watched the moon rise over the Temple of Diana (the Roman goddess of the moon), the ancient monument cast in a celestial glow. In October, it was already dark before I set off, the garden trees rustling brittle leaves in brisk autumn breezes. And then, in late November, the ivy vines that climb the university walls were a deep scarlet red, and the city enveloped in darkness by five p.m.

What mattered most, however, about our time here was timeless. It was the thing that compelled us to stay and to leave. And it was the paradox at the heart of a nomadic life—the richness of relationship to others. In the end, coming and going turn out to be two parts of the same experience. I didn't know how eight years of rootlessness had come to feel like a normal life, but it had. And the foundation of that experience, our own deeply earned truth, was that each place carries its gifts in connection—to ourselves, to others, and the whole of life.

On the night of the going-away dinner, the yoga ladies gave me a modern silver brooch with a circle of yellow spirals emanating from its center to remind me of the Portuguese sun. I recognized it immediately from Andrea's store and the collection of a local artist I admired. I was still grinning ear to ear while tears ran down my face as I stopped, one final time, in front of the Roman temple, the garden beds recently planted with hardy chrysanthemums, before I made my way down the narrow passage of painted houses and home to Hank.

• • •

Three months earlier, Hank and I sat at the kitchen table in the hotel apartment playing a hand of Go Fish with Cristina, Fernanda, and Fernanda's daughter Sophia. It was Sophia's seventh birthday, and we'd celebrated at the hotel pool, followed by pizza and birthday cake in the apartment. Fernanda and Cristina were workmates at the Bakery Lounge where we first met them. Both in their thirties, the two had each come to Portugal from South America: Cristina from Ecuador, Fernanda from Brazil. When Fernanda, a single mother, was suddenly dismissed from the bakery and in limbo while the unemployment office helped her to find new work, I asked if I could hire her to tutor me in Portuguese. She'd accepted, and we'd been enjoying biweekly sessions ever since, with Sophia often joining us. Andrea, who also knew Fernanda from the bakery, had ordered a custom cake from a local woman. A friend, Sandra, delivered it to the apartment and a little gift from Andrea's store. From the hotel reception desk, Pedro brought the delivery pizza to the apartment. He joined us all in singing "*Feliz aniversário*" to sweet little Sophia, who giggled and smiled triumphantly, having trounced us at Go Fish. When Monica stopped by with a card and a small gift, my heart melted at the sight of the gathering of foreigners and Portuguese rallying in celebration of this innocent girl who took us all in stride with our different languages and skin colors and ages. Hank was utterly smitten with Fernanda and Sophia, and I spotted a shadow of sadness in his eyes on this happy day and suspected that he was thinking, as was I, of the day when we would say goodbye.

This time, even if we wanted to, we couldn't stay. Our time as temporary immigrants in Portugal was over.

56

Travel Interrupted

New Mexico, USA

It was December 2019 when we returned to Don and Corinna's guest house in New Mexico, hearts open, full of hope.

The sky was big and blue, the high-altitude sun shimmering on mountains white with snow. Picture perfect. The daily highs were in the high forties Fahrenheit, yet the intense sunshine made it feel much warmer. By ten a.m., we were peeling off the layers, puff jackets unzipped on the morning walk. The nights were crisp and cold, well below freezing, with the Geminid meteor showers active and on full display through the undraped windows and the nightly yip of the coyotes echoing in the surrounding forest.

The guest house, the winter weather, and living communally again with Don and Corinna felt familiar and comforting, like a welcome way station between adventures.

Ingrid seemed to be doing better too. She'd been too busy to talk the last two times I'd telephoned.

"I'm at a wine festival," she told me, picking up the call. I could hear laughter in her voice and the sounds of gaiety in the background.

"I'm at a garden center with a friend," she texted another time. "I'll call you back. Okay?"

It was more than okay.

It was so like Ingrid, I thought, to seize the day. To seek out joy and beauty. She was showing me how to die, I perceived with great sorrow, just as she'd shown me how to live.

It would be three months before we could re-enter Europe again under the Schengen regulations, but Ingrid and I remained close, even at a distance. I sent her Audible books. She sent me photos of herself after she'd cut off her hair in a preemptive strike against the chemo. We traded music tracks. She told me about some of the people she was meeting, the friends from Peru and Europe who were visiting, and shared some writing she was working on as part of a creative writing program offered at the clinic where she was staying in the spa town of Bad Homburg.

• • •

By January 2020, Hank and I were full of new plans, new hopes, new directions to go. With the confidence of seasoned nomads, our dreams and horizons were expanding.

We booked one-way flights for mid-March to St. John's on Newfoundland Island off Canada's North Atlantic coast, with a six-month stay in mind. A spring arrival would put us there in advance of the warm weather. But we also hoped it would provide time to find affordable housing before the seaside town filled up with summer visitors.

From there, we'd chosen New Plymouth, on the west coast of New Zealand's North Island, as a destination for the following six months. A blog article we stumbled across as part of our research described the port city as having: *"a beautiful coastal walkway and pockets of cool—a surprisingly contemporary art gallery, street art, record stores, and artsy design shops, a sourdough bakery in a shipping container hidden down a colourful alleyway, and some excellent cafes for coffee and brunch."* I'm pretty sure it was the sourdough bakery and excellent cafés that sealed the deal.

I was thrilled by the prospect of a year of coastal living in small island cities in Northern and Southern Hemispheres.

Then, without warning, it was over, a decade of itinerant wandering resigned to memory, though we didn't know it then.

In March 2020, when coronavirus cases began to jump at alarming rates, as did hospitalizations and deaths, plans were postponed, flights rebooked for May.

Back then, when we understood relatively little about the disease, and one by one states issued stay-at-home orders shutting down all nonessential businesses, travel, and gatherings, we still thought we could return to travel in a couple of months. The dreadful and deadly long tail of the virus was unimaginable.

When global air travel was restricted in February, the pandemic shattered any hope of international travel. By the end of May, U.S. Covid-19 deaths passed the 100,000 mark.

As cases reached two million in June, and the U.S. became the disease's epicenter, the European Union prepared to open to visitors from fifteen countries on July first, but not to travelers from the United States.

Canada, where we'd hoped to spend the summer, would not open again to vaccinated Americans for another year. New Zealand enforced one of the world's strictest border regimes.

Once again, life as we knew it had been upended. After 3,229 days of nearly unfettered freedom and transcending countless uncertainties, we were back in a New Mexico house on a hill, forced to step out of one way of life and into another.

We'd come full circle—a destination that was both surprising and inevitable.

This time, however, the whole world had been turned on its end. And the stakes were deadly.

57

Staying Still

On a Tuesday morning in September 2021, Hank and I stepped out the door for a walk. The day was crystalline. A pair of ravens swooped low overhead, tumbling through the deep blue New Mexico sky, their trickster moves and gurgling croaks making us smile. It had been more than a year since the pandemic started—over a year of social isolation, eighteen months alone together in the one-room guest house. One year, five months, and sixteen days since Ingrid died in a German hospice.

Hank grabbed my hand as he navigated the two front steps, a habit acquired over the summer when we started walking together as part of his rehabilitation from hip replacement surgery. He groaned at the chill in the morning air, but he grinned as he groaned. He was strong now, his stride loose and exploratory, his gait almost easy again. I watched him in silent wonderment. Four months ago, he wouldn't have trusted his hip. Four months ago, he was lost in osteoarthritic pain.

We rounded a bend in the winding driveway, thick tracks of piñon-juniper, ponderosa pine, and blue spruce trees flanked both sides, the Sierra Blanca peak towering in the distance. Don and Corinna's dog,

Tamzy, the rescue they adopted after their beloved Hershey died three years ago, trotted just ahead, pausing briefly to sniff some animal scat. We stopped to see what had her attention.

"Fox," I told Hank. "I recognize the undigested berry seeds in the poo from the laminated 'Mammal Scat of North America' chart I rescued from storage."

He gave me a quizzical look.

"I also spotted a pair of red foxes scurrying across the driveway the other night at dusk," I admitted. "Their fluffy, white-tipped tails, nearly as long as the animals themselves."

Hank let out a laugh. "You're my favorite wife, you know."

Tamzy wriggled and wrapped herself around our legs. We reached down to pat her head. There we were. Alive. At ease. My favorite husband and me. And Tamzy, the unexpected pandemic bonus.

There had been days, too many, while we sheltered in place in our native country when it hadn't felt this way—days when hope struggled with despair and loss.

At the stroke of midnight on Wednesday, November 4, 2020, the United States became the only country to formally quit the Paris Agreement, the global accord designed to avert catastrophic climate change. On May 25, 2020, Minneapolis police officer Derek Chauvin killed George Floyd by kneeling on his neck for almost ten minutes. On January 6, 2021, Trump supporters stormed the U.S. Capitol in a violent attack that killed five people and forced lawmakers to be evacuated.

I wanted to believe that however ugly things got, justice would prevail. But honestly? Has that been the human story?

I watched in desperation as the days changed chaotically on planet Earth, as Covid killed millions, as willful ignorance fell apart, as Hank endured debilitating arthritic pain with a calm resilience that I never imagined. On October 9, 2021, the day ISIL bombers killed dozens at a Shiite Mosque in Afghanistan, Hank turned eighty-four, equipped, it seemed, for anything the human race—or his body—might throw at him. Even so, the sight of Hank restricting movement crushed me. The sitting all day, the effort it took to get in and out of a chair. After years of roaming, returning felt like death.

I did my best not to show it. Hank was probably protecting me, too. But then, in April 2021, the vaccines blunted the virus enough for a safe resumption of in-person medical care, and Hank began six weeks of physiotherapy in preparation for a prosthetic hip implant.

I could see the weekly changes. Hours after surgery, he was up walking with a walker. He got in and out of the car without assistance to go to physical therapy and resumed exercising. He now joined me for morning walks in the sunshine after coffee.

Hank is courageous in a way I am learning to emulate. But courage barely touches all that I admire in him. The way he faces whatever happens with the confidence that he can handle it, how he intuitively understands what battles are worth fighting without worrying about what any of it means. It felt like something beautiful, unexpected, and inexplicable surged through me as he healed.

Alongside Hank's recovery, late May brought the first monsoon rains of the year and something that resembled hope. The torrential thunderstorms that let loose most afternoons filled wells and aquifers, providing natural protection against wildfire. The earthy aroma of wet conifers and sweetly pungent ozone filled the mountain air. While the typically wet Pacific Northwest baked in a hundred-degree-plus heat wave, the cool summer rains arrived early in New Mexico to transform brown landscapes to emerald green, then yellow with sunflowers. Flowering plants were suddenly everywhere: pale blue Sierra Blanca lupine, scarlet Indian paintbrush, purple thistle, and the blue Rocky Mountain penstemon. It seemed somehow significant that as the land came alive again, so had Hank and I.

Don and Corinna made it clear we were welcome indefinitely and that the guest house rent was helpful. My pandemic workload had shifted into high gear as clients prioritized online alternatives. And while we stayed still, we became reacquainted with the herds of elk and deer and free-roaming horses that bedded down in the tall grasses just off the driveway, that held up traffic downtown and stopped tourists along the side of the road holding their cell phones out car windows for photos. The ladder-backed woodpeckers and stellar blue jays, white-breasted nuthatches and black-headed grosbeaks at the feeders outside felt like old friends now. Tamzy had become a part of us too, wandering in and out of the guest house at her pleasure with her own bed and bowls and accompanying us on walks. I had recently returned to the writings and Zen teachings of Shunryu Suzuki, and whenever I stepped outdoors, the message rang true: "The world is its own magic."

Still, I couldn't imagine that I'd toughened up enough to survive this journey through to the other side of the looking glass that was the current reality. And yet, truth be told, I was holding it together fairly well. I'd grown easy in my skin. I still fell into old resistances and anxieties and melancholic moments, but they passed through me quicker now. I was slower to fret about things beyond my control. More willing, as Suzuki advised, "to leave the front door and back door open, to let the thoughts come and go, but just not serve them tea."

Each year of wandering had left me a little more rooted in self-resilience. And now, in solitude, I spoke less, looked and listened more. Even when what I saw and heard were the weakest and most vulnerable—human and environmental—trapped inside a global emergency nobody wanted to talk about.

I missed Ingrid every, single, day. It was shocking to think she was no longer in the world. The impulse to share a photo, send a text, or call her was still strong. That feeling never stopped. Ingrid had swung open for me a doorway to a world of aesthetics and joy in her singular and irreplaceable spirit of hospitality. She'd left something precious and life-altering in her friendship. She had also taught me the wisdom of asking for help. This was how I'd found the professional estate liquidator who solved the puzzle of the massive, shrink-wrapped bundle in storage by relocating everything to a local warehouse before sorting, staging, and selling it.

One morning not long before the process started, I asked Hank what he wanted to keep. He looked out across the layers of mountains and thick forest spread out before us, his hands wrapped around a steaming mug of Guatemalan dark roast, and said: "Nothing."

Then, after a long pause, he added: "We should get the safe though and any essential documents. I'd also like to keep the Terpning painting we bought in 1994, the summer we eloped. I always liked that one."

Whatever barrier had kept us from getting rid of things for all those years, whatever permanency they once represented or desire to replicate that life was gone now, and letting go felt right. We kept a few special items for the guest house: the Santa Fe kitchen counter chairs, a hand-woven Mexican rug, ceramic dishes made by a local potter friend, and a pair of leather reading chairs. The rest we left to the liquidator to give away, sell, donate, repurpose, or discard appropriately.

One October night, right before bed on the eve of Hank's eighty-fifth birthday, I asked what he envisioned was next for us when this solitary period ended.

He shrugged. "To tell you the truth, it's not something I think about. It's enough, just being with you."

Three minutes later, he was asleep. I lay beside him, thinking about the truth of what he said for a long while. I looked around the moonlit room. The night pulsed with memories as I retraced the decade. I saw Ute, Arlen, Ana Maria, Ingrid, Kate, Mila, and others who had shared this journey with us. I heard the peal of children's laughter in Ajijic, the Oaxacan night air thick with a chorus of insects and tree frogs, Cusco's fireworks, car horns, Andean flute music, the melodic inflections of the Paisa accent in Medellín, and the echoing toll of Évora's ancient church bells. Every recollection confirmed what I now firmly believed—it didn't matter where we lived.

Staying still. Moving on. It didn't matter.

The fear of loss, of the unknown, had lost its menace.

Everything is possible.

Epilogue

Scotland

I opened the small garden gate and a squawk of seagulls let loose. The cottage chimney of the vacation rental was a favored perch of the raucous seabirds.

It had been three months and three days since we arrived in Charlestown, a coastal village in eastern Scotland. More than two years since we'd traveled on an airplane. Thirty-one years since a Fulbright teaching exchange to Scotland inspired a life-altering urge to explore.

I was just back from a walk along the promenade, the road by the waterfront where people jog and walk their dogs and push their babies in waterproof carriages. A widow from across the village green passed by as she does most days, walking two Scottish terriers, one white and one black, with matching tartan collars.

"Will you be along for bowls this evening?" she asked.

I'd never loved lawn bowling, a neighborly *hullo*, cool rain on my face, or country road drives on the wrong side of the road as I loved it now, after the stationary years of the prolonged pandemic pause and a devastating New Mexico wildfire season.

Seeking a peaceful and temperate place to resume traveling, we came to Scotland in August 2022 for an extended stay nearby to Jill, a three-decade-long Scottish friend. Six months in a cozy three-hundred-year-old holiday cottage. The two of us: Hank and me. The bowling club. The Village Green. The friendly neighbors. The abutting estate of the Earl of Elgin, chief of Clan Bruce. It felt like we'd landed in Brigadoon: an imaginary place, unaffected by time and remote from reality. Precisely the desired elixir for the chaotic nature of the times.

That evening, I reached out to Ana Maria in Cusco on WhatsApp with a now-familiar message. *Are you okay? How bad is it? How can we help?* Peru was in turmoil. In the last six years, the country had six presidents. In 2020, Peru cycled through three presidents in nine days. Then, the pandemic hit, devastating Peru with the world's highest Covid-19 mortality rate.

Ana Maria had always been brave and self-sufficient—a single mom, an adventure guide, a risk-taker. So I guess I shouldn't have been surprised when she texted back to tell me she was on a road trip to Lake Titicaca with friends.

"So much chaos and pain in the world," she texted. "Not just Covid and politics, and the horror of Russia's cruel war, but displacement, violence, and corruption on a global scale. But life continues, so shall I."

I understood the sentiment. Life happens now. This moment is all we control. I believe that as never before.

Philosophers and travelers, scientists and seekers, have talked for eons about the ways we are interconnected. It has taken a lifetime of travel and a decade of homelessness to teach me the wisdom of this perspective. What could be more important, in times of crisis or periods of calm, than connection—reaching out, asking questions, learning new ways of communicating and experiencing life?

I thought of Oksana, a Ukrainian woman working at a nearby inn where we often ate breakfast. How she'd been displaced by war and taken in by Scotland. We learned her story gradually over the months as we became familiar. She had a husband and brother back home fighting to defend a democratic Ukraine. Before asylum, Oksana had a fulfilling career as a museum education officer in Odessa and hoped to work again in the profession. She was among the thousands of Ukrainian refugees welcomed under the Scottish Government Super Sponsor visa program supporting displaced people from Ukraine.

I thought of Adriana from Nicaragua once again exiled in the United States as Ortega's tyranny in Nicaragua suffocates her country. And the current surge of foreigners seeking residency and peace in Portugal.

How do you start again and carry belonging within you? What does home mean? Is it possible to feel rooted, deeply and firmly, anywhere? I have been privileged on this journey to contemplate and respond to those questions. Day to day, human to human, soul to soul, life stories overlapping.

This nomadic experience hasn't made me more alone or less of a human being. It's made me a stronger and more connected one.

Acknowledgments

I owe my deepest gratitude to Hank, my unwavering partner and the foundation upon which my dreams have flourished. From the beginning, he believed in me and encouraged me to chase my passions. I am eternally thankful for the life we share.

I extend my heartfelt gratitude to the many individuals whose paths have intersected with ours during this nomadic period and all of the people who helped me make this book possible. In all of you, I honor the power of human connection. It is through these relationships, both enduring and fleeting, that I found inspiration, strength, and a sense of belonging.

To our close friends, who have become a chosen family, thank you for the laughter, the adventures, and the cherished moments we have shared. Your friendship and support—more real than any fixed abode—compose a home.

To those who have touched our lives and moved on, you, too, have made an impact. Your presence, however brief, has left a lasting impression, and I am grateful for the wisdom, perspective, and growth these interactions brought forth.

I wrote much of this book in New Mexico during the pandemic, but the story, recorded in journals and blog articles, was written along the way. I'm grateful to Corinna and Don Zimmerman, who provided us with a New Mexico home base, and to Ana Maria Meneses and Casa Morgado Esporão for welcoming us back to Peru and Portugal again and again. My kindest thanks to Ute Hagen, who brought her artistry to the book cover, and to Kate Armstrong, who helped me wrangle a decade of experiences into a one-page query letter and synopsis.

I'm especially grateful to my editor, Barbara Noe Kennedy, for pushing me to make this the best book possible. Thank you, Barbara, for your intelligence, expertise, generous spirit, and decades of experience. Without you, this book wouldn't be what it is.

I'm deeply appreciative to those who helped me in specific and numerous ways as I wrote this book: Jan Butchofsky, Judie Fein, Laura Bly, Monica Datta, Kerry Gladden, and Kathy Clute. I'm humbled by your trust, faith, and confidence. Thanks also to Dave Houser, Ginny Craven, Jane Watkins, Judy Allpress, Carol Charpentier, and the Adventure Travel Trade Association, whose early mentorship and professional support meant the world to me.

Lastly, I would like to remember Ingrid Zimmermann, whom I wrote about in this book. She died too soon and was a good friend missed daily.

About the Author

Ellen Barone is a writer and wanderer who traded a secure teaching career for a life of creativity and adventure in 1998. Traveling the world as an independent writer and photographer, she parlayed a handful of assignments into hundreds of adventures and co-founded the travel writing website YourLifeIsATrip.com. Since 2011, she's pursued a life of travel that allows her to settle in, dig beneath the surface, and get to know the people and stories behind a place. This is her first book. To learn more, visit EllenBarone.com.

Printed in Great Britain
by Amazon